Within and Beyond the Writing Process in the Secondary English Classroom

Within and Beyond the Writing Process in the Secondary English Classroom

Reade W. Dornan
Central Michigan University

Lois Matz Rosen
University of Michigan-Flint

Marilyn Wilson
Michigan State University

Boston • New York • San Francisco
Mexico City • Montreal • Toronto • London • Madrid • Munich • Paris
Hong Kong • Singapore • Tokyo • Cape Town • Sydney

Vice President: *Paul A. Smith*
Series Editor: *Aurora Martínez Ramos*
Editorial Assistant: *Beth Slater*
Senior Marketing Manager: *Elizabeth Fogarty*
Editorial Production Service: *Whitney Acres Editorial*
Manufacturing Buyer: *JoAnne Sweeney*
Cover Administrator: *Kristina Mose-Libon*
Electronic Composition: *Omegatype Typography, Inc.*

For related titles and support materials, visit our online catalog at
www.ablongman.com

Library of Congress Cataloging-in-Publication Data

Data not available at the time of publication.

ISBN: 0-205-30576-8

Printed in the United States of America
10 9 8 7 6 5 4 3 2 1 07 06 05 04 03 02

To my daughter, Ellen, who was first recognized
as a writer by her sixth grade teacher
R. W. D.

To my children, Michael and Stephanie, whose writing has always
delighted me; and to my husband, Bob Uphaus, who gets high on writing
L. M. R.

To my patient and supportive family and to dear friends who help me see
that life, like writing, is a series of moments lived intensely
M. W.

Contents

Acknowledgments

In the three years that we have worked together on this book, we have enjoyed the support of many people who contributed their expertise. We want to thank the teachers we have worked with over the years who not only inspired this book, but permitted us to draw on their classroom experiences. We appreciate the influence of Kari Molter, Diana Wakeford, and other teachers of the Flint Area and Southeast Michigan Writing Projects, whose classroom activities are mentioned in this book. We especially want to thank Jeanne Larvick, Laurie Lee, and Elaine Porter, who contributed classroom materials for the book. Elling Nielsen-Williams, a high school student, deserves special acknowledgment for his lively writing-process description and example of clustering. The Michigan Educational Assessment Program graciously permitted us to include some of their assessment materials. Our Allyn and Bacon editor, Aurora Martinez, and her assistant, Beth Slater, spurred us on to completion by setting the deadlines every writer needs. They also offered much-needed support and guidance whenever necessary. We are also grateful for the careful reading and excellent suggestions from our reviewers: Elaine V. Batenhorst, University of Nebraska at Kearney; Richard C. Pearson, Idaho State University; Kathleen Quinn, Holy Family College; and Gail S. Taylor, Old Dominion University. They have much to do with the final quality of this book. Finally, we want to thank our long-suffering spouses, David Dornan, Robert Uphaus, and Stuart Wilson, who didn't complain as much as they might have when we disappeared for weekend writing retreats.

Within and Beyond the Writing Process in the Secondary English Classroom

1

Introduction: Writing as Holistic Practice

The students hadn't done much writing in this middle school class, but their teacher was newly enrolled in a writing inservice program, and we'd been invited to visit her class. "Write," she told her students, "write about anything important to you." After 20 minutes of silent writing, scratching of pens and pencils on paper the only sounds in the room, she asked them to stop. Prompted, we were sure, by her first writing inservice session, the teacher asked, "Will anyone volunteer to read what he or she wrote?" One student's hand went up slowly, tentatively. She read to the class, hesitantly at first. Then, as she moved into her personal story, she read with feeling and emphasis about the grandfather she called "her best friend." One day, on a walk in the woods, they found a baby rabbit with a broken leg. They took it home and tried to "fix it," but the rabbit died. When she cried, her grandfather spoke to her of death. Don't be upset, he told her. "All things must die." The paper went on to describe how she learned of her grandfather's illness by overhearing a telephone conversation, her visits to the hospital where they were trying to "fix my grandpa so he could come home," his death, her overwhelming sadness. At the funeral, when she couldn't even bear to see her grandfather's face, her uncle told her to think about what her grandfather had said. She remembered the rabbit. "All things must die," she repeated to herself, comforted by her grandfather's words. We listened in amazement to the power of this piece, its craftsmanship, its language, spilling out as it had in 20 minutes of freedom to write.

****

Michael's father had abandoned the family when he was a baby, leaving him and his two sisters to be raised by their mother, a fact that had been painful to him throughout his growing up years. Recently, his father had returned to the city where Michael lived and they'd arranged to meet at a local restaurant. Michael's first paper of the school year described this meeting in the parking lot where he saw "a man whose faced looked familiar although I'd never seen him before" get out of a pick-up truck. The second assignment of the term was to prepare a piece of writing for a specific audience with a specific purpose in mind, one that could be sent to the intended audience. Michael wrote a letter to his father telling him what he'd missed by not being there for him and his two sisters throughout their childhood. For an assignment on persuasion, Michael crafted a convincing argument addressed to all young fathers, about the compelling reasons a boy needed a father in the household when he was growing up. The paper included interviews with two male friends similarly abandoned by their fathers. Michael's final research paper helped him objectify his personal quest for better understanding of absent fathers by doing research in this area. He gathered statistics on this phenomenon, researched the psychological and social effects of boys being raised by a mother alone, and gathered data on the consequences both personally and for society as a whole.

****

Jan Porter's eleventh grade English class decided to focus a reading/writing unit on the environment. During a general class discussion of the theme, several students complained about the cumbersome, fully loaded trash cans they were responsible for hauling to the curb on their family's weekly trash collection day. After a great deal of good-natured laughter over why this chore was so often delegated to teenagers, five students formed a group to study recycling in their city. Why didn't their community have a recycling program? Would it be possible to initiate one? Could the school begin to recycle its own trash? They gathered information about processes and costs from a nearby city with an active recycling program and wrote a brief report. Then they contacted local community leaders through letters and e-mail messages and wrote to the city council, including a copy of their report on the nearby recycling system. They received polite letters in response, saying this would be considered for the future. Their attempts to initiate a school recycling program met with more immediate success. A letter was drafted to the principal, the school superintendent, and the school's Parent Teacher Association requesting the initiation of a school recycling program. They spread flyers and fact sheets throughout the school to inform students and teachers of this need. Through their efforts, the school did, indeed, start its own recycling program by setting up an arrangement with a nearby program.

****

Jeffrey's final portfolio reflection ended like this: "I spent the whole weekend preparing this portfolio. I reread everything I'd written this term, selected and revised my two best pieces, and wrote this final analysis of my work. I couldn't believe how much my writing had changed since I'd first started this class. When I was finished, I looked at myself in the mirror and said, 'Jeffrey, you're a writer. You're really a writer.' "

****

These scenes of young writers at work illustrate the primary assumption behind this book: writing can and should be meaningful to the writer, a source of personal pleasure and satisfaction, as well as a means for social action and academic success. Writing is a tool that gives students power over their lives. This book will answer the question, "Why write?" in ways that go beyond the typical responses of "to organize ideas, to communicate to readers." We will honor the complexity of the personal and emotional involvement of the writer and the ways in which writing can be empowering rather than merely communicative.

Much of our best writing begins with the personal connection because we write best out of what we know. Writing a long research paper, just because it is assigned, is not going to make students good writers. Writing a variety of shorter papers on topics they feel passionate about may help students learn more. The writing assignment that is most likely to improve students' writing abilities is the one that asks them to think, that forces them to make connections to what they know. Any writing assignment that asks students to stretch as thinkers and writers will be most effective if connected to their personal interests and passions.

The title of this book, *Within and Beyond the Writing Process in the Secondary English Classroom,* points, above all, to the core of writing—the struggle of composing from the point of discovering what to write to the final stages of dotting the i's and crossing the t's so that a reader understands the piece. The writing process is a given in every writer's experience, even if particular steps of the process are not the same for everyone. In addition to talking about the writing process, we hope to convey that teaching the process combines an awareness of the student's need to begin writing with what he knows, to develop a sensitivity to language, and to adopt the rules and conventions of written language. These three aspects—experience, language, and writing conventions—constitute the invisible structures of the writing process. Preceding the moment that the writer puts the writing process into play are years of experience in the composer's life, systems of language and culture the writer has learned, and centuries of rhetorical tradition that the writer must acknowledge in conventions. During the writing process, the writer is discovering his personal connections to others in past conversations, his received knowledge about the topic, and how to express his thoughts. Following the process, he realizes his social connection to others as they read, listen, and consider what he has said. He will often be astonished to learn what his words have added to the total body of knowledge in print.

Within and Beyond the Writing Process in the Secondary English Classroom combines the pedagogies of three instructional approaches to composition: the emphasis on the personal connection from the Expressivists' school of composition, the rhetorical tradition that focuses on the importance of structure, purpose, and audience, and the school of composition that uses writing for social action. The writing process is essential to all three instructional approaches. For further discussion of the origins of these approaches, see "A History of Composition Pedagogy" in Chapter 8. We make the following additional seven assumptions about teaching composition:

1. *Writing is thinking.*

When one thinks briefly about the most fundamental reasons to write, "communication" is likely to appear at the top of the list. Certainly, an ability to communicate through writing over long distances, especially now in the age of e-mail, is crucial to one's ability to function in the contemporary work place and in the electronic world. Also important is a capacity for communicating by notes to loved ones, for being able to express oneself to others, and for telling stories. Writing also helps us record transactions and agreements and facts that we might forget. As important as all of these purposes are, no function is more significant than the use of writing for thinking. Many have wondered which is more dominant—language or thought. Certainly they are bound up in each other and one reinforces the other. Most scholars today agree that thought is bound up with language. Frank Smith, for example, argues that we think without language but "language develops to match the thinking of the people who use it . . . and in turn it shapes their thinking" (116). He explains that we have thoughts that are more complex than capacity to express them in language, so we search for the language to explain our thoughts and to name things for which we have no names. Smith also says that "words are the map of the way we think" (117).

If Frank Smith is right, then writing words down on the page can help a person who is trying to pull her thoughts together to hold the pieces of the map in place, to prevent the words from taking on new meanings and to forestall drift onto a new subject. Writing allows the thinker to work metacognitively with her own ideas as represented by the words, to think about her own thinking processes. In short, writing helps one use language to think. Writing begins with meaning making. It becomes a tool for the imagination, understanding, and learning. As Sondra Perl puts it, ". . . we often begin to compose with nothing more than hunches, inspirations, intuitive pulls, pushes, and leanings. We head in a certain direction, somehow knowing what comes next, but not certain until it comes whether or not it will work. . . . What matters first is to allow the words to come as they do. Sometimes, though, we need to stop and change the words before we can go forward. We must reread, pause, and listen to what's on the page to see if it makes the sense we want it to. If it does, we're on track and continue" (1994, 77). Most writers don't know what they have in their heads until they start organizing sometimes random, often unconnected thoughts into words—on paper or in conversation. The writer draws on ideas, experiences, and language to produce something that did not exist before. Writing thereby depends on past experiences and past experiences of writing. Good writing occurs most easily when students have solitary time to think, to write, to rethink, to rewrite—to draw upon past experiences with the process of writing and past experiences with the world. In fundamental ways, writing is a means of learning and coming to understand.

2. *Writing is a language process.*

Speaking and writing are often considered to be opposites: the first is oral, the second is written; speech is acquired in infancy and early childhood, writing is not mastered until adolescence or adulthood; speaking is acquired naturally without instruction, writing must be taught directly. Viewed this way speech and writing look like polar opposites. But this view is deceptively simple.

As is discussed more fully in Chapter Two, when one considers the fact that speech and writing are both aspects of language and sign systems for meaning creation, their similarities begin to surface. Oral and written are merely two different sides of the language coin; they have similar functions, despite their obvious differences (writing is usually a more permanent record than speech, for example, and writing involves written rather than spoken symbols). Both speech and writing are used for a variety of language functions that transcend differences in their forms. Both operate as vehicles for communicative purposes, for interpersonal reasons, for organizing information, and for creating new worlds through words. As similar processes, speech and writing both operate with a set of complex language rules that are more alike than different, and both are versatile systems that can adapt to the particular context in which they are used. Speech patterns in informal talk, for example, can be quite different from those in more formal speech, just as the rules of good prose shift as the writer moves from a small, familiar audience to a distant, unknown one.

If speech and writing have similar functions and purposes, there are also fundamental similarities in how their functions and forms are developed and learned, despite the fact that oral language is generally acquired in advance of written language. Direct instruction obviously plays a more significant role in the learning of writing, and yet speakers and writers use similar strategies to figure out meaning from the speech they hear and the print they see and to create meaning in those mediums in turn. In both, learners are active participants in the process, taking control of their own learning by using their knowledge of the world and their willingness to experiment with language in order to construct meaning.

Best practice in writing instruction emerges from a fundamental understanding of how learning to write can piggyback off learning to talk. Teachers of writing who take advantage of the connections between oral and written language development provide opportunities for writers to develop naturally with guided instruction. Rather than working at cross-purposes, teachers of writing can use their understanding of language processing and acquisition to help writers see themselves as writers, just as young children see themselves as speakers from the moment they begin to talk. See Chapter Two for a more in-depth discussion of this issue.

3. *We learn to write by writing.*

We don't become good writers by studying about writing; we become good writers by writing—and by reading others' writing. Learning to write effectively doesn't necessarily require help from a better writer; it requires time largely spent in writing and time spent rewriting until it's clear to an outside reader. Good writing develops over time. When we write within a supportive, nurturing environment that encourages risk taking and experimentation with form, language, and ideas, we can accept error and momentary ineptitude as an inevitable part of our writing development.

Good writing develops in subtle ways. Good readers do not necessarily make good writers, but it does help if the writer reads often and widely. As readers of other texts, we see how a friend shapes an argument, how a writer uses examples to support a point, how someone else uses a turn of phrase or a metaphor to clinch an idea, and how another writer uses language to "speak" with a strong voice. We observe style, language, organization to help shape our own use of written language.

Sometimes learning to write is a solitary, individual endeavor, but good writing teachers also recognize that writing is essentially a social process dependent on the cultural context, audience, and purpose. Writers need to exchange ideas, to verbalize concepts, to talk through an issue in order to know what it is they believe. The "talking through" demands an audience, someone who will provide feedback and response. Writers also need to use their own voices and forms of language to have their writing authentic, and those voices may reflect a variety of linguistic and cultural forms not always recognized in the traditional writing classroom. Writers necessarily bring their linguistic, cultural, and experiential backgrounds to bear on the writing process, and good writing teachers recognize the legitimacy of those experiences in the writing of their students and nurture them.

Think/Write #1
Are you a writer? What situations tell you that you are or are not a writer? Describe your experiences with writing that have shaped your self-perceptions as a writer.

4. *Development of our own writing can be facilitated by becoming more conscious of our writing processes.*

Writing is just plain hard work. Most of the time it's not fun. When it goes well, there are certain satisfactions that flow from undertaking the process, but it's still difficult, and good writing is hard to accomplish. Many writers, inexperienced and more accomplished, are not very aware of their own processes. We often write with a focus on what we want to say, largely unconscious of the processes we're using to accomplish our task, but the development of our own writing ability can be facilitated by becoming more conscious of our writing processes. For teachers of writing, making the process more conscious is critical to learning how to help beginning writers, or even writers at more advanced stages, move forward in their own writing. When we think about the writing that we find most compelling, it's often writing for someone other than a teacher—someone real, like a boss, our peers, the editor of the newspaper. Our writing takes on greater urgency when we have real purposes for writing and real audiences who are reading the writing, which suggests that publishing student writing in some form is a critical aspect of the process.

Analyzing our own writing processes also makes us aware that there is no singular writing process—there are multiple processes—and the processes are recursive rather than linear. Despite what some textbooks on writing imply, we don't all start by brainstorming in the same way, or even brainstorming, for that matter. Some of us start writing before we have many ideas at all; some of us revise as we write; others of us do multiple drafts, with specific kinds of revisions in each draft. We don't all wait until the second draft to begin editing, and some of us brainstorm in the middle of the drafting or the revising. Some of us draft and revise at our computers; others write in longhand; some of us write on note pads in bed; others at desks. Our processes, in fact, may vary from paper to paper, from one genre to another, from one audience to another. The writing task itself will largely determine what the process will be. For example, most writers rarely revise e-mail notes to personal friends, but they do lots of revision of e-mails to colleagues. Although their editing of e-mail messages is usually much lighter, regardless of audience, they carefully edit articles they send out for publication.

5. *Writing is a socially constructed process.*

Writers not only learn to write within a community of writers but they also develop as writers within a social and cultural milieu that fosters certain habits of thought and views of the world. Writers use language to create a reality of the world, and these perceptions in turn create them as thinkers and users of language. This reciprocal process—using language to shape knowledge and world views, world views affecting their language and knowledge—suggests that knowledge is socially constructed. Talk radio, chat rooms, and electronic bulletin boards, group work in classrooms, informal discussion with friends about medical problems, a pep rally that encourages certain perceptions of team effort and winning all result in the shaping of ideas and concepts. As teachers we need to recognize that the assignment we give that requires a kind of logical ordering—the persuasive or argumentative essay, for example—has been socially constructed, and we're passing that world view on to our students, who will perpetuate it in their own way. World views become institutionalized and "natural" habits of thought.

6. *We not only learn to write, but we write to learn.*

Given the ability of writing to help organize our thoughts and given the opportunity to produce multiple texts, everything is in place for using writing across the curriculum. It goes without saying that teachers in every discipline should find writing useful in their classrooms to explore new knowledge, to facilitate thinking, to make decisions, solve problems, reason, remember, understand, and imagine. The English teacher can help students discover writing as a tool for all their classes by offering writing in various genres for a variety of purposes, functions, and audiences. The five-paragraph essay as the staple in the writing classroom, with the teacher as reader/evaluator, is simply inadequate.

Writers need a tool kit of strategies, activities, and approaches to draw on as they compose. Learning to write means learning to use a variety of genres and forms: imaginative pieces, poems, letters, research papers, analytic essays, journals, personal narratives, and more. The more opportunities that teachers can provide for attempting personal expression, persuasion, argument, or creative expression, the more young writers can develop their own personal lists of do's and don'ts for getting the job done. Similarly, students need to write for a variety of purposes—many of them real and meaningful. They need to experience the difference between writing instructions for strangers and a business letter asking for a refund for a defective product. Furthermore, the teacher should not be the only reader of this work. Young writers need to write for each other and for readers beyond the classroom—their parents and friends, readers of their local newspapers, and other members of the community.

In this tool kit are therefore lessons learned from the experience of writing and from reading a variety of genres. Reading widely can expand a student's understanding of the world and enhance a writer's experience with ways to shape her ideas.

7. *The young writer benefits from some direct instruction.*

Most of what a writer learns is absorbed on a social level from her use of language and the cultural knowledge she shares with others. On a solitary level, she learns to write from her reading and the writing she does on her own. But there comes a point where she needs help from experts as well. Peer instruction can provide valuable feedback on how a piece is being received and understood by writers who are at the same level as she is. Teacher instruction can provide the response of another reader as well as expertise on a technical level with advice on the mechanics of writing, with reminders about grammatical conventions, and with guidance about specialized forms of writing. Middle school teachers find it useful to offer direct instruction on narratives and descriptive writing. In high school, teachers usually offer direct instruction on the formal essay, on the research paper, and on critical responses to literature. Many high school teachers also offer instruction on the structure of problem/solution, cause and effect, comparison/contrast essays. Direct instruction on how to write for essay tests, too, is helpful for students. In short, the emphasis of the writing classroom is on student-centered learning, but occasional direct instruction is necessary for introducing students to the rules of formal writing as well as new forms and strategies for their tool kits such as methods for generating material and revising rough drafts.

These assumptions about writing and the teaching of composition, consonant with holistic approaches to literacy development, inform, and guide the rest of this book. They encourage an immersion in reading and writing; they *dis*courage the fragmentation of the writing process into a skills approach; and they recognize the interplay between reading and writing. The book is organized as follows:

Chapter Two looks at the intimate connection between oral and written language development as a way of identifying instructional approaches that can foster those processes of writing acquisition most closely connected to the naturalness of language development. In Chapter Three, we describe the writing process in great detail. Based on the strategies that all writers discover sooner or later, the writing process leads young writers to develop their own methods for putting pen to paper. This chapter explores how writing is a recursive act of pushing words ahead, rehearsing and revising those words, then finding new words to push forward once again. It includes discussions on planning, drafting, revising, and editing. Related to issues about language, Chapter Four discusses how to teach grammar through composition—how to edit and proofread papers, how to deal with dialects and the students whose first language is not English, and how to handle touchy issues of correctness. Chapters Five and Six speak extensively about the kinds of writing genres that are assigned most often to students in the English classroom. They offer nuts and bolts advice on how to make the basic essay assignment, often deadly and tedious, become a vehicle for more meaningful self-expression as well as produce a bright, lively, and readable piece that fulfills its rhetorical purposes. The two chapters cover the basic essay and its variations in research writing and responses to literature.

In many of the chapters, specific advice is offered on how to evaluate and respond to student writing. However, Chapter Seven covers writing assessment in greater detail. This chapter gives general guidelines and alternative approaches for evaluation and grading and suggests a basic rubric that may be used as a basis for building genre specific rubrics. Chapter Seven also talks about how to handle the paper load, how to use portfolios, and how to understand the results of national testing in writing. Chapter Eight outlines a brief history of the schools of composition instruction from the days of Aristotle to our time. It situates our suggestions for pedagogy in their rightful contexts, explaining why some modes of instruction are ignored by us and others are privileged.

This text is designed for undergraduate and graduate students taking courses in the teaching of writing, for classroom teachers seeking professional development, and for administrators developing writing programs in schools, as well as for teacher educators and Writing Project participants. Unlike other texts that tend to focus major attention on practice or major attention on writing theory, this text integrates the two as it deals with the intersections of psycholinguistics, writing theory, the writing process, and strategies for the teaching of writing. Important to consider in a comprehensive view of writing theory and instruction are the linguistic foundations of writing development, the historical background from which current writing instruction has emerged, and the sometimes-conflicting theories of writing development and instructional approaches. This text also acknowledges the socio-cultural aspects of writing that have become increasingly important in our multi-linguistic, multi-cultural classrooms.

This is not just a theoretical text. Once the framework for writing and writing instruction is established, the book provides in-depth coverage of classroom strategies for teaching and assessing writing based on these socio-cultural-linguistic principles, centering on writing process methods for classroom instruction. The approaches we discuss include organizing a writing workshop, using peer groups and teacher conferences, teaching revision strategies, responding to student writing, and grading and assessing growth. This text also fills a void regarding research and theory on grammar, correctness, and language variation in the writing of non-mainstream students. Embedded throughout the text are discussions of the role of technology in writing and writing instruction.

Much of the material in the classroom application sections comes from our work with teachers in the schools. Collectively we have many years of experience working with secondary classroom teachers, both pre-service and practicing professionals. We have conducted in-service workshops, consulted in school districts, directed Summer Writing Projects, and participated in the Michigan English Language Arts Frameworks Project developing standards and benchmarks for language arts instruction. This text draws on those experiences and the methods and materials created by the teachers we have worked with over the years.

Each chapter will begin with an overview of the major points and a list of the standards for initial preparation of teachers of English Language Arts for middle/junior high and senior high school teaching that are developed by the National Council for the Accreditation of Teacher Education (NCATE) in conjunction with the National Council of Teachers of English (NCTE). The numbers of the standards correspond to NCATE/NCTE's list of standards, dated 2001. Throughout the chapters are boxed Think/Writes, which offer suggestions for engaging readers by writing in response to the material. Each chapter ends with a summary in a section called "Points to Remember" and a list of books "For Further Reading" on the topics in that chapter.

Think/Write #2
Write about a personally meaningful writing experience you have had similar to those described in the opening vignettes to this chapter. When was writing a source of personal pleasure, satisfaction, social action, academic success? Explain why you found this particular writing experience so meaningful.

2

Psycholinguistic and Social Foundations

Why should we care about literacy? Why should a book on writing assessment begin its discussion with issues of literacy and language? What are the issues of literacy that have implications for the teaching of writing? For one thing, as teachers of writing we need to be knowledgeable about issues related to the quality of literacy in this country. Alarmist views perpetuated by politicians, some educators, and the public have had a major impact on how people think writing should be taught. Mediocre test scores, accurate or not, have strengthened the view that educators in general, writing teachers in particular, haven't been doing their jobs. For another, assumptions that there is one standard for literacy to be met by all students, in every situation, regardless of culture, dialect, or social circumstances have permeated thinking about what good writing is and what good writing instruction entails. These, among the myriad other reasons for considering issues of literacy and issues of language, suggest that writing teachers must be culturally aware of how literacy is defined and how language issues necessarily play a role in writing instruction.

The chapter begins then, with a discussion of "literacy," how its definitions vary over time, and how it is viewed in the current pedagogical and political climate. The discussion then centers on the processes of oral and written acquisition, the implications of writing as a socio-cultural process, and the role of direct instruction in writing. Providing the theoretical framework for the book, these topics specifically address the following NCATE/NCTE standards for writing.

3.1.1 Show an understanding of language acquisition and development, including developmental aspects of writing;

3.1.2 Demonstrate how reading, writing, listening, viewing, and thinking are interrelated;

3.1.3 Recognize the impact of cultural, economic, political, and social environments upon language;
3.1.4 Demonstrate a respect for and a deep understanding of diversity in language use, patterns, and dialects across cultures, ethnic groups, geographic regions, and social roles;
3.1.8 Show the various purposes for which language is used.

Basic Assumptions about Literacy

As a framework for our discussion of writing and writing instruction throughout this text, we outline four premises that undergird our assumptions about literacy: that literacy has been defined differently over time because of changing social, economic, and educational needs; that it is a social activity shaped by the culture in which it is used; that as a political phenomenon it is never neutral and can wield enormous power and authority; and that its acquisition and functions are intimately connected to oral language development, with important implications for its teaching. Studying the process of writing in isolation from oral language ignores the ways in which oral and written are part of the same developmental package and are, in fact, reciprocal processes. Therefore, the discussion of writing development as part of language acquisition is central to this chapter and the book.

Before we launch into our discussion of how literacy definitions have evolved culturally and socially over time, we need to make clear that literacy as we discuss it here focuses primarily on print literacy—not because we want to privilege print literacy over oral literacy—but because print literacy has been the focus of school-based instruction for at least two centuries in this country and is the basis for most of the evaluation occurring at a national and state level. Our focus is by no means meant to imply that writing and reading are inherently superior skills to oral language or that critical thinking is possible only in a print-literate culture, as our discussion further on makes clear. The dichotomy between "oral" cultures and "print" cultures too often assumes a primacy of print, i.e., that orality is inferior to written language and that written histories are more stable than oral ones. Such dichotomous thinking often ignores the transformative power of oral language and elevates print literacy to an unwarranted position of status and authority.

With these caveats in mind, we turn our attention to the issues of print literacy and the premises upon which this text is based.

The Evolution of Literacy Definitions

Our first premise is that the concept of literacy changes over time and is complicated by the specific intellectual needs of each era.

Literacy as Intelligence. In the current educational climate, most teachers use the term "literacy" to mean the ability to read and write at a certain level of expertise. The public, on the other hand, sometimes uses the term to mean something quite different. The most common usage has been its application to a general level of intelligence and/or education, as in "She's a very literate person" or "He's an illiterate boob." The word literacy itself does not appear in any dictionary until the 1920s, although "literate" and "illiterate" date back to the sixteenth and seventeenth centuries in reference to individuals who were learned or unlearned, educated or uneducated (Barton, 1994). These definitions carry tremendous political force because of their positive/negative connotations. To be labeled "illiterate" even now is often to be assumed by some as unintelligent and unschooled. "Illiterate" is almost always a pejorative label, related as much to an individual's social standing in his community vis á vis his level of education or degree of social sophistication as it is to his ability to read or write.

Cultural Literacy. "Literacy" as level of education or social sophistication received major reinforcement with the 1987 publication of E. D. Hirsch's *Cultural Literacy: What Every American Needs to Know.* This book, along with his editions for every grade level through sixth, popularized the notion that to be educated meant to know certain kinds of things, particularly those concepts associated with middle-class culture. It was received knowledge passed along from one generation to the next without question, assumed to be the essence of what it means to be "educated." Among the list of topics, terms, names, or concepts one should know, according to Hirsch, are names like Ginger Rogers and Fred Astaire, Walt Disney, and Carl Jung, along with Rodin, David Copperfield, and Helen of Troy (heavily representative of middle-class culture); lists of concepts such as legal tender, mutual fund, and private enterprise (class-related); and lists of topics likely to be learned in higher education such as penis envy, malapropism, proletariat. These recommended lists have a way of becoming "must know" lists, despite E. D. Hirsch's protestations to the contrary. And despite his assurances that these lists were constructed in consultation with a core of teachers whom he used as consultants, it is apparent that the lists privilege the knowledge of the dominant culture. The section on sayings and phrases, for example, lists 39 common sayings such as "Catch as catch can" and "Rome wasn't built in a day" but not one from the oral tradition in African American communities such as "What goes around comes around."

We don't wish to suggest that some common sets of knowledge aren't important in the secondary classroom. They are. But we *are* arguing that the knowledge that we want to pass on needs to be broadly defined rather than privileging one set of knowledge over others. Unfortunately, presenting this knowledge as lists encourages favoring convergent all-think-alike approaches to knowledge over divergent and complex systems of knowledge. Lists provide no means of connecting ideas, no opportunity to envision complexities, and no opportunities for questioning. And lists recommended for "acquaintance" levels of knowledge frequently lead to cocktail party trivia, precisely what educators interested in developing critical thinking in their students want to avoid.

Because it operates largely without critique, cultural literacy as popularized by Hirsch and others like Alan Bloom (*The Closing of the American Mind*) has become deeply embedded in the theories and practices of our educational institutions. It tends to support textbooks with the "right" interpretation of history, canonical works of literature, traditional genres of writing, and argumentative forms of essay writing. As part of this received cultural knowledge, the five-paragraph essay has been the staple of writing programs for decades. Its "naturalness" largely went unquestioned, and it became the singular structure for the majority of writing in high school classrooms at the expense of other more realistic or natural rhetorical structures.

Functional Literacy. For literacy that relates more directly to the acts of reading/decoding print and writing/encoding print, literacy as "basic skills" seems to have been the longest running working definition. Correctness in oral reading, accuracy in word identification, and the ability to write simple sentences and paragraphs with minimal surface errors were key characteristics of a "functionally literate" person. In an early-twentieth-century society that educated masses of people in a technologically simple world, functional literacy—the ability to read and write at a fourth grade level—was adequate. Higher literacy stakes existed for the college-prep track, but education programs developed to insure a basic level of literacy were often content to help American students reach the minimal level of competence. And as we see in greater depth in Chapter Eight, writing instruction was subsumed by the study of reading and literature and kept to a collection of techniques that further marginalized writing instruction in the English classroom (Myers 94).

Even as demands for higher forms of literacy have increased in schools over the past two decades, functional literacy remains the goal of many programs for students unlikely to go to college. Non-college preparatory students often have limited access to courses that encourage higher order thinking. This group gets "dumbed-down" curricular materials consisting of skills sheets and workbook exercises, while the other group gets to write plays and perform them. Programs focusing on functional literacy often deny kids in lower tracks the same literacy skills that lead to other educational and social opportunities available to middle-class kids.

Critical Literacy. Missing from earlier assumptions about literacy, and growing increasingly more important in a complex technological and social world are critical literacy abilities that enable people to use literacy for their personal benefit and as functioning members of their communities. Our multi-cultural society functioning in an increasingly technological culture demands literacy skills that outstrip the simple definitions with which many school systems have been operating. Writing instruction needs to embrace not only higher-order thinking skills for *all* students but skills that provide students opportunities to use their writing in personally and politically empowering ways. Beyond the five-paragraph essay and the ability to write simple prose error-free, students need to use writing in multi-media formats, to see writing as a way of negotiating their place in society, and to use written language to question and critique and establish themselves as literate, thinking members of society. In later chapters we will discuss assignments like Ira Shor's social action papers that help students find voice and empowerment as they negotiate meaning through writing. We begin to address this need in the following section.

Visual and Technological Literacy. Students in the twenty-first century, with greater experiences with visual media—television, video games, movies, the Internet—have acquired a facility with reading and writing visual texts that sometimes far surpasses their teachers' abilities. Yet, visual literacy as a critical form of literacy needs careful attention in the secondary classroom. What constitutes good information on the web? Are all sources of web information reputable? How can we use the same methods of critiquing visual media that we use for print media? As teachers we need to explore these issues with our students and help them move beyond a simple acceptance of all visual information as equally valid. They must learn to critique visual media by asking questions about what the intentions of the web author or the movie director are, how visual media manipulate their readership, and how visual styles of formatting and use of images influence the reader. How readers read visual and digital texts will play a major role in how they compose them as well. Just as writers of print texts consider issues of audience, purpose, and genre, writers of digital or visual texts must focus on issues that affect their readers/audiences. Literacy in the twenty-first century will necessarily involve this broadening definition of text, reader, and writer. We argue, therefore, for a critique of all texts—visual, digital, and print—as a way of helping readers and writers as consumers and producers of these texts assess them and use them in sophisticated and thoughtful ways.

The Cultural Roots of Literacy

> *Our second premise is that writing—like the other language processes of listening, speaking, and reading—is embedded in the culture of the language on which it is based. It functions specifically within the culture, being shaped by the speech community and occasionally shaping the speech community, in which the writer participates.*

My grandmother, with her eighth grade education, rarely wrote beyond copying recipes, writing messages in Christmas cards, and jotting down notes to the milkman on occasion. I, on the other hand, almost never write letters because of the availability of phones and e-mail, and I spend much of my time writing academic prose. We each adopted the forms of literacy necessary to function in our own personal and professional worlds. To speak, therefore, of a monolithic, one-size-fits-all literacy rather than of literacies is to ignore the fact that literacy beliefs and practices are socially constructed and embedded in one's culture, subject to the conditions under which particular groups of people operate as literate human beings. Literacy is a socio-cultural phenomenon, tied in specific ways to the community's beliefs and practices, dependent for its definitions on the community in which it is learned and practiced. School literacy may be very pragmatic and functional—using writing to accomplish teacher-assigned tasks—while personal literacy may range from writing poetry to keeping a journal. And my neighbor's writing is primarily job-related as she writes company memos, fills out requisition forms, and uses e-mail to make decisions about marketing.

These differences in the uses of literacy are self-evident, but less evident are the cultural differences in the uses of literacy that often go unnoticed because mainstream literacy—the kind that many teachers have themselves experienced as children, teenagers, and adults—often seems "natural"—so natural that it doesn't call attention to itself; it is a given, assumed to be the only kind of literacy that is universal and uniformly valued from one culture to another. It assumes the naturalness of story-book reading, having story-time, learning the alphabet, learning to read environmental print, writing our names, all before formal schooling. It also assumes the continuation of reading and writing into adulthood for a variety of purposes—recreational (magazines and novels), informational (newspapers and the Internet), functional (notes, lists, letters, memos, how-to books).

Seemingly natural and transparent, these values of literacy actually vary from culture to culture. Ethnologists Schieffelin and Cochran-Smith describe two very different literate communities for whom literacy has inherently different values. The Kaluli group of people in Papua, New Guinea, were introduced to literacy by American missionaries in the early 1970s, but after five years of literacy lessons focusing primarily on Bible reading, there was almost no evidence of its having any effect in the social lives of the Kaluli because this traditional kind of literacy did not seem to be relevant to them. They had little need to read and write beyond the school literacy events. Even though the Kaluli were exhibiting literate behaviors during their literacy lessons, few of them used literacy outside the lesson time. Unless literacy provides possibilities for helping new literates have control of their lives in ways that are not possible before literacy, there is little value attached to it, according to the researchers. In much the same way, secondary students who see little value in learning to write in certain rhetorical forms that seem foreign to their own interests and projected life's work may simply go through the motions of acquiring these forms without integrating them into their literacy practices.

However, in another study conducted by Schieffelin and Cochran-Smith of a Vietnamese family living in a West Philadelphia community, for whom there was little literacy in the home and for whom the first introduction to literacy occurred in elementary school, the results were very different. Similar literacy approaches and practices that had little effect on the lives of the Kaluli did, in fact, make important differences in the lives of the Vietnamese family. The son used his literacy skills, learned in school, to help his family fill out job applications, scholarship applications, etc. The researchers suggest that the desire to become assimilated into a literate culture and to reap the benefits of literacy in one's native or adopted language can easily overcome earlier literacy deprivation. The researchers conclude that for an individual to become literate, literacy must be "functional, relevant, and meaningful for individuals and the society in which they live" (Schieffelin and Cochran-Smith 22). Equally important to secondary students is the relevance of literacy to their everyday lives, a fact teachers often take for granted without conscious attempts to make students aware of the connections.

Because literacy is tied to the specific needs and practices within a social structure, it takes on very different shapes from one culture to another, even among different cultures within the U.S., a point that Shirley Brice Heath's studies in the Piedmont Carolinas clearly indicates. Heath studied the language and literacy acquisition of children in three different communities in that region. The African American working-class children in Trackton were able to transmit knowledge through wonderful oral stories full of metaphorical meaning even though that ability was not often validated by the literacy demands of the school and was, in fact, frequently misunderstood. The white working-class children in Roadville, on the other hand, were well-schooled in literal story interpretation and in doing reading workbook exercises, valued in the school, but their relative inability to deal with metaphor and symbol made it difficult for them to deal with anything but literal interpretations. The middle-class town children were best at the academic discourse favored by the school because it more closely matched their own literacy experiences at home. Three different communities, three different cultures, each having its own set of literacy practices that do or do not connect to the schools' expectations about literate behavior. Because literacy is embedded in a culture, a wide variety of literacy practices must count as literacy, determined by the needs and values of the community in which these practices occur.

Think/Write #1

Think about your own literacy practices and make a list of the kinds of writing you do almost every day. Don't forget to include writing grocery lists, leaving a note for a roommate, writing post-it notes for yourself as "to-do" reminders. Then consider the following questions:

1. Should we classify these as literacy practices? If so, why? If not, why not?
2. How might your list differ from lists of people in other cultural groups, or even from your peers, whose literacy practices may also differ in interesting ways?

The Politics of Literacy

Our third premise is that literacy does not guarantee *greater access to power, social acceptance, or job security and that literacy instruction is never a neutral enterprise.*

We must demythologize the common notion that developing literacy/ies—for our specific purposes, developing the ability to read and write—is categorically positive, that it leads automatically to a list of "good" social practices and results. Does learning to read and write always lead to better jobs, greater job security, improvement in social standing? Yes and no. Yes, we can say, for individuals in a literate society, literacy is a necessary condition for functioning fully and well in that society, but it is by no means a sufficient condition for success in society. First of all, the role that literacy plays in an individual's or a community's ability to deal with abstractions is uncertain. We have traditionally ascribed literacy with the ability to increase one's capacity for abstract thought, but there is evidence that some cultures develop this ability without literacy. Sociolinguists Scribner and Cole, in their study of the Vai Mende people in Liberia, demonstrate that the cognitive ability for abstract thought was developed by the Vai Mende through oral language tasks demanding high levels of cognitive ability and that their writing did not contribute significantly to this capacity. Literacy is only one of many cognitive and social variables that must be present.

Second, while we all support the teaching of literacy and view it as essential in our print-oriented society, we must also acknowledge that literacy has been used for ill as well as for good, that there is the potential for ambiguity in the values associated with its learning and use. For some in our society literacy has been the cornerstone of social progress and economic growth, but for others it has been an instrument of oppression and indoctrination. Workers, for example, in the Ford automobile plant in the early part of the twentieth century were controlled to some extent through the propaganda materials used in the required Ford English schools. Designed to teach English to immigrants in order to provide them with the tools necessary for doing their jobs, these programs also had an ulterior motive. Ford's workers learned English by reciting patriotic, moralistic, and work-related axioms that focused on hard work, loyalty, and obedience—all qualities to keep the workers in line, on the line—insuring a smoothly-running and economically profitable system of private enterprise. As educational theorist Michael Apple describes it, entrepreneurs like Ford and other educators of the era formulated educational practices designed to inculcate a set of attitudes, beliefs, and standards that would diminish their "threat" to society, an educational practice that has been repeated across the decades of the twentieth century, systematically attempting to shape ethnic and economic underclasses with middle-class values.

Like the early twentieth century, in the early part of the twenty-first century, some literacy programs are pathways not to opportunity but to limited resources and narrowed visions of possibility. Working-class children encouraged to remain in educational tracks leading to manual labor jobs have different literacy opportunities than students in academic tracks. Literacy becomes a means of gatekeeping, limiting opportunities for some, while opening up possibilities for others. For example, in a study of tracking in middle schools and high schools across the country, Jennie Oakes found that "a student's race, class, or family-based access to knowledge about college and career routes had more to do with what track the student ends up in than does inherent intelligence or actual potential" (Gee 1996, 34–35). Sociolinguist James Gee goes so far as to say that the most consistent thread in the history of literacy through the centuries is its use "to solidify the social hierarchy, empower elites, and ensure that people lower on the hierarchy accept the values, norms, and beliefs of the elites, even when it is not in their self-interest or group interest to do so" (1996, 36).

Students from working class backgrounds whose primary discourse learned in the home environment is different from the dominant academic discourse often find themselves in the unenviable position of being expected to operate in the dominant discourse without knowing how to do so or even how to begin learning the features of that discourse. Gee suggests that this dominant discourse is not just the language features but a whole "identity kit" that comes complete with "the appropriate costume and instructions on how to act, talk, and often write so as to take on a particular role that others will recognize" (1989, 6). Gee goes on to say that the reason dominant discourses—Standard English expectations, for example—focus so much on superficial features of language is precisely because these superficial features

> . . . are exactly the parts of Discourses most impervious to overt instruction and are only fully mastered when everything else in the discourse is mastered. Since these Discourses are used as "gates" to ensure that the "right" people get to the "right" places in our society, such superficial features are ideal (1989, 13).

Using literacy as gate-keeping operates outside education as well. A number of studies provide evidence to suggest that literacy tests in businesses and industries, ostensibly designed to test prospective employees' literacy skills for successful on-the-job performance, in reality are designed to "screen out certain social groups and types" (Street 18), in the belief that more highly literate individuals will not be as antagonistic to new technology, etc. Literacy tests become attitudinal tests used to deny access to the system. If literacy is used to continue the existing social stratification instead of opening up options for people, it is an ambiguous enterprise.

To speak of the cultural roots of literacy, therefore, is also to suggest that literacy in both its teaching and learning is never a value-free, neutral activity. It is rather an act imbued with political consequences. The teaching of writing involves decision-making by teachers that deals implicitly with issues of values, attitudes, and assumptions about language, power, and authority. Whenever we ask our students to write, we are operating with an implicit set of assumptions about who is in control of the writing and what the language standards must be, assumptions that are so deeply embedded in literacy practices that we fail to realize they exist. Are our decisions based on giving students authority and responsibility for their own writing or on our need to control? Are our decisions forced on us by large-scale assessment tests or developed from what will make students responsible writers who care about their writing? Encouraging students to write on topics they care about, to write for real audiences, and to help them negotiate the system for positive change in their lives through their writing is an inherently political act.

Think/Write #2

Teachers often don't think of themselves as political beings in the classroom because they want to remain "objective" in their teaching. And yet the previous discussion has suggested that we can't avoid being political because every instructional decision we make is making a statement about how we position students and how we use the tools of our trade to effect change. Write down three or four seemingly objective instructional decisions or strategies we might make as teachers of writing and list what you consider to be their political nature. For example, what does the use of a red pen for identifying students' writing errors signal? What does the rule that a paper with more than three spelling errors or punctuation mistakes deserves a failing grade suggest about our views of writing?

Parallels Between Oral Language and the Development of Writing

> *Our fourth premise is that understanding literacy and the complexities of writing in an increasingly complicated world demands knowledge of more than just pedagogical tools to foster the development of writing. It demands knowing about the nature of language acquisition, both oral and written, and about the cultural conflicts that serve to complicate the process.*

Understanding the processes of oral and written language development, the difference between conscious and unconscious processes, and the role of direct instruction in the acquisition process is the key to good writing instruction. A successful writing program will consider pedagogical strategies that complement the speaker/writer's natural instincts for language.

Acquisition refers to the unconscious process of gaining knowledge or developing a skill with which to perform a task, without the benefit of direct teaching or instruction (Pinker). *Learning,* on the other hand, refers to more conscious development of knowledge or skills, usually aided by direct teaching, with inevitably greater metacognitive awareness of the process. Many of our abilities are on a continuum, some more clearly acquired, like the ability to walk, others more clearly learned, like knowing the capitals of the fifty states or learning how to tie one's shoes. Children primarily acquire their oral language, a point we will discuss in some detail, but whether they acquire or learn written language is a more complex question.

Humans are biologically wired to acquire language. Contrary to popular opinion, parents don't teach their children how to talk or walk. Both processes develop naturally as children mature physically and cognitively. In fact, the recent discovery of a gene that underlies speech and language provides further evidence of the notion of a biological predisposition for language (Wade A1). Steven Pinker, linguist and author of the *NY Times* best seller, *The Language Instinct,* says:

> Language is not a cultural artifact that we learn the way we learn to tell time or how the federal government works. Instead, it is a distinct piece of the biological makeup of our brains. Language is a complex, specialized skill, which develops in the child spontaneously, without conscious effort or formal instruction, is deployed without awareness of its underlying logic, is qualitatively the same in every individual, and is distinct from more general abilities to process information or behave intelligently (18).

In setting language apart from other forms of human knowledge, Pinker is claiming that, as a biologically determined phenomenon, language is instinctive and natural, that its acquisition is almost impossible to derail, and that it will flourish when the child is in an environment where language is used for a range of communicative purposes. Children acquire it as they participate in social structures. Although linguists may disagree about the extent to which language is biologically determined, virtually all of them acknowledge the basic biological pre-disposition for language. Some linguists liken the process to the germination of a seed. When the conditions are right—the presence of sufficient sunlight, moisture, fertile soil—the genetic code in the seed is activated, and the seed grows and develops. When conditions are right for language acquisition—when the child is in the presence of human language and is included as a participant—the language acquisition device is activated, and language develops.

Assuming that written literacy is also biologically determined is perhaps stretching the point, but clearly a number of characteristics of learning to write are directly related to the processes of acquiring oral language. While a greater degree of learning is involved in the processes of writing than in speech, writing, as one of the language processes, can most easily be facilitated by considering what those natural language processes are and how they play a role in learning to write.

Hypothesis-formation and Generalization. Hypothesizing about how language structures at all levels operate is the key process that speakers use to figure out the forms and functions of language. Arguing against a behaviorist model of language learning, researchers such as Pinker and Chomsky claim that the genetic imprinting of language abilities allows the learner to form a series of hypotheses about language structures at all levels: how sounds work together (phonology), how past tenses and plurals are formed in language (morphology), how the organization of phrases and clauses works to create meaning (syntax), and how the rules for conversation and human discourse operate (pragmatics)—forms of knowledge that go well beyond mere imitation. Do children imitate? Yes, sometimes, but not as a major means of acquiring language. They sometimes repeat phrases or words, but most of their utterances are spontaneous, and what they do imitate is usually less syntactically complex than their spontaneous utterances. What parents and caregivers often overlook is all the cognitive activity going on beneath the surface of those repetitions, which is where the real work of acquisition takes place. A theory of imitation posits the child as a relatively passive learner who acquires language through a system of stimulus-response-reinforcement strategies without much cognitive work.

Many of children's utterances are novel, i.e., they are not direct imitations of the specific structures they've just heard someone else say but rather they are constructions of their own creation based on a generalized set of assumptions about words, structures, and meaning—what forms they take and how they operate. Take, for example, the child who refers to an eraser as an "unraser," a creative response based on a couple of hypotheses related to the meaning of the word and the regular way English verbs are negated. "Un" is, in fact, the prefix before "do" (undo), but it is not the prefix for "rase." The child who calls it an "unraser" is not mimicking a word he's heard; he's creating his own based on rules or hypotheses he's generalized from his observations about language structures. When the four-year-old refers to men as "mans," the "rule" with which she is operating is based on her generalization that we use an "s" suffix to denote plurality. Her hypothesis is accurate to a degree, but it is simply not complex enough to handle exceptions. Rather than imitating language in order to learn it, children develop various theories about language rules, they test their hypotheses and modify them based on other language models that caregivers provide, and over time they gradually refine their hypotheses as they move closer to the rules of adult syntax (Moskowitz). Eventually the five-year-old figures out irregular plurals like "men" and "mice," irregular verbs like "ran" and "went."

Modeling Oral and Written Language. For pre-school children, caregiver language provides a model that they use for forming their assumptions about structures and meaning in oral language. For young writers, environmental writing also provides the data for helping them figure out how to construct meaning through print. In oral language development, caregivers help to structure the environment by providing conversational opportunities, by modeling language, and by providing feedback when children use language. Young children, and even infants, participate in conversations at their own levels, encouraged by the caregivers with whom they are "conversing." The adult provides feedback/response in the course of the conversation that models more adult forms of language and that focuses on the meaning of the child's language rather than on the form—on *what* the child is saying rather than *how.* Thus, a kind of "scaffolding" is constructed by caregivers to provide simple adult models for ongoing conversation. For example, when the two-year-old holds up a sock and asks, "Mommy sock?" the adult may provide a slightly more complex syntactic structure in response, such as "Yes, that is Mommy's sock. Where's Annie's sock?" These conversational exchanges focus on the meaning while providing linguistic data for the child's developing repertoire of linguistic structures. The adult provides the linguistic guidance that enables the child to acquire increasingly sophisticated language rules, an example of what Vygotsky calls the "zone of proximal development," or the space within which adults help children function with greater linguistic complexity than the child would be able to do on his own.

Beyond the acquisition of language structures is the increasing awareness of language functions, both oral and written. Speech, of course, serves a wide range of social functions, including communicating ideas, expressing feelings, establishing and maintaining relationships, asserting opinions, making demands, and learning about the world. Awareness of language functions, in fact, often precedes an awareness of forms. Children learn how to negotiate human relationships through the use of language. "Please gimme that" gets them what they want from an adult more quickly than "gimme that," so they learn to use forms of politeness with adults. They learn how to ask questions in order to learn things; they learn how to negate sentences as forms of refusal or denial.

Similar modeling and scaffolding of written language, both its forms and its functions, occur for young children in their home environments as well. Parents read stories to their children and point out words and meaning; parents write letters and notes and grocery lists that serve as models for young children's own attempts at writing. Children learn the functions of letter-writing or grocery-list making or labeling even as they begin to recognize the forms that those different genres take. Adolescents, like younger children, need models for the forms and genres they are expected to use in writing. For example, the problem with essay-writing for many students is that they often lack familiarity with essays, and without a rich exposure to literature, students don't have models of varied sentence structure and vocabulary. Adolescents learn through exposure to language forms within a variety of different functions—structures of essays, organization of narratives, use of quotations in dialogue, styles of argumentation in position papers. Scaffolding through exposure to a variety of forms and functions is central to writing development for older as well as for younger students.

Writing Development and Risk-taking. Writing and speech are clearly both language processes, similar in many ways, and yet in many respects the latter appears to be effortless, the former much more labored. To ignore the differences, of course, is foolish and irresponsible, and yet the parallels in their acquisitional processes are striking. The impetus for acquiring written forms is similar to the impetus for learning how to talk. Children living in a print-rich environment, surrounded by print, and participating in a print culture become aware of the functions and forms of literacy very early. They begin using the print they see as models for their own writing, trying out shapes to represent meaning, using scribble writing to represent cursive writing, and developing control over letters of the alphabet—at first to represent words or syllables, and eventually to represent specific speech sounds. Like early babbling and speech, early writing forms are matters of trial and error, experimentation and testing. The forms change shape and have varied meaning to the young writer, but at the base of it all is the awareness that print means something. Children are always intent on making meaning. For example, when my son was writing his "autobiography" as a sixth-grader, my four-year-old daughter was "scribble writing" hers on her own piece of paper—"writing" from left to right, scribbles that clearly resembled cursive writing: "I was born in Sparrow Hospital . . ." she said, as she "read" her writing aloud to me, playing with the forms of her "autobiography" once she understood its function. Understanding the function of writing gives children opportunities for trying out the forms. A child wants to write letters to Santa, to write a letter to his grandparents, to write the grocery list for his father. Surrounded by the forms of print—greeting cards, letters, newspapers, stories, books, lists, environmental print—children quickly begin experimenting with the structure. They move from scribble writing modeled on cursive to using the alphabetic principles upon which written English is based (Weaver, 1988). Like children acquiring their oral language, writers rarely participate in imitative behaviors unless they are required to do so, but rather use written language as models for their own experimentations.

When my daughter was five, she left a note for me on the dining room table, written while I was at a conference in California (see Figure 2.1).

What does this child know about written language? Besides knowing how some sounds are represented by letters, she understands directionality in print, the function of letters or notes, the form those letters take, and the appropriate form for this social event. None of this knowledge was "learned" through direct instruction; she figured it out from reading, observing, experimenting with written forms.

Dear Mom
I hope that you got there
safely I love you very
much

FIGURE 2.1 ***Note Written by a Five-Year-Old***

The key concept here is principle-formation, the experimentation that allows children to form assumptions about how writing works, what its forms are, how meaning is expressed symbolically on the page or screen. Teachers of young children who understand this developmental process allow language play in writing just as parents and caregivers encourage it in oral language development. In short, social and literate practices within speech communities provide the model that young children need to acquire the forms and functions of language within their speech communities.

Like young children learning their oral language, older students honing their writing skills need a supportive environment in which experimentation and risk-taking are not only tolerated but encouraged and fostered. Adolescents need to try their hand at writing within a variety of genres, experimenting with language forms and different sentence structures. How else will a middle-school student learn how to master writing good dialogue, more complex sentence structures with sophisticated punctuation, or interesting introductions? Freedom to experiment with language forms and genres, without risk, is critical to good writing development. Writers who fear making mistakes are writers whose writing is likely to be safe, traditional, and dull. It behooves writing teachers to take a chapter from young children's acquisition of language and apply those principles to adolescents and their writing.

The "Messiness" of Acquisitional Processes. The process of acquiring written and oral language is often non-linear, messy, full of what appear to be regressions, not easily modified by direct correction. Children do not first simply learn all the sounds of the language, then all the words, and finally all the possible syntactic rules; rather they must struggle with meaning and syntax at the same time as trying to master the rules of pronunciation. They must struggle with the nuances of meaning as they weave their way through the social context in which they are using language. Developing writers, too, must make connections between words in print and the meaning they represent, between the function of the words they are writing—to tell a story, to thank Uncle Harold for the birthday present, or to write a grocery list that has Coke or Cheerios or Pop Tarts on it. While they are figuring out functions for writing, they are trying to master the design of the alphabet. While experimenting with spelling, they are trying to figure out how to arrange words on the page. Acquisition of writing, like acquisition of speech, never occurs in a straight line from simple to complex, from one level to another.

As part of the "messy" acquisitional process, correction of language, written or spoken, rarely has the effect that caregivers wish; the child needs to acquire new forms by trial and error. Moskowitz (536) cites the example of the child who says to his mother, "Nobody don't like me," to which his mother replies in an attempt to correct the sentence, "Nobody likes me." The child then repeats his earlier version and the mother her corrected version several times until, in desperation, the mother says, "Now listen carefully: Nobody likes me!" at which point the son finally gets the idea and says, "Oh! Nobody don't likes me!" Aside from the mother's questionable reinforcement of a negative self-concept, she is essentially clueless about how language development actually occurs. As Moskowitz says,

> . . . children do not always understand exactly what it is the adult is correcting. The information the adult is trying to impart may be at odds with the information in the child's head, namely the rules the child is postulating for producing language. The surface correction of a sentence does not give the child a clue about how to revise the rule that produced the sentence (536).

In writing for elementary and secondary students, too, until the student is able to conceptualize for herself what the teacher is recommending, correction has limited value. Developing writers, like oral language learners, need to experiment with language without fear of correction. Like young speakers, writers of all ages need opportunities to try out hypotheses about how written language works, what forms work best, what structures are the most effective for negotiating meaning. When secondary students fear that a perfect end product is the only goal of a writing assignment, the naturalness of the writing dissipates and the form becomes the focus of attention. Older writers who worry about getting all the punctuation right in the first draft rarely take chances with their writing, try out more sophisticated structures, or try new genres. There is safety in the tried and true; there is also little learning.

As in oral language development, correction in writing does not always have long-lasting effects. If the writer is not at the cognitive point of understanding the nature of the correction, it is likely to fall on deaf ears—or on silent pencils. Teachers are all too familiar with the lack of transfer from a grammar lesson to the student's own writing. Familiar, too, are the repeated errors writers make from one paper to another, despite constant correction. Until students have the metacognitive ability to generalize from one instance to another, correction may not be very effective.

Risk-taking in written language also involves learning, relearning, and restructuring old assumptions to form new ones. A case in point is the tendency towards "regression" in language development. Those predictable movements forward to more complex structures in writing or speech sometimes suffer what appear to be setbacks, in which adult-like forms are rejected in favor of structures conforming to the child's internalized system of language (Moskowitz). For example, at one point children often use irregular forms of very common past tenses and plurals accurately: "went" and "ran," "feet" and "men." Yet, *at a later stage,* when they are acquiring the regular past tense and plural rules, they may "regress" from using forms like "ran" and "feet" to using "runned" and "foots" or "feets." This regression, of course, is not really a movement backward to a less sophisticated form but rather an indication of their developing ability to generalize the rule system for past tense and plural. "Regression" is a result of rule development that in its early stages may be overgeneralized and applied too liberally before exceptions to the rules are mastered at a later time. Young writers, too, whose early sentences are short enough to each fit on separate lines, may seem to regress in their understanding of writing from left to right as they begin to realize that on-going writing can flow over onto the next line. After writing very short sentences from left to right (using his own form of creative spelling), my five-year-old son wrote his letter to Santa, starting from left to right for the first line, then right to left on the second. This "regression" was momentary, but a clear sign of his having moved ahead in his understanding of written language.

Many young writers with the ability to use commas and periods correctly in simple syntactic structures begin to struggle with punctuation all over again when their written syntax becomes more complex. What may appear to be regressive behavior in the use of punctuation is actually a reflection of the demands of greater syntactic complexity. Errors, as Constance Weaver (1996) suggests, are frequently signs of progress. As elementary and secondary writers' ideas become more complex and as writers grapple with issues they are still in the process of understanding, their cognitive confusions may result in confused syntax, awkward word choice, and inappropriate writing conventions. For example, as writers begin to use embedded clauses and phrases to deal with causal relationships, their attempts to express these complex ideas may for a while result in awkward syntax, increased use of sentence fragments, dangling modifiers, more convoluted sentences. Teachers unaware of these patterns may see these errors as regression without realizing that more sophisticated errors are replacing less sophisticated ones (Weaver 1996, 72).

The writer who has discovered the effective use of subordinate clauses in writing may use them for a time ad nauseum. The child who discovers the use of the apostrophe and applies it appropriately in possessive nouns may also use it indiscriminately with all words that end in "s." It's not unusual for second graders who've discovered the joys of the exclamation mark to use at the end of every sentence, sometimes even in mid-sentence! and sometimes in multiples at the ends of sentences!!!

Part of this written language play results in idiosyncratic forms that sometimes strike terror in the hearts of parents or teachers: if we allow invented spelling, for example, in first grade, won't those "incorrect" spelling patterns become habitual? If we encourage new complex sentence structures that sometimes result in sentence fragments and run-on sentences, won't they become structures of habit? If we encourage experimentation with vocabulary, won't students fail to learn the "correct" form? The answer, for the most part, is no. Children and adolescents, through more reading and writing, begin to modify those patterns in the direction of traditional spelling patterns, syntactic patterns, and vocabulary choices. Giving them freedom to experiment encourages developing writers at any age to try new forms, to take risks, and to play with language as a way of discovering what does and does not work stylistically. Much of this cannot be taught; it must be acquired through writing.

Think/Write #3

We learn to write by doing a lot of writing, and often our writing is a reflection of our reading. Write a brief description of how you developed as a writer. What impact did the reading you participated in as an elementary student have on your own writing? For example, do you have any samples of your early writing that reflect the structure or the plot of one of your favorite stories? Did you write poetry because you loved the poems of Shel Silverstein? What kinds of writing models did you have? Or write a description of your development as a user of oral language. What "cute" childhood stories have your parents passed along to you as you developed oral language?

Cultural Differences in Literacy Development

While the processes of acquiring the functions and forms of language are similar across speech communities and cultures, the specifics may differ. Negative forms may differ between Standard English and African American spoken and written patterns; verb forms may differ between Appalachian vernacular speech/writing and northern vernacular speech/writing. However different in form, they are not different in quality. All speakers operate with a fully-formed, rule-governed system of language. No dialect is an impoverished version of an ideal standard (which doesn't exist anyway). All dialects are linguistically complex systems of communication.

The functions of language, too, may differ operationally across communities. Question-asking/answering, which is a universal speech act, operates in different ways in different speech communities, as Heath's study in the Piedmont Carolinas indicates. Roadville children (working-class European Americans) are socialized partially through their participation in answering known-answer questions that their caregivers ask, such as: "What color is that?" or "Where's your nose?" as a way of demonstrating the child's knowledge, while caregivers in the Trackton community (African American) see little purpose in asking questions that have obvious, known answers. Instead they provide language models rich in metaphor and storying. Because the role of conversation with young children, therefore, varies from one community to another, children have different experiences with the function of language, with the role of participation, and therefore with differences that may be contrary to middle-class school expectations when children reach school age.

The stories kids want to write may also differ in structure and genre across speech communities because of how stories are represented in different cultures. Episodic narratives favored by many young African American writers are different from the more tightly structured narratives favored by most middle-class teachers. The uses to which writing is put may also vary culturally, because those forms and functions are acquired by observation and participation in the community. Children growing up with computers will be much more at ease with e-mail structures and chat-room formats than children without easy access to technology. Some children learn the format for writing personal letters because they send and receive them; others learn the format for informal journals because parents keep a travel journal on family vacations; and still others learn the structure of newspaper editorials because Sunday mornings are filled with parents reading editorial comments to one another from the *Morning Gazette.* Just as our oral language structures reflect our linguistic environments, so our interest in particular kinds of writing mirrors our exposure and experience to those genres of writing.

Direct Instruction and Issues of Writing Development

It stands to reason, of course, that younger writers write more grammatically simple sentences than older, more experienced writers do. As is true of oral language development, writers develop greater fluency in writing as they develop increasing ability to hold several ideas in mind within a single, complex sentence or group of sentences, their vocabulary gets more sophisticated, and they are increasingly able to make stylistic choices that are marks of writing maturity. Most of these abilities develop, less as a consequence of direct instruction, and more as a result of cognitive development and growing conscious awareness of structures, forms, and purposes of writing. Wide reading, of course, aids the development of writing, so every good writing program will include lots of reading and lots of talk. (A more detailed discussion of developmental issues in writing fluency is found in Chapter Four.)

The forms and functions of writing, too, develop in increasingly sophisticated ways. James Britton, et al., in their massive study of writing development in Great Britain, suggest that younger writers often start naturally with expressive forms of writing—verbalizations of writer's needs, preoccupations, and feelings; personal letters; personal journals; notes and letters to familiar persons in the writer's life. It is this function of writing—the expression of personal opinions—from which more sophisticated forms of writing occur. In developmental terms, the authors state, "The expressive is a kind of matrix from which differentiated forms of mature writing are developed" (83).

If, as we have seen, much of writing acquisition—both the forms and structures of writing and the functions of writing—occurs indirectly and naturally as a result of participating in a literate environment, what is the role of direct instruction in the writing classroom? Obviously some direct instruction in the process of writing development is necessary and important. We see the teacher's role as three-fold: 1) to create a supportive environment for those natural processes of writing development to occur; 2) to provide encouragement, coaching, and guidance; and 3) to provide developmentally appropriate direct instruction about structure, form, audience, and purpose. The first two roles provide support for the acquisition of writing to occur, and the third provides learned knowledge that enables writers to consciously manipulate language for effective writing. Teachers who guide and coach their students are aware that writers need support structures in the curriculum that foster good writing practices; opportunities to use writing for a range of real audiences and self-sponsored purposes; continued experimentation with written forms and functions and opportunities for language play; and a focus on the links between their own writing and local literacy needs. Writing letters to the city council for constructing roller blade facilities, writing for the school newspaper, researching health issues that affect young people or senior citizens, contributing to a class magazine or newsletter for parents, writing expressively or poetically to explore issues and ideas are all authentic writing experiences with real purposes and audiences, and with real consequences.

Direct instruction can be effective at certain developmental stages—and at various stages in the writing process. Writing teachers who see a particular need for direct instruction in the forms or genres students are developing or in the appropriate use of the semi-colon can develop mini-lessons at the point of need, directed toward the writing issues emerging from student writing. Direct instruction will be most effective in the appropriate stages of writing—during the revision and editing stages of the process. With the teacher as guide and coach, initial feedback to student work should focus on the ideas; matters of correct word choice, punctuation, and writing conventions are better left to the editing stage near the end of the process. Despite our reluctance to endorse direct correction too early in the stages of writing, we do want to stress that some direct teaching about sentence structures, writing conventions, and organizational patterns will be an important part of the writing classroom when students are cognitively ready to deal with this information. Knowing the connections between oral and written language development and seeing writing as a language process will encourage the appropriate kind of direct instruction. Our discussion in the following chapters, we believe, provides a rich, comprehensive view of writing development across secondary grade levels that will help writing teachers make good decisions about the kind of guidance young writers need.

Points to Remember

Literacy is a complicated concept going well beyond simply the ability to read and write. Part of the complexity lies in differences among different speech communities and cultural groups who may use literacy in different ways from one another. Literacy is also complicated by the growing demands for critical literacy that require readers and writers to do more than express personal opinions. Critical literacy demands an awareness on the part of readers and writers that they have power individually and collectively to make political changes through their literacy. When readers/writers use their abilities to negotiate positive change for personal and public reasons, literacy becomes an instrument for individual and social change.

The acquisition of literacy, like the acquisition of oral language, is less the result of direct instruction than it is the opportunity to regularly participate in meaningful reading and writing activities, self-sponsored as well as school-imposed. The reading that children and young adults do provides the models for writing: reading poetry inspires its writing; seeing the effects of writing published in school newspapers encourages others to write in response; and learning the structures of acceptable written forms occurs most naturally when students have lots of reading to serve as models. Direct correction of writing, like the correction of oral language, has a limited effect, unless the writer is at the point of understanding the nature of the correction and can see the application to further writing. Lots of correction is less effective than lots of continued writing.

And finally, schools need to rethink the focus on the dominant function of writing to demonstrate knowledge. Writing to learn, to explore ideas, to develop habits of critical thinking is equally important—and necessary—to help students develop a wide range of writing functions within a variety of print and nonprint media in order to operate effectively in our society.

For Further Reading

Barton, David. *Literacy: An Introduction to the Ecology of Written Language.* Oxford, UK: Blackwell, 1994.

Gee, James Paul. *Social Linguistics and Literacies: Ideology in Discourses.* 2nd ed. London: Falmer Press, 1996.

Heath, Shirley Brice. *Ways with Words: Language, Life, and Work in Communities and Classrooms.* Cambridge: Cambridge University Press, 1983.

Moskowitz, Breyne A. "The Acquisition of Language." *Language: Readings In Language and Culture.* 6th ed. Ed. V. Clark, P. Eschholz, and A. Rosa. New York: St. Martin's Press, 1998.

Pinker, Steven. *The Language Instinct: How the Mind Creates Language.* New York: HarperCollins, 1994.

3

Teaching Writing as a Process

Writing in the schools has undergone a tremendous change in recent years. Teachers have been encouraged to re-think both methodology and goals as composition instruction shifted from a focus on the finished written product to the process writers use to achieve that final product. Consequently, the classroom environment for writing has changed dramatically. So has the teacher's role in writing instruction and expectations for student writing behaviors. This chapter will chronicle that change, describing the theoretical influences and research that pointed out deficiencies in previous writing instruction and promoted more effective classroom strategies for young writers. We will then move on to describe a full array of methods and approaches for teaching writing as a process in the secondary classroom.

The information in this chapter will prepare teachers of English language arts by addressing the NCATE/NCTE standards listed below.

3.2.1 Demonstrate in creative and innovative ways through their own work and teaching the influence of language and visual images on thinking and composing;

3.2.2 Integrate on a consistent basis writing, speaking, and observing as major forms of inquiry, reflection, and expression into all of their coursework and teaching;

3.2.3 Demonstrate skill with composing processes to create various forms of oral, visual, and written literacy of their own, and show evidence of teaching those processes to students;

3.2.4 Demonstrate through their own learning and teaching the functions and purposes of writing, visual images, and speaking for a variety of audiences and purposes;

3.4 Gain knowledge and understanding of different composing processes;

3.4.1 Use a wide variety of writing strategies to generate meaning and clarify understanding and incorporate that knowledge into their teaching;

3.4.2 Demonstrate their ability to produce different forms of written discourse and teach them to students;

3.4.3 Demonstrate on a regular basis throughout the program how written discourse can influence thought and action and incorporate this knowledge into teaching;

3.7.1 Use major sources of research theory related to English language arts consistently to support their teaching decisions.

The Traditional Writing Classroom

For the better part of the twentieth century, writing instruction at the secondary level typically looked like this:

The English teacher would assign a topic or list three or four alternative topics on the board, then spend a few minutes explaining what was expected, perhaps encouraging students to use detail and description or organize clearly or write in an interesting way. After she answered questions students had—usually of the "how long does it have to be?" and "can I write in pencil?" variety—students would write for the rest of the period while the teacher busied herself at her desk, stopping occasionally to admonish anyone who dared whisper to a neighbor ("Do your own work, please.") or answer a student's question about spelling. Ten minutes before the period ended, the teacher would remind students of the time, suggesting that they try to finish quickly in order to go back over their papers to find and correct errors. The papers were turned in at the end of the period as students filed out.

The conscientious teacher's job began here: with red pen in hand, she laboriously combed through each essay, marking each error, making brief generic comments in the margin such as "good!" "confusing," "awkward," "well done," putting a grade and final comment at the end of the paper. Before returning the graded set, the teacher often read one or two of the best papers to the class while students listened restlessly, worrying about their own grade or trying to figure out who wrote the selected papers. Sometimes students would spend the rest of the period correcting the errors the teacher had pointed out.

In effect, every writing assignment was a test of the student's present writing ability rather than an opportunity to develop further as a writer and thinker. Note the grim atmosphere in which any talk was forbidden, the need to get it right the first time, the lack of support, response, or instruction from the teacher or classmates while writing was in process. Under these circumstances, every paper the teacher marked was a rough draft, the student's first thoughts on the topic, spilled out with little time to ponder or plan, check spelling or grammar, get response from a reader. Yet teachers marked these papers meticulously even though they were the product of a hasty 40 or 50 minutes of silent writing. Sometimes a teacher would assign a paper on Monday for students to write at home and turn in on Friday, which ostensibly gave students more time to think through the topic and produce a more polished paper. But students were still completely on their own as they wrote unless they drew on the help of parents and friends. The teacher not only controlled the topics students wrote about, but was also the only audience for the paper.

Composition instruction centered on two kinds of activities: 1) grammar and usage lessons accompanied by practice exercises with artificial sentences and canned errors from a grammar and composition textbook; 2) instruction in forms and formulas: the five-paragraph theme; the compare/contrast paper; notecard, footnote and bibliography format for research papers; the importance of "showing, not telling." Students were also expected to learn how to write a better paper next time from seeing the comments and grades on their marked papers, perhaps the major reason teachers spent so much time on this even though numerous studies of paper marking gave clear evidence that intensive marking of student writing had little effect on writing improvement (Braddock 1963; Haynes 1978).

Charles Cooper, describing writing in the schools for the Foreword to Applebee's 1981 research report *Writing in the Secondary School: English and the Content Areas,* labels this approach "a writing program certain to fail" (12). And that really was the end result. The majority of students came to dislike writing, even fear it, an attitude that spilled over onto the writing teacher, who was accused of "red-pencilitis" and "error-hunting," giving writing instruction negative associations, drawing groans even today from adults when asked to write.

Throughout almost three-quarters of the twentieth century, writing instruction was in a state of alchemy. Based on the study of Latin and Greek grammar, focused on appropriate form and mechanical/grammatical correctness as if these were the sole characteristics of effective writing, composition as construed in secondary classrooms and writing texts did little to support *the writer*—emphasis was on the finished product, the paper with all its flaws corrected. Teachers had little knowledge of how to help their students become better writers other than to keep on teaching out of the grammar book with the assumption that if you teach form and correctness, content falls into place. Laments from teachers like "How can I expect them to write a paper when they can't even write a correct sentence?" betray a serious lack of understanding about how writers write, how thoughts become language on the page, and how teachers can influence effective writing behaviors.

The belief that grammatical knowledge and correct form were crucial to effective writing can be seen in Figure 3.1, the section on writing from the Table of Contents of Warriner's *English Grammar and Composition: Complete Course,* 1957 edition, a text series for grades 7–12 widely used in secondary schools for decades, in many editions.

Part Six, Writing Compositions, is preceded by the following five sections in this order: 1) grammar review, 2) writing correct sentences, 3) writing clear sentences, 4) writing smooth sentences, and 5) using the library. It is followed by a section on speaking and listening and a final section on mechanics: capitalization, punctuation, manuscript form, and spelling. This organization suggests that a thorough study of grammatical terms and sentence construction must occur before students write. Note also the emphasis on the final product that permeates Part Six: organizing and outlining are paramount as are topic sentences (a construct

PART SIX

Writing Compositions

24. The Effective Paragraph
The Topic Sentence • The Concluding or Clincher Sentence • Development of the Topic Sentence into a Paragraph • Adequate Development of the Topic Sentence • Unity in the Paragraph • Coherence in the Paragraph • Arrangement of Details • Linking Expressions and Connectives

25. The Whole Composition
Selecting and Limiting the Subject • Assembling Materials • Organizing Materials—Outlining • The Topical Outline • The Sentence Outline • Rules for Form in Making an Outline • Writing the First Draft • The Introduction • Paragraphing • The Conclusion • Revising the First Draft • Preparing the Final Draft • Summary • Suggested Topics for Composition

26. Clear Thinking
Inductive Reasoning • Deductive Reasoning • Reasoning by Analogy • Thinking Clearly About Cause and Effect • The Irrelevant Fact—"Off-the-Subject" Arguments

27. Exercises in Composition
The Garbled Paragraph • The Précis • The Essay of Opinion • The One-Paragraph Factual Report

28. Narrative Writing
Recognizing Story Material • Writing about What You Know • Learning by Writing • Planning a Narrative • Narrative Style • Building a Plot • Exercises in Narration

29. The Research Paper
Selecting and Limiting the Subject • Preparing a Working Bibliography • Preparing a Preliminary Outline • Reading and Taking Notes • Assembling Your Notes and Writing the Final Outline • Writing the First Draft • Writing the Final Draft • Footnotes • Bibliography

30. Letter Writing
The Friendly Letter • Social Notes • The Informal Invitation • The Informal Reply • The Thank-You Note • The Bread-and-Butter Note • The Formal Invitation and Reply • The Business Letter • The Order Letter • The Letter of Inquiry or Request • The Letter of Adjustment or Complaint • The Letter of Application • Business Letter Exercises

---

FIGURE 3.1

From the Table of Contents, *English Grammar and Composition* by John E. Warriner, copyright 1957 by Harcourt, Brace & World, Inc., reprinted by permisson of the publisher.

that research shows exists only in composition textbooks, not in real world writing). Nowhere are writers encouraged to develop or explore their ideas, consider readers, or seek response to what has been written. Writing is construed as a solitary occupation focusing on getting the forms and formulas right.

The idea that writing was a matter of transcribing ideas already mentally formed and organized pervaded instruction. As an example, here are the steps students were to use for writing a personal narrative given in a 1958 curriculum guide used by teachers in the Philadelphia schools:

A. Decide upon an experience that is worth writing about (unusual, exciting, amazing)
B. Jot down notes as to what should be told
C. Arrange your notes in logical order
D. Think of a topic sentence to give the key to the meaning
E. Think of a forceful closing sentence
F. Choose a title that attracts attention
G. Write the paragraph
(*A Guide to the Teaching of English Composition Grades 7 to 12,* 4)

According to this formula, students were to be taught that everything, from the title to the closing sentence, should be worked out before they wrote the paper. In an accompanying parenthesis, the teacher was also advised that "Pupils should strive to write clear, entertaining compositions in good taste and technically correct as to form, punctuation, spelling. Enriching the vocabulary should always be kept in mind" (4).

One of our own experiences teaching writing to tenth graders in the 1960s from this "assign and mark" product-centered paradigm illustrates the frustration many teachers felt at what seemed like a labor-intensive yet ineffectual component of the English curriculum since students improved so little despite the teacher's arduous efforts:

> After a 45-minute in-class writing session, a student turned in a stunning description of a street fight he'd witnessed. Vivid, detailed, full of dialogue and description, it was the kind of rich and fluent narration readers hunger for. But the only punctuation on two full pages of prose was a capital letter at the start and a period at the end. I didn't know how to grade it, how to respond to it (circling all the errors was out of the question), how to help the student harness his considerable power as a writer. In response to the same assignment, another student turned in a perfectly punctuated, perfectly correct, perfectly empty half page of writing. When she asked me why she only got a "C" even though she had no errors, all I could answer was, "It should have been longer." I didn't know how to help her either. All my teacher training courses, all the books I'd read about the teaching of English, hadn't given me the methods I needed to help these students become better . . . writers. (Rosen 1992, 6)

We talk of a "product emphasis" in the past teaching of writing in contrast to the present "process emphasis," but past writing instruction had more serious problems than simply a focus on the product. We were teaching writing without understanding what it meant to be a writer, focusing instruction on characteristics of the final written product with no attention paid to the processes, knowledges, and support necessary for a writer to compose. Unfortunately, some classrooms and school writing programs are still based on this current-traditional model despite the groundbreaking research of the 1970s and 1980s leading to a new model for teaching writing. The historical roots of the current-traditional model, discussed in greater detail in the final chapter, make it particularly tenacious even into the twenty-first century.

Think/Write #1

Think about your own writing experiences in middle school and high school. Jot down what you remember. How were writing assignments made by your teachers? What kinds of writing instruction did you receive? Is the pattern just described familiar to you or were you taught methods to help you with the process of writing? What assumptions about writing appeared to shape the approaches your writing teachers used?

Now reflect on your responses to the writing instruction you received. When you were in middle school and high school, how did you feel about school-based writing? Why?

A New Model Emerges

Although the seeds of change in composition instruction had been sown throughout the twentieth century, the event that most influenced our thinking about language and composition was the Anglo-American conference on the teaching of English, held at Dartmouth College in the summer of 1966, reported in John Dixon's *Growth through English* (1967). The British emphasis on a personal growth model for English instruction, one based on the students' needs, interests, and linguistic growth, rather than on a prescribed curriculum, dominated the conference. The act of writing, the importance of classroom talk, the need to foster students' creativity as well as their intellectual ability made a lasting impression on the U.S. conference attendees. They began to think about using writing for self-discovery and self-expression, a concept virtually foreign to composition instruction in U.S. schools at that time. A statement made by James Britton, a writing researcher from the University of London, that "the writing may be the act of perceiving the shape of experience,—not the evidence that it has [once] been perceived" (Dixon 45) stands in sharp contrast to the formula described earlier that assumes the act of writing is a matter of transcribing one's already-known thoughts. These new ideas were embodied in an innovative writing text by James E. Miller, whose *Word, Self, Reality: The Rhetoric of Imagination* (1972) invites writers to use language to better understand and shape their world. The following assumptions upon which Miller bases his text introduce concepts that now form the core of contemporary writing instruction.

According to Miller, writing must be motivated from within, tapping personal feelings, needs, and experiences, whether the piece is a research paper driven by a problem of special interest to the writer or a poem to a loved one. When writing is motivated by such inner needs, students will draw on their own rich store of linguistic resources to find language to say what they mean. In order for writing to be highly motivated, it must be a meaningful task for the writer, serving real purposes such as self-exploration, discovery of new ideas, or communication of the writer's thoughts to others. Finally, Miller believed that writers will pay attention to correctness when they have a strong desire to reach readers who care about this (Miller 3). These ideas provide a foundation for our contention in this text that good writing comes from the writer's sense that the work is purposeful, personally meaningful, and written to be read by an audience beyond the teacher with a grade book.

Another innovative text from this period was Donald Murray's *A Writer Teaches Writing: A Practical Method of Teaching Composition* (1968). A Pulitzer Prize-winning journalist as well as a writing teacher at the University of New Hampshire, Murray based this text on what he understood about composing from his own considerable experience as a practicing professional writer and teacher. Focusing on the writer and the process of composing, the text was another groundbreaking move toward a new writing curriculum. The Table of Contents shown in Figure 3.2 illustrates Murray's radical new approach.

Note the emphasis on what the *writer* must do: discover a subject (not write about one handed out by the teacher), think about a possible audience (not write to please the teacher), collect material for the writing, plan, write, revise. The teacher's role is altered, too: listener, coach, diagnostician, fellow-writer. Compare Murray's approach to the assumptions about writing implicit in the Table of Contents from Warriner's 1957 composition handbook shown in Figure 3.1 to get an even clearer sense of how original his ideas were. Murray is one of the first to talk about the importance of a positive and supportive climate for writing in which "the student speaks and the teacher listens" (103), and to recommend having students write for real readers, not just for the teacher. Perhaps Murray's most important contributions to a new way of thinking about composition were his emphasis on revision as a process of rethinking and rewriting—"All good writing is rewriting" (230)—and his belief that writing is a process of discovery, that the writer generates new ideas and discovers new meanings through the act of composing. Note the similarity here to Britton's concept that the act of writing leads to "perceiving the shape of experience." The title of Murray's brief essay, "Teach Writing as a Process not Product" (1972) became the motto for this new model of writing instruction.

Ken Macrorie's *Writing to Be Read* (1968) and *Telling Writing* (1970) added to the growing movement toward change by introducing free writing, the unstructured, unfocused, tapping of inner ideas and resources to explore what a writer knows and can write about. He recommended that writers keep a journal and try to develop a strong personal "voice" in their writing, avoiding what he termed "Engfish," the phony, pretentious language of the academic establishment.

Contents

FIGURE 3.2

Table of Contents from *A Writer Teaches Writing* by Donald Murray, Houghton Mifflin Company, 1968. Reprinted with the permission of Donald M. Murray.

Macrorie's description of the Helping Circle in which students read their drafts aloud to a small group for responses led the way toward peer critique groups and collaborative writing projects.

We must not omit Peter Elbow here as another composition theorist challenging the tradition. His 1973 writing guide, *Writing without Teachers,* elaborated on the values and purposes of free writing, urging writers to start writing before meaning is clear to them and to use the processes of composing and revising to clarify their thinking. He called this "a way to grow and cook a message" (15). Elbow felt it was crucial to separate composing from editing: writers should first write freely to get their ideas down in an unrestricted fashion and only then become critical evaluators of their own work for rewriting and final editing. Building on Macrorie's idea of the Helping Circle, Elbow devised methods and procedures for writers to use when sharing their drafts. Several of these will be described later on in this chapter.

Think/Write #2

Examine the Table of Contents of a composition textbook presently used in a secondary English classroom or look at the one you used for your college freshman composition course if you still have it. What assumptions about writing has the textbook's author made in selecting and organizing material for the book? What does the student learn to do? What role does the teacher play? Compare the Table of Contents in your text to Warriner's and Murray's: which text is it most like?

Would you like to take (or did you like taking) a writing class based on the ideas in this text? Why or why not?

As composition instructors developed new models for the classroom based on a fuller understanding of how writers write instead of on the prescriptive approaches of composition textbooks, researchers studied writing in the schools and the composing processes of writers. Three research studies that came out about the same time as these textbooks furthered the changes in thinking and teaching that were beginning to occur.

In 1971, Janet Emig's case studies of six high school writers, reported in *The Composing Processes of Twelfth Graders,* fueled interest in developing a better understanding of what happens when a writer writes and led the way to a series of studies aimed at helping us better understand the writing process. Emig taped her young writers composing aloud and collected autobiographies of their writing experiences. Her analysis showed two distinct modes of composing used by these twelfth graders:

Reflexive Writing: Self-sponsored

- Writer focuses on thoughts and feelings about experiences.
- Audience is the self.
- Domain explored is usually the affective .
- Style is tentative, personal, exploratory.
- Process takes longer; steps include pre-writing, thinking, stopping and starting, reformulation, aesthetic contemplation.

Extensive Writing: School-sponsored, assigned

- Writer focuses on conveying a message.
- Audience is others, beyond the self.
- Domain explored is usually the cognitive.
- Style is assured, impersonal, reportorial.
- Writing process is truncated, dominated by attention to stylistic principles. (3–4)

Comparing students' writing and thinking processes in these two modes, Emig was very critical of writing in the schools. Self-sponsored reflexive writing done outside the school setting allowed time for reflection, personal involvement, and aesthetic pleasure in the final product. By comparison, school-based extensive writing assigned by teachers who were usually not writers themselves oversimplified the writing process. Pre-writing and planning were reduced to outlining; revision was a matter of correcting "minor infelicities." Emig concluded that school-based writing for secondary students in the U.S. was "a limited, and limiting, experience," dominated by the five-paragraph theme, and perpetuated by teachers "interested chiefly in a product [they] can criticize rather than in a process [they] can help initiate through imagination and sustain through empathy and support" (97). She called for major changes in the way writing is taught in schools, recommending that writing teachers write themselves in both the extensive and reflexive modes, which would lead them to offer broader writing opportunities to their students.

Donald Graves (1975) also studied the writing process, using naturalistic observation and case studies of seven-year-old children in two classroom environments, formal and informal. He found that when children are permitted to choose their own topics and decide for themselves whether or not to write, they write more and in greater length than when given specific writing assignments. Graves divided the writing process into a Pre-writing Phase (including what he termed "rehearsal" of ideas by drawing or talking to others), a Composing Phase, and a Post-writing Phase. Even with such young writers, he claimed "the writing process is as variable and unique as the individual's personality" (35).

Partly as a result of these studies, interest in the composing process grew, leading to numerous other case studies exploring various aspects of the writing process. Researchers analyzed the composing processes of unskilled college writers (Perl 1979), compared the revision strategies of student writers and experienced adult writers (Sommers 1980), studied writer's block (Rose 1980), studied pausing and planning during the composing process (Matsuhashi 1981), and analyzed Donald Murray's writing process to learn more about how professional writers compose (Berkenkotter 1983). This research, contributing heavily to our understanding of what happens when a writer writes, brought new ideas and methodologies to the composition classroom.

A third study of writing in the schools that merits attention was the work done by James Britton and his colleagues at the University of London. They created two classificatory systems to categorize the 2,122 samples of student writing they collected, devising ways of looking at writing that still influence our thinking today.

The first of these classifications deals with audience—the relationship between writer and readers. For this they devised the following audience categories:

1. Self
2. Teacher
   child (or adolescent) to trusted adult
   pupil to teacher, general (teacher-learner dialogue)
   pupil to teacher, particular relationship
   pupil to examiner
3. Known wider audience
   expert to known layman
   child (or adolescent) to peer group
   group member to working group
4. Unknown audience
   writer to unknown public readers (66)

Note how these categories move in a continuum outward from a personal, private, and known audience to a more general, public, and unknown audience.

The second of these classifications is the function or purpose for writing, a response to the question "Why are you writing?" (74). They categorized writing in three ways: expressive, transactional, and poetic. *Expressive writing*—personal, informal, exploratory writing—is seen as the foundation for the development of the more public and formal writings in the transactional and poetic modes. The purpose for expressive writing is *to think aloud on paper,* to use writing as a process of discovery in order to explore ideas and express thoughts and feelings. Expressive language is often informal, unpolished, and unstructured—a means for discovering what one has to say rather than attempting to communicate it to readers. Journals, diaries, notes, lists, free writing, and exploratory first drafts are examples of expressive writing. More formal, structured, public forms of writing develop from the expressive in two dimensions: poetic and transactional. The British researchers describe *poetic writing* as *a work of art made of language,* whose purpose is to create an aesthetic object pleasing to the reader in which the form is part of the substance of the message; for example, poetry, stories, novels, and drama. *Transactional writing,* they define as writing *to get things done,* to communicate ideas to others, transact business, record facts, transmit knowledge, and exchange opinions. The language of transactional writing is formal, structured, and usually error-free. This form of writing includes essays, literary analysis, business letters, memos, reports, editorials, and all manner of argumentative and persuasive writing. By its very nature, transactional writing is rhetorical in its focus and implementation, situating the writing within an authentic context that will require the writer to make rhetorical judgments based on the purpose of the piece and the needs of readers (88–91).

The findings of these researchers about the state of writing in the British schools echoed Emig's conclusions about writing in U.S. schools. In the audience category, almost 50 percent of the papers were written for the teacher as examiner, with the second largest category the teacher-learner dialogue. Painfully little writing was done for the self or for wider audiences both within and beyond the school setting. Writing was a way of proving to the teacher that the student had done the work and knew the material. As for the functions of writing, transactional writing predominated, especially informative writing, increasing steadily over the four age levels of the sample papers. Poetic writing tended to be limited to English classes in the earlier years of the study. Expressive writing was rarely used in school, much to the disappointment of the researchers, who believed it to be "the key to developing confidence and range in using written language" (142). Britton argues, therefore, that discrepancies exist between the ways writers work naturally—using expressive writing for exploring and understanding—and the way many teachers and composition texts advise or require students to write.

A final factor in initiating change in writing instruction was the Bay Area Writing Project, started in 1975 and now federally funded as the National Writing Project with sites throughout the United States. Based on the premise that a teacher of writing must be a practicing writer in order to understand the writing process first-hand, these projects also introduced teachers to the newest theory and research in writing and provided a forum for the rich exchange of ideas about classroom practice. All of these forces for change, coming from researchers and teachers, theorists and textbook writers, led to what Maxine Hairston (1982) has termed a "paradigm shift" in the teaching of writing: the writing process model.

Teaching Writing as a Process

What do we mean by "the writing process"? What do you teach when you are using a writing process approach? What does a writing process classroom look like? This section will answer these questions and provide multiple methods for teaching students to do what practicing writers do as they work their way to a finished piece of writing.

Underlying this approach to teaching writing is our belief that writing is "meaning making": these processes stimulate the kind of "thinking on paper" that leads to discovery of new meaning and the shaping of experience. Jotting down rough ideas, revising, rereading, reshaping content and language, all help produce not only better writing, but also new ideas, clearer ideas, more meaningful pieces for both the writer and the reader. Teaching writing as a process develops students' abilities to think on paper (or with a computer keyboard) in order to create something that didn't exist before. The writing process is more than just a set of mechanical steps; it is a cluster of thinking and writing behaviors that lead to the making of meaning.

The Writing Process

Research into the composing processes of practicing writers shows that most pieces of writing go through some version of the following stages: pre-writing, drafting and revising, and post-writing. The chart in Figure 3.3 illustrates various components of these phases:

FIGURE 3.3 ***Stages of the Writing Process***

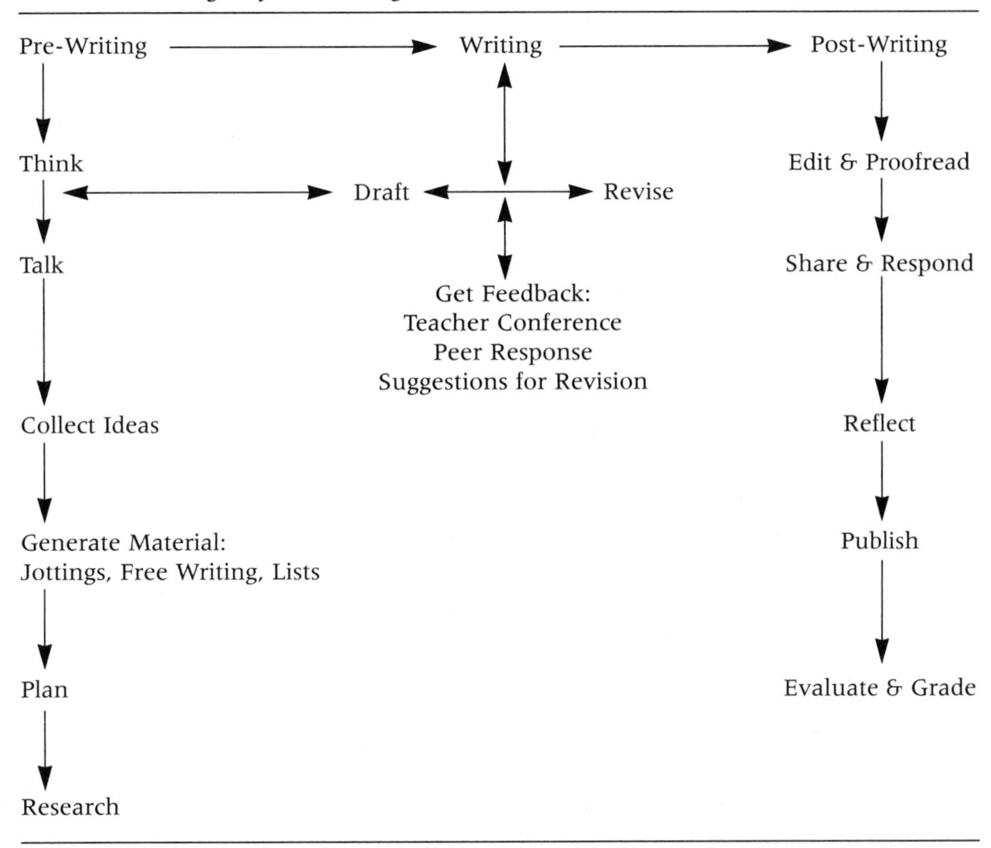

These stages of writing are not linear like a train on a track heading single-mindedly for its destination. Rather, they are "recursive": they repeat, recur, as writers move back and forth, thinking and writing their way through a piece, shaping and re-shaping it until it expresses their meaning, and then preparing it for a reader by editing and proofreading. This process varies from writer to writer and from piece to piece. The process of producing a personal narrative may differ drastically from the process for a twenty-page research paper. Yet certain features remain constant for experienced writers: a phase of thinking, planning, jotting notes, and collecting material; time spent drafting and revising; a final "clean-up" phase to prepare the piece for readers. The actual activities each phase entails are personal and contextual, depending on such variables as available time, kind of writing, audience, purpose, and even the mood of the writer.

Eventually, writers find a process that works for them, making writing less intimidating, easier to control, even more pleasurable. The three authors of this text have widely dissimilar writing processes yet it's easy to recognize the steps and stages described above. Here's Lois at her writing desk:

> Getting started is sheer misery; a dreadful period of anxiety, marked by a sense that this time I just can't do it. I jot notes, free write, scribble incoherent sentences and bits of ideas, eventually draw up a "game plan," sometimes filling up several pages with rough notes and planning ideas before I actually begin to compose the piece. Finally I force myself to start a draft, pushing words on the page or computer screen no matter how awkward they sound. The language soon starts to come, and I find my opening paragraph, revise it, and move on.
>
> Composing and revising occur simultaneously as I work my way through the piece. My written drafts are a mess, full of crossed out sections, new thoughts inserted between the lines and scribbled down the sides of the page, language changed again and again. Each time I set the piece aside and then resume work on it, I re-read from the beginning, revising what I've already written, before I add new material. By the time I've reached the end of the piece, it's finished. I've done all I can to revise it while I was in the process of writing it. I may solicit reader response here or just do a final proofreading and polishing. I never do a full re-write; the piece becomes shaped and formed as I write, the "center" emerging while I think my way through the piece and reread each time from the opening sentence. Any final revision is more stylistic than anything else—finding a better word or varying sentence structures.

Reade has this to say about her composing process:

> I begin by thinking for several days or weeks about what I want to say. Sometimes I'll read extensively till I have an overview of the topic and am ready to write. Then one morning I wake up with the first sentence in my head. I write this and all my ideas down until I've played out my thoughts.
>
> Then I jot down a skeleton outline in capital letters. This outline is so crude that another reader would think it was a loose arrangement of phrases, but these phrases frame the piece. If the argument is complex, I might even write out a thesis statement that contains all the pieces of the outline to establish the order of the argument and the logic that guides the argument through tangents. The outline prevents sidetracking and acts as a checklist for what must be said next.
>
> I write around three pages a day on the assumption that at least a third of the pages will be discarded. As I write and I think of new ideas, I make note of them in capital letters at the bottom of the manuscript. If I have to research an idea, I don't stop the flow of writing; I insert a place marker that says RESEARCH AND EXPAND. At the end of each day, I head the TO DO list with all the unfinished ideas from that session in capital letters, so the undeveloped ideas will pop out at me when I sit down to write the next day. As I complete a section, I delete it from the outline.
>
> Each new day of writing begins with revision. Everything from top to bottom gets revised, unless the piece has grown very long. I re-examine diction, grammar and punctuation, but mostly I question the order of ideas and the placement of large chunks of information. I think in terms of blocks of material rather than a continuous narrative. As the piece grows and grows, this process becomes in-

> creasingly important. I write in chunks, read more research, and add new chunks. These become the building blocks for the whole. They are malleable, moveable, and easy to delete. When I hit a dead end, I look back to where I began to get stuck and delete material or I read more on the subject. Sometimes I sleep on the problem, because a solution often occurs to me in the morning.

Marilyn's writing process illustrates yet a third approach:

> I delay writing until I feel the pressure of the deadline looming. By the time I put words on a page, I've cleaned my bedroom closet, arranged my recipes in alphabetical order, cleaned the lint trap on the dryer, and dusted my plants for mites. I write best under conditions of few distractions: no pressing engagements to think about, no papers to grade. I also work best when seated at my computer, in my office, away from the refrigerator or snack bar.
>
> I start by putting down ideas in random order—sometimes lists made on the computer, often notes placed randomly on a yellow pad. Occasionally I'll begin to see the connections among ideas and may do circle diagrams showing their interrelatedness. At other times, I simply begin writing the opening paragraph.
>
> Writing, for me, involves thinking through the keyboard. I never write in longhand, except for those initial notes, and I never know exactly what my thesis is until I have written several paragraphs or sometimes until I've completed most of the first draft. Early drafts are "think-alouds"—too wordy and not always coherent, in need of trimming and tightening and greater coherence. Drafting and revising, revising and re-drafting are recursive, sometimes simultaneous events.
>
> My habit of revising and editing as I write is a distraction to efficiently honing my ideas. Reared to believe in tidiness and order, I rarely practice what I preach to my students—"Just get your ideas down on paper and then worry about the editing details." I correct spellings in mid-sentence and check for subject-verb agreement before I end the sentence.
>
> Finally, if I allow myself enough time, I'll use the last hour or so to check for active voice, clarity of expression, sentence variety. My writing is never finished, and when I submit it to my co-authors or editor, I know that other drafts will necessarily follow.

Elling Nielsen-Williams, a high school student who has taken classes based on the writing process, describes his process this way:

> My writing style is a subject I have never really put much thought into. I don't mean to say that teachers have never told me how to write. It's just that when they did, I stopped paying attention. Taking directions is never fun and being told how to become inspired has never appealed to me, especially when it involved more work.
>
> I've been taught to use cluster grams, idea charts, brainstorms, and a million other ways to get thoughts on paper. I never use any of them. Instead, say I have a short story due in three weeks; I'll wait until two and a half of those weeks have gone by, then start thinking about it. Two days before it's due I'll have a good idea on what to write about. The morning of, I'll be revising what I wrote three hours earlier.

> As a freshman in high school I had a teacher who told me it didn't matter what you write in your first draft as long as it is in the ballpark of what you want to say, and then sit down and revise, revise, revise. I think this worked for me the best, because of all the possible things there are to get one inspired this involves the least time. It may take more thought, but it's drawn out so you can't tell how much time it's taking.

A close examination of these four descriptions reveals not only differences but also similarities, the overlaps, the methods all writers learn to rely on when they write. We can recognize pre-writing strategies; drafting and revising methods; editing, proofreading, and polishing techniques in these descriptions. Yet each writer has a distinctive process. Elling really doesn't do much pre-writing because he's thought through this stage internally. Faced by school deadlines, he considers pre-writing too time-consuming, although he's been taught several pre-writing strategies. He does, however, spend considerable time thinking about a piece before he writes his first draft. Reade and Lois consider pre-writing strategies the most significant way to enrich a paper and discover what they have to say. They do a great deal of jotting and planning in preparation for their first draft and throughout the writing of the piece. Reade starts with "a skeleton outline in capital letters" before she begins her first draft while Lois is content with a much rougher "game plan." Marilyn, on the other hand, does some listing and clustering of ideas but basically uses the initial draft to discover what she has to say without any formal planning. The one theme that runs consistently throughout the process descriptions of all four writers is "revise, revise, revise." Even here we find differences as Elling revises furiously right before the assignment is due, while the three authors of this text are more likely to revise over and over again, starting at the beginning each time they pick up the piece again to continue writing.

As we've illustrated above, each writer has developed a unique process that works for him or her. This should be a central goal of the writing classroom. The best writing teachers equip their students with a tool kit of writing methods, letting each young writer select what works for him or her. They don't force *every* student to march through *every* stage of a fixed writing process for *every* paper. They teach multiple methods, encourage students to find what works for them, share successes and processes with the whole class, and prod students into reflecting on their own writing process, bringing the unconscious to conscious awareness. Classroom talk about "how I write" becomes a recurrent and inspiring activity.

Think/Write #3

Write a paragraph describing your own writing process. You might think of this in general terms: what do you usually do when you write? Or you could describe how you went about producing a recent piece of writing. Compare your process to the four descriptions above. Which one is closest to yours? Does your own process reflect any or all of the elements in the writing process chart of Figure 3.3?

The Importance of Classroom Environment

In order for students to flourish as writers, they must feel safe enough to take risks with their writing and share it with others, not just the teacher. The writing classroom must be a safe haven, a place where everyone's best efforts are accepted, hard work is rewarded, risk-taking is encouraged, and students are taught to respect one another's work. We are reminded of a message we saw posted on a writing teacher's classroom door: "No panning allowed in here."

The first few weeks of the semester are crucial for creating this supportive classroom climate. Here are some ways a teacher can work with the class to develop an environment where writing students may thrive.

- Use questionnaires or informal writing to find out about students' past experiences with writing; talk about these; share both good and bad writing experiences.
- Allow students to choose their own writing topics.
- Show genuine interest in students' ideas.
- Model intense concentration when listening to student writing read aloud.
- Model positive response and constructive suggestions (See Praise, Question, Suggest later in this chapter).
- Refuse to allow any kind of verbal or non-verbal put-downs of anyone's writing.
- Show respect for young writers and their writing; encourage your students to do the same.
- Openly enjoy what your students *can* do; build on this to develop further writing skills.
- Share and celebrate good writing, that of your students as well as professional writers.
- Praise, encourage, and reward what works much more than you criticize what doesn't.
- Write with your students and share your pieces with them.

The writing strategies discussed below all reinforce a positive and supportive climate for developing writers.

Finding Topics and Developing Fluency: The Journal

Students respond very positively to an opportunity to write often and informally in an ongoing journal. Here's a chance for them to use writing to spill out ideas and feelings or respond without pressure to writing topics suggested by the teacher. Ideally, students should write in a journal daily except when they are working on a piece of more formal writing. Many teachers set aside the first ten minutes of class each day for students to write in their journals.

Journals have many benefits above and beyond the fact that students enjoy writing in them. Journals build fluency as students become accustomed to moving from oral language and thought to words on paper or a computer screen. Early in the school year, inexperienced writers may have difficulty writing more than a few sentences, but with continuous opportunity, encouragement, and responses from the teacher, journal entries usually become noticeably longer and richer as the term goes by. Some young writers become deeply attached to their journals, begging for more time to write in them, even writing over the weekend or during vacations. Journals can also help students find topics for more formal writing. Reading through his or her journal, a student often finds the kernel of a paper, poem, or story. Students can also use the "j" to experiment with new forms of writing, to take risks without fear of failure: try some poetry, write a dialogue, plan a story. Reading and responding to journals give teachers an opportunity to get to know students more personally through their writing and communicate with them one-to-one, a rare occurrence in most secondary classrooms.

Many different kinds of journals are appropriate for a writing classroom, running a range from the personal journal to those assigned for a specific purpose such as responding to literature. Perhaps the most common is the journal used for daily writing, almost like a daily log. Sometimes teachers list possible topics on the board each day but often students are permitted to write about anything they choose as long as they spend the allotted journal time writing in their notebooks. See NCTE's *What Can I Write About? 7000 Topics for High School Students* by David Powell (1981) for ideas.

It is important to understand that privacy may become an issue when personal journals are assigned. Some schools have policies forbidding or limiting the use of personal journals, sometimes as a result of parents' complaints that they don't want their children revealing personal family matters in their journals. In addition, teachers may discover abuse, drug use, potential suicide, or other dangerous situations revealed in a student's journal. Under these circumstances, the teacher has a responsibility, spelled out in some school districts, to report this to the counselor or principal. The journal writing may be a cry for help when the student has nowhere else to turn. Before assigning a personal journal, it is best for the new teacher to ask about the school's policy. A teacher who strongly believes in the value of this type of writing can discuss appropriate versus inappropriate journal topics and caution students that the teacher is legally obligated to report anything in the journal revealing a dangerous situation. Teachers can also suggest that students protect their own privacy by folding in half and stapling any pages of writing they don't wish the teacher to read. But the teacher who wants to use journals can also avoid the privacy issue by assigning journals for more specific purposes: keeping a writer's journal, writing in response to literature, using the journal as a log for a research paper or as the place for write-to-learn jottings. Several different types of journals and purposes for their use are described in more detail below.

The journal is a good place for students to generate topics to write about. We know of a very successful writing teacher who starts off the semester by having students title a journal page "Treasures Within Me." Students are instructed to fill the page with every topic they could possibly write about. The message behind the title is a good one: we are all filled with many "treasures" that writing will bring to the surface. Another exercise for finding topics is to have students fill out a "What Can I Write About?" list like the one in Figure 3.4. Students should store these lists in the front of their journals, keep adding to them when new topics appear, and refer back to them frequently for writing ideas.

An "Outward Focus" journal can be especially helpful in expanding students' perceptions and attention to detail. This one is like a journalist's notebook. The student carries it around outside class and tries to find at least one thing each day to describe in the journal, then comment on. This develops a young writer's awareness, building descriptive as well as analytic writing skills.

Practicing writers often use the journal as a writer's notebook, collecting ideas for writing that can include dialogues, memories, short pieces, items cut from the newspaper, interesting quotes or song lyrics, language from billboards, ads, and television. Similar to the artist's sketchbook, this is a collection of writings and ideas about writing that can be drawn on in the future. Donald Murray begins each day by writing in what he calls his "daybook," an eight-by-ten spiral notebook that is narrow ruled and has a margin down the left side. In it he records questions that need to be answered and notes from lectures, ideas for articles, poems, books, papers, diagrams, titles, odd lines that strike his fancy, observations, newspaper clippings, notes on his reading, quotations from his reading, pictures, interesting letters, lists. In *Crafting a Life in Essay, Story, Poem* (1996) he describes how he uses it:

> I plan and outline, note and predraft in my daybook, in which I paste pages printed out from my computer that I may want to edit, quotes from writers, pictures, poems, whatever helps in the conversation I carry on with myself about what and how I write. . . . It is a workbook similar to what a scientist might have in a lab (20).

When Murray is ready to write, he reads through the past daybooks, photocopies the pages he'd like to work with, and uses them to stimulate his thinking. Students can be instructed to use their journal in a similar fashion, collecting materials, ideas, and thoughts for future writing projects.

Students can also keep a literature response journal when the class reads literature or a research log of data-collection activities and responses when writing a research paper. The journal can be used to store in-class jottings, answers to questions, collaborative learning assignments, and other writings whose purpose is writing to learn. These journals are described in more detail in Chapters Five and Six.

Some teachers like to store students' journals in plastic crates kept in the classroom. Students pick theirs up as they enter class and return them as they leave. Other teachers find that more interesting writing occurs when students are also able to write in their journals during the rest of the school day or at home. Of course, the problem here is that journals taken home may never make it back to the classroom. Decisions about this depend on the teacher's knowledge of how responsible the students are and also the purpose for the journal.

Grading journals doesn't have to be a chore if the teacher keeps in mind that building fluency, thinking on paper, and collecting ideas for writing are the

FIGURE 3.4 ***What Can I Write About?***

Your own experiences, ideas, opinions, and concerns are the best starting points for writing. Work through the list below, filling in as many of the blanks as possible. Leave empty spaces if you run out of ideas for a category. Afterwards, go back through your lists and place a check or asterisk beside topics you would enjoy writing about.

PEOPLE: List the names of some people, friends, enemies, family members, people you admire, people important to you personally.

a.	b.	c.	d.
e.	f.	g.	h.

PLACES: Write down the names of some places.
Places where you spend a lot of time

a.	b.	c.	d.

Places where you would like to spend time if you could

a.	b.	c.	d.

Places you've visited on vacation or would like to visit

a.	b.	c.	d.

Places that are special to you

a.	b.	c.	d.

MEMORIES: List some experiences you have really enjoyed—happy times, friendly, warm times, free times.

a.	b.	c.	d.

List some unhappy memories—sad experiences, frightening experiences, disgusting events.

a.	b.	c.	d.

CONVERSATIONS: List some things you often talk about with friends or family members.

a.	b.	c.	d.

List some topics you sometimes argue about with friends or family.

a.	b.	c.	d.

AMBITIONS: Write down some of your aims, goals, or ambitions—for this term, this year, next year, thirty years from now. What plans to you have for your future? What are your hopes and dreams?

a.	b.	c.	d.
e.	f.	g.	h.

ACTIVITIES: What do you like to do in your free time? What are your hobbies, sports, musical interests, other personal interests?

a.	b.	c.	d.
e.	f.	g.	h.

FIGURE 3.4 ***Continued***

KNOWLEDGE: What do you know a lot about? What do you know how to do really well? What could you teach others?

a.	b.	c.	d.
e.	f.	g.	h.

HUMOR: What are some really funny things you have seen, felt, or experienced?

a.	b.	c.	d.
e.	f.	g.	h.

MISCELLANEOUS: What are some of the other things you know about, have thought about, or have seen? Don't forget pizza, basketball, toothbrushes, rap music, ice cream, pagers, plumbers, punk rockers, pink shirts, and bad movies.

a.	b.	c.	d.
e.	f.	g.	h.
i.	j.	k.	l.

These lists should help you come up with topics to write about. Remember, any topic can be used in many ways. Take "pizza," for example. That topic may lead to a recipe, a short story, a one-act play, a personal experience, a description (can you make your reader hungry?), a poem, an advertisement, and lots more.

---

primary goals. No need to read every page—this would be a good path to teacher burnout. And journals are not the place to correct grammar or spelling errors or insist on Standard English. This kind of close attention to writing skills should be saved for more formal pieces that students have a chance to revise and edit for correctness.

If the writing is done in class, some teachers don't read journal writing at all but give just a participation grade. Others grade by numbers of entries, specifying a minimum number of entries of a given length for an A, B, C, D, or E. We like to collect and read student journals occasionally, mainly skimming pages but reading and responding to one or two entries more fully. We might ask students to put an asterisk at the top of the page for the entries they want us to be sure to read. This gives students an incentive to continue to use them and also gives the teacher some useful insights into their students' thinking and writing. Using the journals in class to spark discussion or occasionally asking for volunteers to read an entry aloud also rewards students and keeps them writing. Interest will decline unless a real effort is made to make journals a valuable addition to the writing of the class. We suggest that journals of any type be used for a limited time period such as six to eight weeks, then set aside while the class turns to other activities. The journal can be resumed for a variety of purposes at other times throughout the school year. This keeps the students from journal burnout, too.

Pre-writing Strategies

For many writers the hardest thing is to face a blank page or an empty computer screen when given a formal writing assignment. Informal pre-writing techniques provide ways to get ideas down on paper before actually starting to compose a draft. Writing spurs thinking, leading to more writing. Often, the piece starts to write itself as the writer jots notes about it. Students benefit from learning to use several different pre-writing techniques, then choosing what works for them. Both the type of pre-writing strategy and the time spent in the pre-writing stage may vary widely based on the student's needs for any particular piece. These techniques are also useful for finding topics to write about. Here are directions for several typical pre-writing assignments. Most of these can be done with pen and paper or on the computer. Chapter Five also describes invention and topic-generating techniques that work especially well for formal essays and other write-to-learn assignments.

Free Writing. Tell students to write freely for ten minutes about whatever comes to mind. The only rule is that you can't stop. If your mind goes blank, write "I can't think of what to write about" or "hippopotamus" over and over again until new ideas come. "What's On Your Mind?" is a good title for this exercise. Many writers find this a good way to start writing; it's a warm-up exercise similar to that of an athlete and gets the writing juices flowing.

Focusing free writing is a method for generating material about a specific topic such as the main point of a paper. To illustrate the value of this kind of free writing, we recommend the "Six Objects" activity described in Figure 3.5.

Brainstorming. Instruct students to jot down the longest possible list of everything they could possibly say about their topic. Tell them, "Don't censor yourself; jot it down no matter how mundane, far-fetched, or silly." This can be a mind-expanding exercise that opens a student's thinking to new ideas or turns the topic in an unplanned direction. Brainstorming can be done independently or pairs can brainstorm together on paper or on the same computer screen. Students can do this on the chalkboard as a class if all are writing about the same topic.

Listing. Have students make a list of everything that comes to mind about their topic: things they already know, questions to investigate, memories, sensory images, bits of dialogue. This should lead to a rich set of details and ideas for a paper.

Talk. Never overlook the power of talk to spur thinking and writing. Students can take their lists into small groups or pairs and chat briefly about what they plan to write. They can question each other and make suggestions for three to five minutes before they start a draft. This again works as a warm-up, an especially effective one for more oral students.

Clustering or Mapping. Visual learners benefit from this non-linear graphic display of their thinking, a form of brainstorming. Gabriele Rico in *Writing the Natural*

FIGURE 3.5 *Six Objects*

Come to class with a brown paper bag containing six common objects students are familiar with or simple childhood toys: an uninflated balloon, a rubber band, a dollar bill, a Band-Aid, a water gun, a needle and thread, a stick of gum, a set of keys, a map, a chocolate bar, a comb, a tube of lipstick. Before you reveal the objects, tell students they must choose one object to write about for fifteen minutes—only one. Then slowly, with great drama, take the objects out one by one, wave each in the air, chat about it for a second, and line it up with the others on your desk where students can see all six. Once all are revealed, give students a few seconds to select one and tell them to start. They must write without stopping for the allotted time, trying to stay on the object they've chosen. They may write anything about it that comes to mind. No stopping. Quantity counts. Write with your students for this one and be ready to share yours if asked.

When the allotted time is up, call "stop" and insist that everyone put down his or her pen or pencils. Shake your hand—it probably aches a bit from the pressure. Compare quantity. How much did most students write? Who wrote the most? Praise that person for speediness. Ask for a show of hands from those who chose each object. Which one had the largest number of writers (usually the first one or two objects); which one the least? Ask for volunteers to share what they've written—whole pieces or sections. After the writer reads, discuss each piece for a few minutes: What do you especially like? What do you remember? Could this freewriting be shaped and revised into a short piece of writing? Could it be turned into a poem? Be sure to thank each volunteer profusely for being brave enough to share this informal piece with the class. Share yours. Invite responses to it. Have students re-read and underline their favorite section or word or sentence. Have students share these "bits" in pairs or once again ask for volunteers to share these with the whole class. Conclude by asking how many students feel they had something of merit in this free write. How many could turn it into a short finished piece on their object?

Students enjoy this activity because it often produces some good writing on a topic they would never have chosen to write about. What's to be said about a set of keys? A lot if you're a middle school student eager to drive or a 15-year-old with a temporary permit or a 17 year-old who just lost a friend in a driving accident. Enough said. This writing activity really works to demonstrate the power of free writing for generating material for a paper.

Way (1983) makes a case for using this technique to stimulate creativity, "releasing the inner writer" in all of us. Directions are to put a single word that represents your topic in the middle of a sheet of paper, circle it, and let your mind carry you where it will in thinking about the central word. Jot down each new idea, circle it, and connect it to the center with a line radiating outward. Continue to make branches from each new idea until you have exhausted it. When you think of another idea, connect it to the central word and branch outward from there with further associations. See Figure 3.6 for an example of clustering by a high school student assigned to write about his own writing process. New ideas emerge from this activity, and sometimes the organization of the piece becomes clear because each main branch from the central word can become a paragraph or section of the paper.

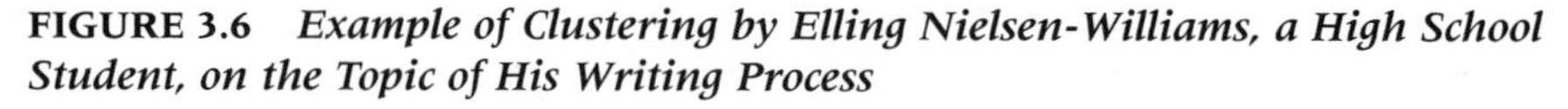

FIGURE 3.6 ***Example of Clustering by Elling Nielsen-Williams, a High School Student, on the Topic of His Writing Process***

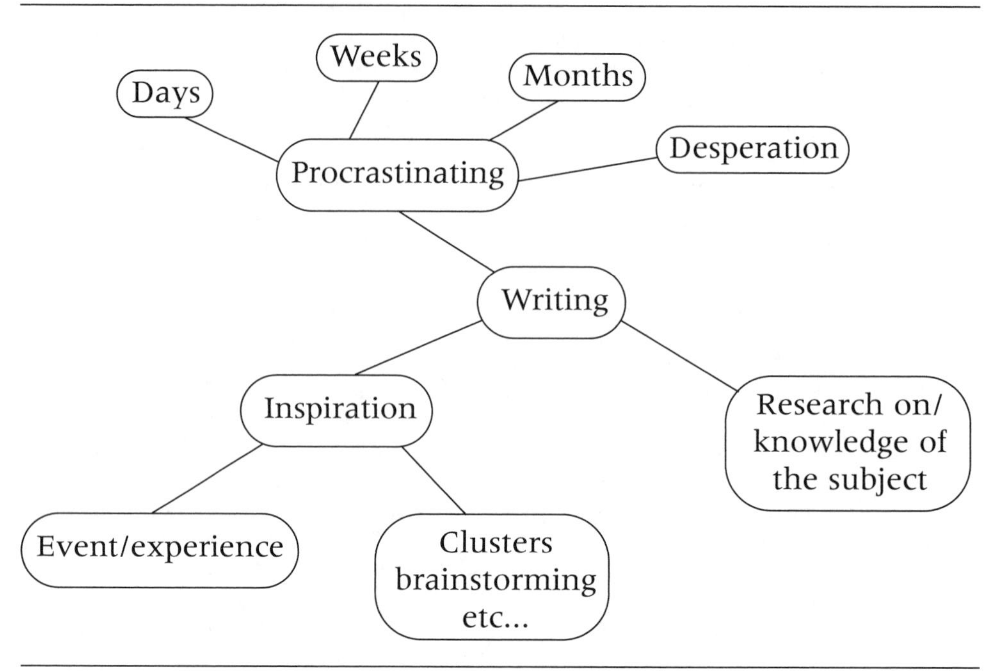

Visualization. Ask students to close their eyes for two or three minutes and make a mental picture of whatever they are writing about. This works especially well for personal narratives or descriptive writing, but it can also be useful for writing about literature (visualizing scenes and people in the story) or other topics that invite illustrations or examples. It's a way for students to enter into the world they are creating in their writing.

Write Before Writing. Teach students to "write before writing," to fill up some blank pages or a computer screen with language and ideas in order to generate material they can then use in their writing or build upon for a complete piece. Students will learn how powerful it can be to spin out language without worrying ahead of time about getting it right or finding that perfect first sentence before you can begin the paper. When teaching students these strategies, be sure to explain why and how they are used. A free writing or other pre-writing activity is the initiation of a piece of writing, not the finished piece. Sometimes parts of a pre-writing activity can be used directly within a paper. Sometimes a piece of writing grows right out of a brainstorming or free writing session, with adept cutting, revising, and re-arranging of material. More often pre-writing activities start the thinking and planning process, providing ideas for the piece that has yet to be written. Spelling and sentence structure don't count in any of these pre-writing exercises. This is James Britton's "expressive" writing (89) at its most informal:

- thinking aloud on paper
- writing to explore feelings, moods, and opinions
- writing to plumb the depths and spark surprises
- writing that generates new ideas as well as recalling what is already known

Getting Started

After students have spent some time writing in their journals and experimenting with pre-writing techniques, we like to do one or both of the exercises in Figure 3.7, Significant Experience, and Figure 3.8, Writing about an Accident, to help students generate their first piece of writing by drawing on these pre-writing strategies.

FIGURE 3.7 *Significant Experience**

1. Make a list of six significant experiences in your life—good ones or difficult ones, large and important, or small but unforgettable. (You might want to give some prompts here to get students thinking—a special vacation, summers in the family cottage, birth of a brother or sister, sports or musical or theatrical activities, etc.)
2. Look at your list. Check off three things you might want to write about; look at those three and check off your two favorites; look at the two remaining and check off the best one.
3. Free write for ten minutes about the last one you checked off—or you can always change your mind and go back to anything else on your list. Set this free writing aside.
4. The next step is to find a "key moment" in your significant experience. Thinking about the whole experience, try to find one central, most important minute in your whole story. In *After the End* (1993), Barry Lane describes this as a "snapshot," a zoom lens that moves in on one particular scene to capture it with great sensory detail. Visualize that minute, using all your senses to see it, feel it, smell it, hear it. Now take a new sheet of paper and write only about that key moment, again for ten minutes. Use all your senses to describe it as fully as possible—colors, movement, dialogue. Set this free writing aside.
5. On a third sheet of paper, write for a few minutes in answer to this question: Why did you write about this significant experience? Why choose this one?

After all the free writes are completed, the teacher can work with them in several ways. Ask for volunteers to read one section aloud. Have students pair up and share one or two sections; remind them to talk about what they like and what they remember, to praise the good parts. Discuss possible arrangements and rearrangements of these three free writes. Have students move them around. See what happens if they start with the key moment as the opening paragraph or start with the reason for choosing this piece. Point out how free writing was used to general material for the draft of a full paper. Did this make writing easier? Were they surprised at how much they wrote? Now give students time to connect these three pieces, revise, shape and form the piece.

*We are indebted to Dick Koch of Adrian College for the original version of this exercise, one that we used for many years with teachers enrolled in the Flint Area and Southeast Michigan Writing Projects.

FIGURE 3.8 ***Writing about an Accident****

1. Think about an accident—your own or that of someone you know well. Have students share some of these—just the topic, not the whole story—save that for writing. This sharing is sure to spark some memories for those who might be struggling to find an accident to write about. (3–5 minutes)
2. Visualize—direct students to close their eyes and try to see the accident as it occurs. Start with a minute or two before the accident and then move your mind through it. Try to use all your senses and really "be" in that moment. (3 minutes)
3. Now open your eyes and jot a list of things that came to your mind; make it as long as you can. Jot quickly so you capture everything you visualized. (5–8 minutes)
4. Pair up with someone and talk about your accident for a few minutes. Share your lists if you want to. Ask questions about each other's accidents. (5 minutes)
5. Write a full draft of a paper about your accident. (30 minutes)

Usually these four pre-writing techniques lead to well-detailed writing and help students move easily into the composing phase. By the time they've shared topics, visualized, jotted notes, and talked about their topic with a partner, the piece practically writes itself. When most students seem to have completed a draft, have students share their writing in pairs by exchanging papers or reading aloud to each other. Have students tell each other what they liked best about the piece or what they thought was the best part of the story. You can also ask for one or two volunteers to read their papers aloud to the whole class. Encourage the rest of the class to point out the best parts of each paper. Thank these writers for sharing their work with the class, acknowledging how difficult that can be but also how rewarding to hear readers' responses to the piece.

*Adapted from *A Writing Project: Training Teachers of Composition from Kindergarten to College,* Zemelman and Daniels, 1985.

Think/Write #4

Do one of the writing exercises described in Figures 3.7 and 3.8, either Significant Experience or Writing about an Accident. Try to complete an entire first draft using all the steps outlined above for pre-writing, drafting, and sharing for feedback. Pair off with another person for the pre-writing activities and then share your full draft with the same person. Respond to each other's writing by pointing out what you like best about the piece.

Write a paragraph about your reactions to the various pre-writing elements of these activities. Did they help you generate ideas? Did they make the actual drafting easier? How did you feel when you were sharing your draft? Did you expect the responses of your reader or did they surprise you? What could you do now to revise?

Planning

Sometimes writers benefit from drawing up a rough plan for their paper. We call this a "game plan" rather than an outline because it's freer in form and, like all plans, likely to change as the writer drafts the piece. A game plan can be no more than a list with a possible beginning, the material the writer wants to be sure to include, and a possible ending. Jotting responses to the following items can also be useful in planning a paper.

- What's your paper about? State it in one sentence.
- What's the main idea you want to be sure to get across to readers?
- What do you want your readers to learn from your paper?
- How would you like your readers to feel after reading your paper?
- Write three different opening sentences for your paper.
- What's the most important or most interesting thing you want to be sure to include in your paper?

Mapping is another good planning device, especially for visual learners. The student puts the title or topic in the center of a piece of paper and uses one line radiating from the center for each main idea or section. We don't recommend teaching students to write a detailed formal outline before they write the paper. This inhibits the thinking on paper that emerges during the composing process, seriously cutting down on the flow of ideas and the new ideas that the act of writing stimulates. Students seem to know this intuitively. In our experience, when outlines are required, students more often write them after the paper (and the thinking) is completed.

Drafting

Pre-writing and planning activities must eventually come to a halt as writers face deadlines. Sometimes a rough draft begins to take shape during pre-writing and planning activities. Other times, the writer has to determine that it's time to begin a solid first draft. Time is necessary here, time to think and write, draft and revise. The writing classroom must provide blocks of time for this intensive work plus reader response and constructive feedback on works-in-progress.

The Writing Workshop

The best way to provide both time and support for young writers is to organize the class as a writing workshop. Mary Ellen Giacobbe, a writing teacher and researcher, says writers need three basics: time, ownership, and response (Atwell 1987, 54). A workshop format provides for all three, as well as for planned mini-lessons on the craft of writing, revising, and editing. Similar to the artist's communal studio, the carpenter's workshop, the scientist's laboratory, the writing workshop environment is structured so each person has all the tools at hand, can work independently at his or her own pace, and can seek feedback at any time from others engaged in the same creative work.

The key to success in a workshop environment is organization: patterns and procedures established early in the term, clearly communicated to students, and reinforced throughout the semester. A stranger walking into a writing workshop may consider it chaotic—some students write quietly at their desks; two students compose a piece together, whispering back and forth as they jot notes; in each back corner of the room, a pair of students sits on opposite sides of a small table, heads bent together, conferring over their drafts; four students have gathered chairs into a close circle to pass revised pieces around for peer editing and proofreading; the teacher holds an individual conference with a student at a desk in front of the room. The class has a buzz of voices while students are engaged in many different activities; yet everyone is busily involved in some stage of writing.

When planning a writing workshop, teachers may be concerned about losing control of the class or having students waste time chatting. A common question is "What is the rest of the class doing while I'm holding individual conferences?" When teachers plan in advance, setting goals and procedures, and when students know what's expected of them during workshop time, most of these problems disappear. As with any new classroom methodology, it may take time to discover what works, what to tell students, what forms to design, what procedures to follow. But workshop sessions are the heart of any successful writing program.

Here is a typical daily routine for a 50-minute workshop class. Students pick up their writing portfolios as they enter class and decide how they will spend the class session: writing, revising, conferring with peers, conferencing with the teacher, etc.

5–10 minutes:	Mini-lesson
1–2 minutes:	Status of the class: quick questioning of each student's plans for the class period, noted on a record-keeping form. Some teachers may prefer to have students do this themselves by signing in when they enter the class.
20–30 minutes:	Writing time
10–15 minutes:	Group sharing

Mini-lessons early in the semester can focus on procedures and forms for writing workshop and finding topics to write about. Later they can deal with all aspects of writing from modeling pre-writing and revision strategies to brief lessons on grammar and usage that can then be applied to students' drafts. During writing time, tell students to do any of the following activities.

- Select topics to write about and do pre-writing activities independently or in pairs.
- Develop a rough plan for a new piece of writing.
- Do research to gather material for an essay or research paper.
- Draft new pieces of writing or work on revision and final editing of a work-in-progress.
- Write in a journal, using one of the journal varieties described earlier in this chapter.
- Hold a conference with the teacher over a draft.

- Work in peer response groups or pairs, conferring over drafts or proofreading final papers.
- Work on editing problems by studying grammar guidebooks or conferring with other students.
- Write collaboratively.
- Illustrate their own writing.
- Use a computer if available to find a topic to write about, gather material for a paper, or prepare and embellish a finished product.
- Read the writing of other students in class publications or on bulletin boards for models, ideas, and inspiration.
- Prepare a piece for publication.
- Review his or her own portfolio to reflect on progress, consider pieces worthy of further revision, find more topics to write about.

Group sharing is an invaluable part of writing workshop, a chance for each writer's voice to be heard and for the class to celebrate both writing in progress and final pieces. Students soon begin to look forward to having this activity conclude writing workshop time.

The Appendix contains the beginning framework for developing a writing workshop in a middle school classroom, including daily plans for the first four weeks. The following sections of this chapter offer more specific information and guidelines for the various components of a writing workshop.

Supporting Young Writers at Work

Teachers have important roles to play while students are working on their writing during writing workshop time: coach, consultant, collaborator, editor, fellow-writer. During this phase of writing, teacher intervention can be the difference between success and failure. Many student writers are not used to focusing for long periods of time on developing a piece. They may have difficulty getting starting or run out of ideas in a very short period of time, declaring themselves "done" long before the paper is finished. Sometimes they get stuck and don't know how to proceed with a piece or they're so unsure of themselves as writers that they dismiss everything they write as worthless. A brief conference with the teacher can provide a turning point, giving them confidence, support, and ideas when they are most needed—while writing is in process. Responding to drafts almost always leads to a better final product, one which can be read and graded much more quickly. Better individual papers and demonstrable writing growth are more likely to occur when the teacher puts his or her time into working with drafts rather than copious marking of final papers. Kirby and Liner note in *Inside Out* (1988), "Extraordinarily successful teachers of writing have one thing in common: they spend very little time in isolation, reading and marking papers, and a great deal of time responding and discussing student writings with the writers themselves" (234).

The Teacher-Student Content Conference. While students write, the teacher can work with students who seem to be struggling or those who directly request help. These can be a brief three or four minutes to answer a question or check to see if a student is on track with the writing assignment. We have visited a classroom in which the teacher went up and down the aisles during the period, checking every student's paper for a "focusing sentence." As he leaned over shoulders, skimming drafts, those who were fulfilling the assignment got a few words of praise: "fine, keep going." He spent a few minutes longer with students who were having difficulty, asking questions designed to help them better focus the paper: "What are you trying to say about this topic? Can you tell me what your paper is about? How could you re-phrase this section to be clearer about your main idea?" Another method teachers use is to hold conferences at a designated table or the teacher's desk where they can oversee the rest of the class while they talk to individuals. Students sign up for a teacher-student conference at the beginning of class or add their name to the sign-up sheet when problems arise.

Teachers are sometimes intimidated by the idea of working so closely with writing-in-process, especially if they don't do much writing themselves (a good reason for writing with your students!). They may be unsure about whether or not they can give students the help they might need or doubt that the rest of the class will work independently while the teacher confers with individual students. It has been our experience that students hunger for one-to-one attention from the teacher and are willing to follow class rules for a quiet writing time as long as they know they will eventually have their own turn for a conference.

Student Ownership and the Teacher's Role. One of the authors of this book, in the very early weeks of teaching composition, held a conference with a freshman composition student whose paper was disorganized. Recognizing how the paper needed to be re-arranged for clarity, the teaching assistant took scissors and tape to the student's writing, cutting it into pieces and taping it back together, all the while chatting about why this would work better. With a triumphant "see," she handed the re-organized piece back to the student, saying, "Isn't this easier to follow?" Of course the student nodded yes, but the look of dismay and bewilderment on his face showed his real feelings. The student didn't learn very much from this conference, but the graduate assistant learned a lot about what *not* to do when conferencing over drafts.

Asking questions, pointing out areas that are hard to follow or unclear, making careful suggestions, and listening to the student's responses, are all more effective conference strategies. The goal of a conference is for the student to learn something about the paper and come away with a good sense of how to proceed for revision. Ownership should remain clearly in the student's hands. The teacher's role is coach and facilitator here, not an evaluative judge or "fixer-upper" of the paper. On the other hand, the teacher shouldn't hesitate to use his or her own expertise to help the student think about how to proceed. "Have you thought about doing X?" or "Let's brainstorm for other ways you could work with this idea," are good ways to guide students toward revision without robbing them of ownership. Here is some advice for holding one-to-one conferences with students.

Guidelines for Effective Conferences over Works in Progress

1. Whenever possible hold conferences around a table or side by side at a desk where you can both look over the paper together, sitting at the same level. This makes the conference a more personal experience than if you loom over a paper while standing beside a student's desk or take it away from the student altogether to make cryptic remarks in the margins while the student anxiously watches and waits.

2. Use open-ended questions to start the conference.

"How's it going?"
"How can I help you with this piece?"
"What do you like about your piece?"
"What kinds of problems are you having with this piece?"

3. Try to keep conferences brief so you can see a number of students in a class period. Center your conversation on a specific area of concern and watch the clock. Covering too much at a single conference will only overwhelm young writers. The student can always work on the problem you've discussed and then return for further feedback at another conference. You don't want students to rely on you to solve all their writing problems but instead to learn to work things out themselves or confer with other students for response and suggestions.

4. You don't always need to read the entire paper. Ask a student to tell you about the paper or read only the section the student is having trouble with. You can also ask the student to read the paper aloud to you. There's nothing more satisfying than having a student stumble over a weak spot in the paper and recognize on his own that work needs to be done to clarify that section. Students will sometimes read with a pencil in hand, correcting their own errors as they find them and making notes where they want to work on something. When a student's paper is long, requiring more time and attention, take the draft home to read and respond to more fully. A brief conference with the student on the following day can clarify your written comments.

5. When working with first drafts, focus on content, organization, clarity, and development of ideas with details and examples. Save attention to correctness for later drafts after the piece has been revised. Don't confuse the student by commenting on sentence level problems and mechanical errors when the paper still needs work on the larger issues of content and organization. What's the use of correcting a spelling error if the entire sentence is thrown out when the paper is revised?

6. Read and respond as a human being, not a teacher-corrector. Give specific praise for good parts of a piece of writing. For example, "You do a really fine job describing your boss with his food-specked tie and rumpled jacket. We can see how insensitive he is in the dialogue between the two of you over your request to change your hours so you can study for a test." "I like the way you do X" is also a good way to give honest praise that encourages the student to do more of the same kind of writing in the future. It can also be helpful to say, "I'm not sure what you mean here. Can you explain this to me?"

7. Ask questions to get the writer talking rather than tell the writer what to do. Writers can often solve their own problems as they talk about their papers. All you need to do is confirm that they are on the right track or suggest the writer write down what he or she is telling you to include it in the paper.

8. Be a good listener; let the student do most of the talking.

9. Sometimes a conference can be used for a brief mini-lesson, for example, the need for a transitional phrase to guide the reader as the paper moves from one idea to the next. You can explain the concept of the transitional phrase and then demonstrate its usefulness by working with the student to add one at a critical point in the paper where it was missing.

10. Trust yourself to learn how to be a better responder to student writing as you gain more experience with conferences. Writing time/conference time can soon become the most pleasurable part of teaching writing. It gives you a chance to help students when they need it most, resulting in changes that can move a mediocre paper right to the head of the class. It's also just plain fun to hold conversations over drafts. You learn a lot about your students and have the satisfaction of watching their writing skills and confidence increase as they begin to produce successful, meaningful pieces of writing.

During conferences, the teacher often recognizes what's problematic about a paper, especially since we are experienced readers and writers ourselves. But telling the student what's wrong and how to make it right doesn't facilitate growth in the student's own ability to evaluate and revise his or her own work in progress. Good questions can do much more by guiding the students' thinking and encouraging effective revision. We have found the following questions helpful in dealing with some of the most typical problems found in student writing.

Questions to Use in Writing Conferences over Writing-in-Process. For unfocused papers with no main point, ones that just give a list of events and information, ramble on in a disorganized way, or have too many unconnected ideas:

- What are you trying to tell your reader in this paper?
- What's the main point or most important point of this paper?
- Several things seem to be happening (or you seem to be making both point A and point B). What's the most important thing you're trying to say?
- Are there parts you could leave out?
- Tell me what your paper is about.
- Why is this important? Why did you decide to write on this topic?
- What did you learn about X from writing this paper?

If meaning is unclear:

- Set the paper aside and tell me about X.
- Can you explain what you mean here? What's happening? What are you saying about X?

When the paper is undeveloped, needs more detail, examples, or explanations:

- Tell me more about X.
- What else happened here?
- Are there places where you could describe more?
- What else can you tell me about X?
- What's an example of X that would *show* the reader what you mean?
- Was anyone talking in this part of the paper? What did you see, hear, or smell? How were you feeling when this was happening?
- What research could you do to learn more about this topic? Where could you gather more information?

If the paper is disorganized, hard to follow:

- I'm not sure I fully understand what you're saying here. Can you tell me about this?
- Why did you decide to put your ideas in this order? How else could you arrange these ideas?
- What could you do to help the reader understand where you're headed as you move from one idea to another?

The paper needs a better opening or conclusion:

- How else could you start this paper? Write three different possible openings and then decide which you like best.
- What could you put in your lead that would capture the reader's attention right away?
- What do you want your reader to think or feel after reading the paper?
- Could you sum up what your paper is about?
- How else could you conclude your paper? Write three possible endings and then decide which you like best.

One of the teachers we work with in the schools keeps these questions on a clipboard carried with her during conferences so she can refer to them when she's not sure what to say to students.

Peer Response

Teachers may hesitate to use peer response in their classes for fear that students will not be able to help each other or will waste time chatting instead of working at the task. This may well be true if the teacher suddenly announces, "Get into groups of three and help each other with these papers," expecting the class to know what to do. This is where many teachers leave themselves open for failure; they blame the students for not working productively and end up believing that peer response groups are a waste of time. In order for peer response to be effective, students must be taught how to read and respond to each other's writing. Once they have a better sense of how to work together over drafts, students can be of great benefit to each other. They are, after all, readers and can respond to unclear meanings, ask questions when they need more information, and make helpful suggestions based on their own reading and writing experiences. But they won't do this without direct instruction and guidance from the teacher.

Students will learn a lot about peer conferencing from the one-on-one conferences they hold with the teacher. They will ask each other the same questions and even use the same phrasing for their suggestions. But they also need more specific training in peer response methods. The best way to accomplish this is through modeling effective peer response with the whole class, using the papers of volunteers or those written by previous students.

The model for responding to student writing with which we have had the most success is Praise, Question, Suggest or PQS (a strategy modeled after Bill Lyons' Praise, Question, Polish or PQP). It goes like this:

1. The writer reads the paper aloud.
2. Listeners respond first by giving specific *praise:* What do you like about this paper? What stands out? What do you remember?
3. Then listeners ask *questions* they have about the contents of the paper: What would you like to ask the writer about the paper? The writer does not answer these questions but should take notes on the questions asked in preparation for revising the paper. Readers' questions often reveal areas needing clarification, examples, or further development.
4. Finally, readers make *suggestions* for further work on the paper: What suggestions can you make to help with revision?

PQS is both positive and constructive. Students get the praise all writers hunger for, are guided to think about answers to readers' questions, and are given some specific suggestions, which they may or may not choose to follow. This process should be modeled several times with the whole class before putting students into pairs to try it for the first time on each other's papers. It also helps to put the questions into a handout, leaving spaces for the responder to write answers. The writer will then have something in writing to refer to when revising a draft. One caution here. Students have often been well trained by previous teachers to search for mechanical and grammatical errors instead of focusing on content. Unless the purpose of the peer conference is final editing, students should focus on meaning in early drafts, just as the teacher does. When modeling PQS, teachers should discuss this concept, helping students differentiate between revision for content and organization and final editing for mechanical/grammatical correctness. There will be plenty of time for correcting errors once the paper has been revised for content.

Peer response groups for writing-in-process work best when teachers take the time to prepare students for them by modeling, talking to the class about their purpose, and carefully structuring the group process. Here are some guidelines for making peer response groups a success.

Guidelines for Effective Peer Response Groups

1. Model constructive, non-judgmental response to writing in student-teacher conferences and by critiquing student writing with the whole class. Use a "fishbowl" if possible to show students how small groups work together to give feedback on a piece of writing. To do a fishbowl demonstration, ask a volunteer to read his or her draft aloud to a group of three or four students. This group sits in the middle of the room with the rest of the class in a larger circle around them. The writer reads the draft aloud while group members jot down their responses informally or on a Reader Response Form. The writer then asks questions of the small group, guiding an oral discussion of the paper that focuses on positive features of the writing and explores possible ideas for revision. We recommend that writers use the PQS questions above, but it may also be helpful to have writers generate their own questions. Thomas and Steinberg, originators of the fishbowl strategy, recommend asking students to answer this question before the fishbowl takes place: "If you had access to the most wonderful editor in the world who would give you just exactly the help you needed, but who wouldn't give you that help unless you asked the right questions, what would you ask?" (26). The teacher then lists these questions on the board, asking each student writer to select three or four to use when they read to their peer group. Discussions inevitably lead to other ideas beyond the writer's questions, but these initial questions put the writer in control of the group response session and get the conversation started. As the group responds, the writer can take notes or simply listen, asking further questions if necessary to clarify the group's feedback. At the end of the session, the Reader Response Forms should be given to the writer to help with revision. The final step in the "fishbowl" is a debriefing with the rest of the class, discussing whether the writer's questions elicited useful feedback, which suggestions seemed most valuable, and general observations on the group process, including ways to improve it.

Do this modeling several times throughout the school year to reinforce effective response. Guide students away from empty responses like "Good," "Great." Focus these modeling sessions with drafts on responding to what they "hear" in the writer's piece and making constructive suggestions for the content of the paper.

2. Prepare students to work cooperatively. Discuss the need to be sensitive to one another's feelings and to focus comments on the writing, not on each other. Don't allow negative comments: give helpful suggestions or ask questions instead. Students who are disruptive or insensitive to others in the group should be removed from the group and denied the privilege of this kind of interaction.

3. Start with pairs. Move to small groups of three or four when students are working well together. You might let students pair off themselves at first or even form their own small groups. This provides a certain "comfort level" with friends early in the school year. Eventually you may want to re-group students so less productive groups are disbanded or do this just to vary the group structures. You might also form groups by putting one very good writer and one weak writer in each group and distributing the remaining students throughout the groups. In some classes this distribution works well because it offers support for the weaker writers and gives the better writers a chance to develop their skills at reading, listening, and responding.

4. Structure group critiques. Give explicit directions for what is to be accomplished and why. Set a time limit. Directions might go something like this:

> Move into your peer response groups and pull your chairs close together. Remember to keep your voices down so you don't interfere with the discussions going on in other groups. You will have the entire class period to work with the papers of all four group members. Please allow no more than 15 minutes for each writer to read the paper aloud and lead a discussion on it. Someone should watch the clock to be sure everyone has an equal amount of time. The writer should read his or her paper aloud to the group while members jot notes on the Peer Response Form to help them give useful feedback during the discussion. When the reading is completed, finish filling out the forms and then discuss your responses. The writer should take notes on the comments, questions, and suggestions of group members. The writer may also ask other questions about his or her paper. When your discussion of the paper is complete, give the Reader Response Forms to the writer to help with revision. The purpose for this class session is for everyone to receive feedback on what's working in the paper and suggestions for revising the content and clarity of the paper. Please save comments on grammar and mechanics for an editing workshop once these papers are revised.

5. Make students accountable for accomplishing the work. Some teachers like to give specific group responsibilities to each student. One is the timekeeper and must see to it that equal time is spent on each member's paper. Another is the discussion monitor, making sure everyone has a turn to speak. A third manages the written critiques, insuring that everyone does one and collecting them to give to the writer.

6. Use response sheets. Ask students to write their responses and then discuss the paper. Early in the semester use simple ones based on PQS; later in the term design more complex ones to focus discussions on specific points. See Figure 3.9 for some examples of peer group response sheets.

7. Understand that social interaction is a necessary component of successful groups. Peer response is a social process, dependent as much on group dynamics as on the writing skills of its members. Time spent settling into the group work mode is a natural and necessary phenomenon. If the group is to function comfortably

FIGURE 3.9 ***Three Examples of Peer Response Forms: PQS, Significant Experience, Argument***

Reader Response Form Based on PQS

Writer's Name ______________________________

Title of Paper ______________________________

1. What did you like about this paper? What do you remember? What stands out?

2. What questions would you like to ask the writer about the paper?

3. Do you have one or two suggestions to help the writer revise this paper?

Reader's Name ______________________________

Peer Response Sheet
Significant Experience

Name of Writer ______________________________

Title of Paper ______________________________

1. What did you like about this paper? What do you remember? What stands out?

2. Does the paper have a clearly described central event or experience? Do all the ideas in the paper deal with this central event? Can anything be omitted? Has anything been left out that you would like to see added?

3. In a sentence or two state what you think the significance of this event or experience is for the writer. What ideas or feelings was the author trying to get across to readers? Does this need to be clarified, sharpened, or expanded?

4. Does the writing begin and end well? Any better ideas for either spot?

5. What questions would you like to ask the writer about this paper?

6. Please make one or two suggestions to help the writer with revision. If this were your paper, what changes would you make?

Reader's Name ______________________________

(continued)

FIGURE 3.9 ***Continued***

Peer Response Sheet
Argument

Writer's Name ______________________________

Title of Paper ______________________________

1. What do you like best about this paper? What is working well? What did you respond to?

2. Please state what you believe to be the position the writer is proving in this paper.

3. Do you have any problems following or accepting the reasons for the writer's position? Would you make any changes in the reasoning?

4. How persuasive is the writer's evidence? Is there enough evidence? Is the evidence explained with detail, examples, and description? Can you suggest evidence the writer has overlooked?

5. Has the writer considered the opposition and shown why the opposite viewpoint is not as good as the one the writer is taking?

6. Has the writer provided sufficient transitions to guide you through the paper, especially before and after the opposing argument? Can you follow the argument clearly or do you need more guidance as you read?

7. If this were your paper, what would you work on before turning it in?

Reader's Name ______________________________

---

together, they must chat, make or renew relationships, and prepare psychologically for the task at hand. Peer group work on tasks requires concentration and focus; but it is also a social activity, one that should be pleasurable and supportive. Don't expect the group to spend 100 percent of its time focusing on papers.

8. Circulate about the room while the pairs or groups are at work. Visit the groups to answer questions and keep them on task. If the groups are functioning well on their own, the teacher might remain with one of the groups for the discussion of a paper but try not to dominate the group with your own comments. Relax; trust the students to help each other.

Revision: Re-seeing the Work in Progress

Revision can't be taught with the same ease that one teaches pre-writing activities, for instance; but the teacher can do many things to create an environment that encourages students to re-look, re-think, and re-write their pieces. We are talking about global revision for content here, focusing on the paper's ideas, organization, clarity, logic, coherence, detail and examples, and attention to purpose and audience. Attention at the sentence level to the surface features of writing and stylistic changes are best saved until after the paper has been revised for content. Many of the strategies discussed earlier in this chapter promote a revision-oriented attitude toward writing: teacher conferences, peer group critiques, modeling. All of these activities for feedback and suggestions on drafts help make content revision a normal and routine part of the writing classroom. Here are some other things teachers can do to encourage students to revise:

- Use a "rough draft" stamp to indicate to both students and their parents that a given piece is in its early stages, still needing more work. This also emphasizes that writing is a process with several necessary stages before a piece is completed.
- Have students keep all their work together in a writing folder. Some teachers like to use two folders for each student—one for works-in-progress and another for finished pieces. When writing is stored in a folder, students can browse through their own work, selecting pieces to work on after drafts have had a chance to sit for a while so the writer can get some distance and "re-see" the piece. Even pieces in the "finished" folder are sometimes revised yet one more time when the writer revisits the folder after several days or weeks.
- Model revision using student papers on the overhead projector. Have students suggest possibilities for revision:
  —places where information could be added or rearranged;
  —alternatives for the opening or conclusion;
  —places where irrelevant material, tangents, or repetitions should be removed;
  —words and phrases that might be omitted to tighten the language.
- Teach mini-lessons on the writer's craft—good "leads" to grab the reader's attention, use of detail and description, the value of examples, ways to use dialogue, methods for concluding papers. Barry Lane's *After THE END: Teaching and Learning Creative Revision* is full of ideas for teaching students how to craft pieces using the techniques of published writers. Chapter titles indicate some of these methods, any of which would make an excellent mini-lesson leading to revision of an existing draft: "Explode a Moment and Shrink a Century," "Snapshots and Thoughtshots," "Voice and Choice." Ask students to apply these techniques to their own writing-in-progress.
- Display examples of student papers that have gone through multiple drafts. Ask the student writer to explain to the class how and why revisions were made.
- Read published writing and discuss how the author achieved certain effects. It can also be valuable (and fun) to ask students how they would revise a published piece if it were their own writing.

- Let students choose their own topics or offer options broad enough to appeal to the majority of students. When students write about personally meaningful topics, they are willing to invest time and effort on revision.
- Encourage the collaborative and social aspects of writing to create a classroom community in which drafting and revising in collaboration with peers is both valued and respected by everyone.
- Have students write for a variety of audiences both in and out of school. When real readers are involved, students are motivated to do their best work and to reshape their pieces to meet the needs of their audience.
- Make sharing a regular part of the classroom environment and publish student writing in as many ways as possible—powerful incentives for revision. The section on publishing writing later in this chapter suggests multiple ways for sharing and publishing students' work.
- Write with your students as a practicing member of the classroom writing community. Share your struggles and successes so they can see that all writers go through the same difficult but rewarding process of drafting and redrafting a piece until it is just right. Read your drafts to your students and ask for feedback to help you with revision; then share the final results with the class.

Editing, Proofreading, Polishing

The final stage of all finished pieces focuses on correctness—the scrupulous attention to mechanics, grammar, and usage that marks the accomplished writer. Style may come into play, too, with work at the sentence level on language, vocabulary, and sentence construction. The following chapter focuses with much detail on these issues, offering both a theoretical stance and practical classroom strategies. However, some significant points can be made here about this stage of the writing process.

First, and probably most critical, classroom time must be set aside for this final phase of writing. It is not sufficient, and rarely effective, to send students home to make a final copy of their paper. Incorporating editing, proofreading, and polishing into the classroom schedule creates an invaluable chance to teach the grammatical and mechanical skills of Edited Standard English. We firmly believe attention to these skills should be separated from revision for content. Writing is an extremely complicated process, perhaps the most complex of all our uses of language. Students who are developing the writing skills necessary for lifelong competency will learn best if the various components of the writing process are staged out for them. In this way they can focus on one thing at a time instead of trying to compose, revise, edit, and proofread all at once.

Second, not every piece of writing has to go through a final editing stage. Students may decide that some pieces in their folders are not worth investing more time and effort to polish. For other pieces, it may be totally appropriate to ignore error and focus solely on meaning; for example, write-to-learn assignments, journal-writes, informal exercises, and experiments.

Finally, editing and proofreading should be an integral part of every formal graded or published piece of writing. We suggest that teachers spend time marking only papers that have gone through the revision process and then been edited and proofread by the students first. Otherwise, teachers may find themselves focusing most of their marking time on grammar and correctness rather than responding to students' ideas or frustrated by poorly written work that obviously needs to be revised, yet is handed in to be graded. We recommend that such papers be returned to students with instructions to "revise and re-submit" or "edit, proofread, correct errors, and re-submit."

Assignments that do not move through a full writing process to the final editing stage can be given participation credit, points, or assessed with a check plus, check, or check minus. In this way, students can do a great deal of writing without overburdening the teacher with grading and correcting unpolished work. Teachers should save their efforts for marking papers that have truly been prepared for grading and publishing.

Think/Write #5

Examine the entire process, including all the drafts, that a piece of multi-draft writing has gone through. Use a piece of writing done by a secondary student or something you have written yourself. Analyze the changes that occurred as the writer moved the piece through early pre-writing stages and from draft to draft to achieve a finished final product. What kind of revision was done to the content and organization of the paper? Why do you think the writer made these revisions? What effect did these changes have on the quality of ideas in the paper? Also examine any changes made for stylistic purposes or to correct mechanical/grammatical errors. When did these occur? What effect did these have on the paper? Finally, reread only the first draft and the final version of the piece. Did the multiple drafts improve the overall quality of the paper? How?

Reflection

When a piece of writing is completed, students benefit from a chance to reflect on what they have accomplished, focusing on why and how they wrote this piece and what they learned in the process. This metacognitive activity—thinking about their own thinking—brings to conscious awareness the student's writing process, building a student's sense of self as a writer engaged in the writer's craft. We ask students to attach a short piece of reflective writing to the extended pieces they write, addressing some or all of the following questions.

- Why did you choose to write about this topic?
- How did you go about writing this piece? What steps did you go through? Did you conference with fellow-students or the teacher? What kind of revision did you do? What kind of editing and proofreading did you do?
- Was this piece difficult to write or easy? Why?

- How do you feel about the piece now? What do you like best about it? Are there any parts you still feel unsure about?
- What did you learn from doing this piece of writing? Did you experiment with any new writing techniques, apply something from a lesson we had in class, or work on a particular editing skill?

Students who are asked to reflect on their work frequently throughout the semester become aware of their own writing strengths and weaknesses and the strategies that have helped them. They develop a clearer sense of what to focus on to become more effective writers because they are asked to think about themselves as working writers. Reflective writers also learn to become more objective about their work, developing the critical thinking and self-evaluation skills that eventually lead to more independent composing and revising. A final benefit, according to Cooper and Odell, is that ". . . self-reflection or self-evaluation in writing enables students to consolidate and remember longer what they have learned about writing" (2).

Publishing Student Writing: From Sharing in Class to Professional Publication

Sharing, publishing, and celebrating student writing is one of the best ways to strengthen writing development. Knowing that their writing will be published may spur even the most reluctant writers to produce a piece, and it encourages all students to put more effort into their work. Writing that has a real purpose in kids' lives with the potential for being read by an audience beyond the classroom is highly motivating. Publication has many benefits:

1. It gives the student a meaningful reason for writing.

2. It provides authentic audiences for students to imagine as readers when they shape and revise their work. They can ask themselves such questions as
"Will my reader understand this?"
"Have I given readers enough information?"
"Is my language and tone appropriate for those who will be reading this?"
"What do I want my readers to feel, think, and remember when they read this?"

3. It motivates students to edit, proofread, and polish their work until it is relatively error-free or is appropriate for its intended purpose and audience.

4. It provides real incentives for writing, not just a grade to fulfill an assignment.

5. To use James Britton's phrase, published writing is not a "dummy-run"; it's the real thing. No matter how hard we try to shape school assignments into meaningful work, without readers except for the teacher, writing remains a "dummy-run," often sapping motivation from all but the most dedicated young writers.

6. Publication induces pride in seeing one's work in print, on display, or the subject of discussion by others. It's great for ego building, self-esteem, or just plain feeling good about school and oneself as a student.

For all these reasons, multiple forms of publication should be a regular part of the writing program. On an ongoing basis, teachers should be on the alert for real purposes for writing: editorials about a school issue that could be sent to the school paper or the local newspaper; letters of inquiry, complaint, or thanks that are actually mailed; projects that fulfill a genuine need such as flyers, pamphlets, brochures, leaflets, and information sheets; letters, poems, stories, and articles in response to local events that could be sent out for publication or to specific people; responses to political issues affecting students' lives that could be mailed or e-mailed to members of state or national political bodies.

Beyond the search for meaningful reasons to write for real audiences, we like to think of "publishing" in the broadest sense of the word—providing a receptive readership for student work. Teachers can publish all manner of student writing in ways ranging from the simplest—sharing in class—to the most public—entering contests or submitting pieces to national student publications.

Suggestions for Publishing. Regularly schedule "read-alouds" as part of writing workshop time. An Author's Chair makes this a special event, no matter what the grade level—an old rocker from the Salvation Army or the teacher's desk chair works fine for this. Older students might appreciate a chance to stand behind a Writer's Podium to do a reading of their work. Encourage the writer to introduce the piece, talking about how and why it was written. Students can also share their work in reading groups or with a regular reading partner.

Ask each student to select his or her favorite piece of writing, staple a blank sheet of paper to the back, and pass it to other readers who are invited to write a response, indicating what they liked about the piece or what associations it brought to mind.

Post papers on a class bulletin board used solely for this purpose. Sometimes post only especially fine pieces; other times post one piece from every student. Allow some class time for students to browse the board for the latest postings. Occasionally, post a piece with all its pre-writing, drafts, and revisions right up to the final polished version.

Display research papers or other extended writing projects on a table in the room so students can read one another's finished work. Or fill a display case or bulletin board in the school hallway with students' work for others in the school to read.

Put together a class anthology once each semester—a best piece from each student in a looseleaf notebook or spiral binding. Or publish a poetry or short story anthology at the end of a unit on this genre. Students can act as an editorial board, publishing team, and illustrators to select pieces, design the format, and assemble the publication. Display these in the classroom for others to look through in search of possible topics or just to read and enjoy. Make a second copy for the school library and ask the librarian to set aside a special area for anthologies of student writing. If funds permit, duplicate a copy for each student in the class. A simple spiral binding machine may be the best piece of equipment any English Department with an active writing program could invest in!

Divide the class into groups, each assigned to create a publication of some kind such as a newspaper, anthology of writings, series of articles on a theme, newsletter, pamphlet, or magazine. Publish these works within the classroom, in the school library, or in other appropriate places.

Have students make individual bound books of their own writing, illustrating their pieces with drawings or art cut from magazines or computer sources. In our experience, writers of any age right up to adulthood and beyond respond with pleasure to this activity. These make splendid gifts for parents as well as personal mementos for the students. See the Appendix for some easy bookbinding directions.

Encourage students to submit their work to the school newspaper or literary magazine. If no literary magazine exists, consider starting one with your students to provide a venue for all students and teachers in the school to publish their work.

Diana Wakeford, a high school teacher in Tecumseh, Michigan, holds an annual Celebration of Writing with her graduating seniors. The assignment is for each student to select a favorite piece to illustrate with a visual, often three-dimensional display. Students work on this throughout their spring term, developing projects that range from desktop displays and three-dimensional scenes to expressive artwork and multi-media presentations, turning key themes of their work into visible images. The writing itself is central to the display. For example, a series of poems about color and mood are tacked to yards of fabric batiked in colors to match the poetry. A short story about senior prom night is hung on a senior prom gown accompanied by other artifacts of the night. A table filled with photos, ballet slippers, and programs documents a paper on the ballerina Margot Fonteyn. Sports equipment is artfully arranged in a three-dimensional collage surrounding an essay on sports. Toward the end of the semester, as graduation approaches, students fill the school library with these works and invite parents, administrators, and other students to spend an hour reading, viewing, browsing, and joining them as they celebrate their own multi-dimensional creativity.

Desktop Publishing and the Internet. The Internet offers opportunities for students to see their work published in a new communication mode. The easiest way to do this is to create a class website on which students regularly publish their work. Just as with any in-class publication, an editorial board, design team, and website publication staff can give students ownership over the site. Work published this way becomes available to audiences worldwide and creates a library of materials for use by future students. Some computer-savvy students can even publish personal websites filled with their own writing and other creative products. Many public sites are also now available to teens for self-publishing opportunities.

Desktop publishing software makes all kinds of classroom publishing projects possible from class newsletters to illustrated magazines or informal "zines." Templates for some projects are often bundled with newer word processing programs, but more sophisticated publishing software is relatively inexpensive when purchased for educational purposes. Many young writers thrive on the opportunity these offer to both write and design on the computer. At a more basic level, we find that students of all ages enjoy embellishing their writing with computer-generated art, clip art, photos, and decorative designs.

Suggestions for Publishing Beyond the Classroom. Local businesses—banks, shops, supermarkets—are sometimes willing to let teachers and students set up a display of student writing for the public to read as they wait in lines or visit these places. We've seen some wonderful poster displays of student writing in the windows of local stores and hung on walls in local banks, often illustrated by the student, each with a snapshot of the young writer.

Investigate writing contests designed especially for students. The National Council of Teachers of English offers an annual Promising Young Writers Program for eighth grade students and Achievement Awards in Writing for high school juniors. See their website http://www.ncte.org for further details or write to NCTE, 1111 Kenyon Road, Urbana, IL 61901-1096. Scholastic Art and Writing Awards are another reliable source of awards for student writing. Each year 50,000 students nationwide receive regional awards and 1,100 become national award winners. Their website gives details and entry information http://www.scholastic.com/artandwriting/index.htm or contact Scholastic at 555 Broadway, New York, NY 19912. Local newspapers and magazines regularly sponsor writing contests, often dedicated to special occasions or holidays. *The Flint Journal* holds an annual Martin Luther King Writing Contest with a different topic each year, such as "brotherhood," something teachers in the Flint schools anticipate as they plan their writing assignments for the semester. Some newspapers have a weekly or monthly section for publishing student writing from surrounding school districts plus an annual writing contest.

Many magazines exist that publish student writing. Encourage students to send their best work to these magazines. Even if the work is returned with a polite letter of rejection, it's a valuable experience for an aspiring author to prepare a piece for an editor, write the accompanying letter, and send it out. Acceptance can be the impetus for a lifelong passion for writing! *Merlyn's Pen,* an annual publication of student work by teens 12 to 18, has a website with a list of 30 magazines and newspapers that publish student writing, including information about how to contact each one. Their site also provides a list of writers' resources, books, magazines, and websites useful for aspiring teenage writers. In addition, *Merlyn's Pen* offers a critique service providing a personal editorial review of stories, poems, and essays submitted by teens. See http://www.merlynspen.com for further information.

For serious young writers, Kathy Henderson's *The Young Writer's Guide to Getting Published* (2001), offers tips, warnings, and resources plus directions for preparing and submitting pieces. The book also lists 48 magazines that publish student writing and 58 student writing contests.

One Final Note

It is especially important to point out that the writing process and workshop methods discussed throughout this chapter are beneficial for all secondary writing classrooms, from seventh grade General English to twelfth grade Advanced Placement English, and for all forms of writing, from personal and descriptive writing to expository essays and the research paper. Teachers sometimes relegate these methods to personal narratives and descriptive writing, reverting to forms, formulas, and outlines for essay writing. But workshops based on the writing process support writers who are at work on all kinds of writing. The Appendix contains two examples of the writing process used for formal essays: 1) a two-week workshop for high school students assigned to write a persuasive paper; and 2) a one-month unit on the research paper for senior level students.

A story bears telling here. An experienced teacher of college preparatory English for seniors was "converted" to a belief in the writing process by participating in a summer writing project for teachers. In the fall, she wanted to change her methodology, but was afraid she might fail to prepare her students for college if she did. So she compromised. She spent the first half of the school year on essay writing and the research paper, using her normal methodology. In January, she switched gears to more personal writing and engaged her class in writing process activities, eventually moving into a daily writing workshop. She wrote with her students, they engaged in peer response groups, she conferenced with them, they published. About mid-semester, the students began to ask her why they hadn't been allowed to do this throughout the first term. "We would have written so much better papers if we could have worked together and revised," was the repeated complaint. The following year she reversed the sequence, establishing a writing workshop approach with her seniors early in the semester and using such strategies as pre-writing, revision, conferences, and peer response groups throughout the year. The students had been right, she reported at a recent teachers' meeting; students' essays and research papers in her college-bound class really were much improved when she implemented these methods early in the school year.

Points to Remember

1. Writing instruction has undergone a significant change in recent years, moving from a focus on the form and correctness of the final product to an emphasis on the process writers use to produce a finished piece.

2. The new paradigm for writing instruction, "teach writing as process, not product," means teaching students to do what practicing writers do: pre-writing and planning, drafting and revising, editing and proofreading to prepare a piece for readers.

3. The writing process is not a set of mechanical steps to march students through; it is a cluster of complex thinking and writing behaviors that lead to the making of meaning as the writer works to produce a finished piece.

4. A safe, comfortable, risk-free environment where young writers are both supported and challenged is crucial to writing development.

5. Writing workshop provides the time, ownership, and response all writers thrive on.

6. Teacher conferences and peer response groups give students feedback on their writing to aid revision and also provide readers. Students need training and modeling in order for peer response groups to be effective.

7. Grammar, usage, and correctness are best taught as part of the writing process with a special focus on the editing and proofreading stages of writing.

8. Writing teachers must write themselves in order to understand what young writers need to grow and develop. When teachers write and share their work with their students they demonstrate the value of writing and also provide models of the hard work all writing requires.

9. Sharing, publishing, and celebrating students' writing has powerful motivating force in the writing classroom.

For Further Reading

Atwell, Nancie. *In the Middle: New Understandings About Writing, Reading, and Learning.* 2nd ed. Portsmouth, NH: Boynton/Cook-Heinemann, 1998.

Kirby, Dan and Tom Liner with Ruth Vinz. *Inside Out: Developmental Strategies for Teaching Writing.* 2nd ed. Portsmouth, NH: Boynton/Cook-Heinemann, 1988.

Lane, Barry. *After THE END: Teaching and Learning Creative Revision.* Portsmouth, NH: Heinemann, 1993.

Murray, Donald. *Learning by Teaching: Selected Articles on Writing and Teaching.* Portsmouth, NH: Boynton/Cook-Heinemann, 1982.

Rief, Linda. *Seeking Diversity: Language Arts with Adolescents.* Portsmouth, NH: Heinemann, 1992.

Romano, Tom. *Clearing the Way.* Portsmouth, NH: Heinemann, 1987.

Zemelman, Steven and Harvey Daniels. *A Community of Writers: Teaching Writing in the Junior and Senior High School.* Portsmouth, NH: Heinemann, 1988.

4

Grammar, Correctness, and Style

No topic in writing instruction garners more public debate, more educational research, or more headaches for writing teachers than grammar and correctness and the role they play in the writing process. No topic reported on in the scholarship of writing instruction is ignored more than this one. And no topic strikes terror in the heart of young writers more than this. The intensity of the emotions surrounding the topic of grammar and correctness is, in large part, attributed to the myths and misconceptions embedded in these issues. Grammar and correctness issues are often inflamed by intuition rather than by reason, by misunderstandings rather than by knowledge based in research. As part of the introduction to this chapter that focuses on writing issues related to correctness of language and effectiveness of style, we want to explore these common myths and provide an overview of the research on the relationship between direct grammar instruction and the development of writing. This theoretical framework can then be used to discuss when and how teachers can deal with the correctness issue in more rational and practical ways. The chapter will then move to the more practical issues of what to do about grammar, correctness, and usage in the classroom, including non-mainstream dialects. The concluding sections will focus on sentence combining and other stylistic issues at the sentence level.

The following NCATE/NCTE standards are addressed in this chapter.

2.1 Demonstrate respect for the worth and contributions of all learners;
3.1.1 Demonstrate understanding of language acquisition and development;
3.1.2 Demonstrate how reading, writing, speaking, listening, viewing, and thinking are interrelated throughout all aspects of the English language arts curriculum and draw upon both theory and practice in doing so;
3.1.3 Demonstrate that they understand the impact of cultural, economic, political, and social environments upon language and can convey that understanding to students by drawing upon both theory and practice;
3.1.4 Demonstrate a respect for and a deep understanding of diversity in language use, patterns, and dialects across cultures, ethnic groups, geographic

regions, and social roles and show consistent attention to accommodating such diversity;

3.1.6 Demonstrate a knowledge of English grammars and use that knowledge in teaching both oral and written forms of the language;

3.2.5 Demonstrate knowledge of language structure and conventions in creating and critiquing print and non-print texts of their own and their students;

3.7.1 Use major sources of research theory related to English language arts consistently to support their teaching decisions;

4.5 Create and sustain learning environments which promote respect for and support of individual differences of ethnicity, race, language, culture, gender, and ability.

As we suggest later in this chapter, pendulum swings in the formal teaching of grammar have been occurring over this past half century. Not all teachers entering the new millennium are assuming that formal grammar instruction is necessary; in fact, as we suggest later, many have given up the study of grammar altogether. Nevertheless in many schools and classrooms, grammar instruction remains a major area of study within the English curriculum. Weaver (1996, 7–9) suggests that the systematic teaching of grammar persists in those classrooms for a number of reasons: 1) unfamiliarity with the research or a refusal to believe the research; 2) the claims made by some of the good writers in their classes that their writing ability is a result of direct grammar instruction; 3) the belief that direct, systematic instruction is necessary in order to apply the principles to writing; 4) the belief that the study of grammar is good mental discipline; 5) or the belief that national standardized tests mandate overt knowledge of grammar. Complicating teachers' attitudes toward the teaching of grammar is the widespread public perception about the importance of systematic grammar instruction. Politicians, parents, and the public in general see systematic grammar instruction as the way to self-discipline and the way to writing effectiveness, particularly if they feel that their own writing ability corresponds to their experiences of studying grammar in school. Even teachers who question the efficacy of its instruction get caught up in the political impact of these arguments. The following comments by teachers indicate the knotty issue grammar instruction has become:

> "I don't understand why good students leave out possessives when I've taught it, reinforced it, quizzed it. . . . Yet even after all this, there are those errors in the title, in the very first sentence!"
> "Do I read a paper and ignore all punctuation? What good is that for them?"
> "I put 5X on their papers and they have to write it over five times. It's so stupid, obviously. But I can't reinforce this by doing nothing" (Rosen 1987, 139).

Grammars Defined

Before we can consider issues related to grammar instruction in any detail, it is important to specify what we mean by the term "grammar." On the one hand, linguists use the term to refer to the linguistic knowledge that speakers of a language operate with, for the most part unconsciously—the internalized system of rules by which we operate in our production and comprehension of language (Grammar I). For example, all speakers operate with a rule that allows a verb particle to shift to the end of a sentence: "She turned down the offer" or "She turned the offer down." Speakers can choose either option: "turned down the offer" or "turned the offer down." But speakers feel obligated to make the shift when a pronoun replaces the direct object "offer": "She turned it down" rather than "she turned down it." Speakers know this rule unconsciously and operate with it consistently: when it's a noun phrase, the shift is optional; when it's a pronoun, the shift is obligatory.

On the other hand, grammar is sometimes defined as the descriptions of those rules that linguists have constructed from observing the language in use (Grammar II). When we say, therefore, that speakers of a language operate with a grammar of that language, we are referring to Grammar I; when we talk about a description of those rules as they are outlined in a traditional grammar book or a transformational grammar text, such as how adverbials or verb tenses operate in English, we are referring to Grammar II, which merely reflects the internalized knowledge (Grammar I) of speakers. Grammar II is always descriptive rather than prescriptive; it describes how speakers actually use language rather than how someone thinks they *should* use language. Descriptive grammars, therefore, are non-judgmental. They theoretically acknowledge variation from dialect to dialect, simply recording how speakers operate with the rules within their dialect system. A description of the rules of one dialect would reflect a different system for negation, past tense formation, and verb forms from the system used in a neighboring dialect, much like the grammatically different structures in Spanish and English for noun modification, where in the former the adjective follows the noun and in the latter it precedes the noun. For example, one dialect may have a rule allowing for double negation, as evidenced in the usage found in many English vernaculars such as "He didn't do nothing to earn it." A neighboring dialect, on the other hand, might operate with a rule that disallowed most double negatives: "He didn't do anything to earn it."

Grammar III is the study of usage—the table manners of language—that focus on "correctness" of usage, that prescribe some features and proscribe others: "Plural subjects take plural verbs" and "You should never end a sentence with a preposition." Usage texts, therefore, violate the linguistic definition of Grammar II by their assumption that what is worthy of description is only the rule system operating in some kind of ideal language or dialect—Standard English, for want of a better term. What usage texts consider to be "correct" usage primarily reflects the language patterns of some idealized version of "Standard English" and the non-stigmatized usages of dialect patterns of middle-class speech, even though few speakers of any dialect operate with all the usage rules of "Standard English" consistently. What is considered "correct" usage has evolved over time from historical precedents regarding usage, usually based on the linguistic forms most commonly used by the speech communities with the greatest economic and political power. Considering something as "incorrect," therefore, is a matter of social convention rather than an inherent "flaw" in the linguistic structure itself.

"Correct" usage often changes over time because of shifts in attitude towards various usages. In fact, "hisself" was a perfectly respectable usage in the eighteenth century that eventually fell into disfavor; multiple negation was a regular feature of Middle English speech until the eighteenth century, when the age of rationalism suggested that linguistic features should be symmetrical and logical, for example, and that two negatives make a positive. Double comparatives were considered just fine until the eighteenth century when "more gladder" was rejected in favor of "gladder" or "more glad." The imposition of prescriptive rules for language use in the eighteenth century coincided with the growth of a middle class eager to change their dialects to reflect a new gentility (Thomas and Tchudi 1999) and to use language rules as a means of identifying those who "belonged" to the middle class. The fascination with Latin as the "ideal" language encouraged usage rules such as never ending sentences with a preposition, never splitting infinitives, etc. Never mind that the radically different way verbs operated in Latin prevented infinitives from being "split," unlike English, whose verb system easily accommodated it. "Rules is rules," Latin predominated as the model language, and the "middle class" cheerfully adhered to the rules as a way of maintaining their position, prestige, and power, on the one hand, and as a way of making middle-class membership inaccessible to those whose language didn't match up, on the other.

In short, when we speak about "grammar" we need to clarify which of the definitions we're using, and we will regularly refer to Grammar I, II, and III as a means of identifying the definition to avoid confusion. Much of what goes on in English classrooms related to grammar study is a combination of Grammars II and III—some focus on descriptions of syntactic elements such as kinds of phrases, clauses, verbs, and parts of speech, and some focus on prescriptive usage rules that attempt to get speakers and writers to avoid stigmatized forms of English usage.

Reviews of studies based on the teaching of Grammar II, traditional descriptions of grammar (H. A. Greene; DeBoer; Searles and Carlson; Braddock, Lloyd-Jones, and Schoer), uniformly report not only the lack of positive effect on writing ability but the potential for negative effects if time spent on writing is taken up by the formal study of grammar. And despite the fact that newer methods of linguistic analysis, such as functional grammar and transformational grammar, held some hope that their formal study would yield more positive results, these approaches, too, have proven to be disappointing. Carryover to student writing from grammatical analysis seems minimal (Elley et al.; McQuade). Sentence combining activities seem to be the one exception. Some evidence exists that writers who participated in sentence combining exercises used more syntactically complex sentences in their own writing. Yet even here, the positive results occurred only when students actually did some writing, not when they merely studied the structure of language (Weaver 1996). Weaver indicates that "there is little pragmatic justification for systematically teaching a descriptive or explanatory grammar of the language, whether that grammar be traditional, structural, transformational, or any other kind" (23). As Weaver suggests, it's the guided application, not the formal study of grammar, that's important (24). In other words, marching students through eight-week units or twenty-week school semesters identifying grammatical structures, studying Standard English usage, and doing workbook exercises is not as effective as we'd like to believe. Instead, students need to be immersed in a writing and reading environment in which language study has a direct application to their own composing, where the usage skills they are taught are immediately applied to the papers they are writing, and where the grammatical structures they study help them become responsive readers and flexible writers. Later in this chapter we present suggestions for how teachers can accomplish the guided application of grammar to student writing by incorporating grammar and usage study into a well-planned writing program.

The Developmental Nature of Syntactic Complexity

Before we discuss the principles and practices of guided application to student writing, it is critical for teachers to understand both the developmental nature of writing and the complexity of issues related to what we mean by "error." The development of writing is an on-going process, just as oral language development is, a point discussed in Chapter Two. Being able to articulate the nature of writing development for their own students, for parents, and for the public enables teachers to deal with the notion of error in writing that moves the discussion beyond the polarity of mere correctness versus incorrectness.

Like oral language, children's written syntax becomes increasingly more complex over time, primarily from opportunities to write for a variety of purposes and a willingness to experiment with new forms and structures. Trial and error is a natural part of the process. Studies over the past several years tracing children's syntactic development suggest that all the basic English sentence patterns in oral language are developed by the end of kindergarten, and major kinds of subordinate clauses such as nominals, adjectivals, and adverbials are used frequently by kindergartners, as in the following examples:

> "I want whatever he wants" (nominal clause);
> "Sally is the girl I like the most" (adjectival);
> "If she chases us, let's hide" (adverbial).

Combining simple sentences into more complex ones can also be accomplished by coordinating elements. In their writing children first coordinate entire sentences ("The bunny ran across the front yard, and then he went under the evergreen."), which eventually gives way to coordinating elements within sentences ("The bunny ran across the yard and went under the evergreen.") These two major forms of sentence combining—subordination and coordination—at first result in increasing sentence length, but eventually those sentences become shorter and more efficient as writers reduce clauses to phrases, replace coordination with phrases, and use syntactic patterns that require fewer words. Weaver cites the work of Hunt as he describes, through example, how young writers become increasingly more efficient—using fewer words but more syntactically complex structures:

In grade four, says Hunt, the following sentences, not very syntactically complex, are typical:

> Bauxite contains aluminum and it contains several other substances. Workmen extract these other substances from the bauxite. They grind the bauxite and put it in tanks. Pressure is in the tanks. . . . (qtd. in Weaver 1996, 125)

By eighth grade, writers are more likely to use more complex syntax by conjoining and subordinating ideas:

> Bauxite contains several other substances. Workmen extract these from bauxite by grinding it, then putting it in pressure tanks. . . . (qtd. in Weaver 1996, 126)

As Weaver suggests, writers say more, in fewer words.

We should note here that oral language seems to be more syntactically complex than written language until approximately grade seven, when it begins to reverse. By high school, students are capable, for the most part, of using complex coordination and subordination and various kinds of phrases and clauses in their writing, even if they are unable to identify the types or kinds of clauses and phrases used and unlikely to use them in their oral language. What is evident in their writing is that the syntactic complexity moves beyond any descriptions of grammatical constructions they have studied overtly in their English grammar classes. For example, it isn't unusual to find a junior writing something as syntactically complicated as "His attitudes toward the governor, strengthened by the time he spent working in the governor's office, became increasingly negative." Chances are excellent that no grammar book asked for sentence diagramming of such a linguistically complex sentence or even asked students to identify all the clauses and phrases embedded into this one complex sentence.

At the same time, we must understand that the syntactic complexity evident in the writing of high school students is not always well structured, clear, and graceful, so that many writers still have considerable work to do to make their prose polished and articulate.

Although we encourage the use of sentence combining activities (see later discussion in this chapter) for developing fluency in writing, our discussion of developing syntactic complexity and the research on its effectiveness must be tempered with the following caveats. First, some of the work on which these results are based involves out-of-context sentence combining exercises (Hunt), problematic for two reasons. Writing resulting from such exercises may not always reflect the free-writing of children at these ages, and even if sentence combining exercises encourage children to create more syntactically complex sentences as part of those exercises than they might do naturally in their writing, there is not always the carryover from syntactic complexity in out-of-context exercises to their own natural writing. Furthermore, sentence combining exercises out of context are less valuable than direct guidance in helping writers expand, combine, and reorganize sentence structures within their own writing (Weaver 1996, 81).

The second caveat is that it may be neither desirable nor possible to hasten syntactic growth, which is more often a matter of maturation and writing experience than something that can be induced artificially through writing exercises. Such growth occurs for most writers naturally through continued writing opportunities. Focusing students on complexity at the expense of clarity and sentence variety can lead to inflated, awkward prose. As Weaver suggests, syntactically complex sentences can be

> . . . awkward, convoluted, even unintelligible; they can also be inappropriate to the subject, the audience, and the writer's or persona's voice. Conversely, relatively simple sentences can make their point succinctly and emphatically. Often, of course, sentence variety is best (1996, 130).

And the third caveat is that syntactic complexity varies considerably from one genre to another. Exposition and argumentation often call for greater syntactic complexity than does narration, for example. Assuming that all genres should have similar levels of complexity is to overlook the inherent differences among them. Furthermore, students asked to write in these more complex genres are often stretching their linguistic ability, which may produce errors, as we will discuss below.

The Nature of "Error"

Because so much grading energy traditionally has gone into the "error hunt," looking for "violations" of Grammar III usage rules, we wish to question, and complicate teachers' notions of error within the developmental process of syntactic and linguistic maturity. Not all errors are simple violations of a Grammar III usage rule, as Murdick asserts, despite the fact that traditional textbooks often imply just that—that error is an obvious deviation from a set of rules easy to describe and apply to one's writing. The result is that a set of easily identified mistakes such as agreement, comma splices, dangling modifiers, leads to the mistaken notion that error hunting and error correction are easy goals to achieve. Murdick complicates this notion by citing Krishna's 1975 article in *The Journal of Basic Writing* which points out that the

> clear-cut and predictable errors that are most precisely described and categorized in the grammar books . . . dwindle in significance next to problems of incoherence, illogicality, lack of conventional idiom or clear syntax—amorphous and unpredictable errors involving the structure of the whole sentence (qtd. in Murdick, 41).

Murdick's examples of such syntactic difficulty include the following (41):

1. Due to the problems of discipline and general apathy arise largely from the boredom of students who have no interest in academic matters.
2. They suggested to make the course easier.

Neither sentence is easily "correctable" from prescriptions of usage rules found in most grammar books or handbooks. Both sentences suggest the need to look beyond the traditional kinds of errors cited in grammar books and to consider the broader developmental, rhetorical, and usage matters that affect writing fluency, a point we discuss in the next section. Both types of problems in the writing need to be dealt with through teacher-conferencing, working with the student on reshaping the sentence to make it more idiomatic. (See below for a fuller description of how these sentences can be revised.) Graceful, idiomatic, articulate writing comes only with considerable practice, opportunities to write, and guidance by teachers on an individual basis.

Our discussion of error in this chapter deliberately excludes the issues of typos or performance errors that result from momentary lapses in writing: inadvertently reversing two words or deleting a word, etc. Error, from a linguistic and rhetorical perspective, falls into four general categories: 1) developmental errors resulting from experimentation with more complex syntactic structures and vocabulary; 2) rhetorical errors that may simply be inappropriate for the context, voice, and purpose of the writing; 3) dialect or usage features that, when they appear in writing, may be social markers that identify the writer as using features considered to be non-standard; and 4) errors in the use of writing conventions such as punctuation, capitalization, spelling. Particularly the first three categories suggest the need to give up the polarities of correct/incorrect, good/bad, right/wrong views of language. Not all errors are violations of rules, not all errors are categorically bad, and not all errors need to be red-penciled as signs of writing failure. "Good English," we would like to echo from a number of linguists, is appropriate to the writer's purpose, appropriate to the context, and comfortable to the speaker/writer and the listener/reader (Andrews). And we might add, good English is language that is also age-appropriate. Such a definition complicates the simplistic notion of correct and incorrect and has implications for the nature of the "error hunt" in which some teachers participate.

The following section describes each of these kinds of errors and provides examples:

Developmental Errors. Developmental errors and inappropriate language for the context, voice, or purpose of writing evolve from attempts of writers to try out new forms, to move beyond familiar ground, to write within new contexts and with a variety of purposes. In Chapter Two we argued that "error" is not categorically negative—that as speakers and writers begin to use more sophisticated syntax and sentence organization, they make errors as they experiment with structure and vocabulary. Because growth in language, both oral and written, is accomplished through a certain amount of trial and error, what may appear to be errors or regressions are often indications of progress. The syntax of young writers may consist primarily of simple sentences, all punctuated correctly, but when writers begin using more complex sentences containing dependent and independent clauses, they may also use sentence fragments for the first time, reflecting the growth of syntactic complexity of their writing. "I hate peanut butter and jelly sandwiches, but my mom made me eat it anyway" may become, "My mom made me eat a peanut butter and jelly sandwich. Even though I hate them." Similarly, when complex sentences with modifying phrases are first used, writers may have difficulty knowing where to place the phrases. For example, "We flew over Washington at night. The Capitol was all lit up" may become, "Flying over Washington at night, the Capitol was all lit up." When writers first begin to use subordination, they may over-use or over-generalize the appropriateness of this structure, as in the following example: "Soccer coaches sometimes favor certain players, who might not always be the best ones who can get the job done, which really angers other players on the team who want a chance."

Sometimes the less-than-fluent use of language involves idiomatic usage—new vocabulary that takes a specific grammatical structure unfamiliar to the writer, as in the previously cited sentence, "They suggested to make the course easier," in which the writer is unaware of the need to use a gerund following the verb "suggested": "They suggested making the course easier." Similarly, problems with word choice and diction often reflect writers' attempts to use vocabulary that they are not fully comfortable with as they move beyond simple topics and ideas to more complex ones requiring a degree of sophistication not yet achieved, as in: "Euphemism is the desire to use words in an imprecisive manner purposively to create false impressions of precise word meanings."

Occasionally developing writers " 'back into' their sentences, putting the heart of their idea into prepositional phrases, object noun clauses . . . or other ancillary parts of the sentence, wasting the subject" (Krishna, quoted in Murdick, 41), as in the sentence quoted earlier: "Due to the problems of discipline and general apathy arise largely from the boredom of students who have no interest in academic matters," which can be revised as, "The problems of discipline and general apathy arise. . . ."

While such "errors" may be pointed out to writers as places for revisions, they should be considered by-products of a necessary stage in the development of more sophisticated syntax. Similarly, as writers try out new forms and more complicated sentences, their writing may temporarily develop problems with punctuation and sentence fragments. Perfectly punctuated simple sentences give way to more complex ones that sometimes involve difficulties with punctuation, sentence fragments, and awkward structures that may appear to suggest slippage in writing ability rather than as a necessary part of the developmental process of syntactic complexity.

Learning new grammatical structures is a gradual process. Because acquiring control of a new structure requires multiple attempts at using it, writers need these intermediate stages between no control and full control to learn the tricks of the trade. Writing fluency develops most easily when teachers make a conscious effort to protect these stages for their students' experimentation with writing by creating risk-free writing environments, by encouraging revision, and by not grading drafts.

Rhetorical Errors. The second category of "error" is the inappropriateness of the structure or diction for the purposes of the writer or the audience—using the rhetorical context of the writing for decisions about voice, tone, and usage within the writing. From an early age, children and young adults are aware of the social context of oral language and modify their use of language to fit the particular social situation. Even five-year-olds know that direct demands are inappropriate in some social contexts, and they soon learn that polite forms of request are going to be more effective than direct demands in getting what they want. "May I have that?" gets them more than "Gimme that" does. But the nature of audience and appropriateness in writing is a difficult concept because often the audience is either a distant one, unlike oral conversation, or the real audience is actually the teacher, the real reader of the writing, despite attempts to "imagine" an audience beyond the classroom. Imagined artificial audiences sometimes make it difficult for writers to use the expected, appropriate diction because they write with the teacher or their peers in mind, especially if the writing is not to find its way beyond the classroom walls. Using slang in a paper may be acceptable to the writer's peers but not to the teacher. At other times writers imagine that all their writing must be formal structures and diction, resulting in awkward, stilted sentence structures, inelegant and sometimes inappropriate for intended audiences. The student who writes "If the college of your choice is a highly-reputated one . . ." is attempting to approximate the academic discourse community he wishes to become part of. These scenarios reflect more the inexperience of young writers than their violation of a set of "rules." Sometimes these reflect misguided notions of appropriateness, sometimes the lack of awareness that different registers exist for different purposes and audiences, and sometimes the assumption that all writing should be written for the teacher. Writing for real, varied audiences beyond classroom walls provides opportunities for writers to explore varying structures and forms, writing in different registers, writing for specific purposes.

Dialect Features or Usage Errors. The third issue related to error deals with usage or dialect features in student writing. All speakers of English speak a dialect of English, and the features of any given dialect systematically follow the rules and conventions of that dialect. Any usage that conforms to the speaker's internalized system of language and abides by the rules of that system is grammatical from a linguistic perspective. Double negation, as in "I don't want none," is grammatical for speakers of some speech communities. No rule has been violated within the constraints of this dialect; rather the double negative conforms to the internalized structure of that linguistic system. As speakers of English, we do not consider Spanish speakers for whom adjectives follow nouns—"casa grande" (big house), for example—to be violating a linguistic rule when placing the adjective after the noun. We recognize Spanish as a different linguistic system. The same is also true of different dialects. All dialects are fully-formed linguistic systems with some patterns unique to those systems.

Why is it, then, that some English speakers make negative judgments about dialect speakers when they don't make those same judgments about speakers of other languages? Negative judgments about dialects within the same language system (Appalachian English versus New England English, for example) are usually social judgments reflecting social class attitudes and assumptions. Linguistic differences become the basis of social judgments, not for linguistic reasons but for social reasons—a way of laying claim to greater power and authority, a way of maintaining social distance and superiority. Valuing certain linguistic forms over others ("I saw" rather than "I seen"; "I don't have any" rather than "I don't have none," etc.) reflects the social attitudes of some middle-class speakers towards the speech patterns of working-class speakers—a "we-them" phenomenon fostered by the simplistic dichotomy of "good" and "bad" language, "correct" and "incorrect" language. As we stated earlier, these features become social markers and the basis for classifying speakers in terms of social position and power.

Linguistic judgments rooted in social class differences have an even more negative impact when these social markers appear in student writing, for one reason because most teachers and many laypeople are more willing to accept dialect differences in speech while resisting acceptance in writing. Often home discourses, or primary discourses, as James Gee refers to them, differ from the academic discourse patterns in print, and when the primary discourse includes features considered to be non-standard, they are often targeted for elimination in writing. The "sacredness" of writing and its potential permanence encourage the attitude that these social markers in writing are errors to be eliminated at all cost. The issue is a difficult one. While teachers knowledgeable about the linguistic validity of all dialects recognize these features as grammatical within the writer's linguistic system, they also know that the social judgments are very real, that most readers will impose a set of traditional linguistic standards on what they read, regardless of the validity of the speaker's dialect. For all practical purposes, then, they view these social markers as features that need to be eliminated because they are judged by the reading public as errors.

It is important to point out that the social markers in writing, although they reflect social markers in oral language, are nevertheless more limited: all writers modify their written usage in favor of more expected forms. Speakers who use double negation, "ain't" as a verb form, or the habitual "be" in AAVE (African American Vernacular English) rarely use these forms in formal writing. Many speakers are code-switchers, able to use one set of linguistic rules for oral use within the community and for informal writing, another set of linguistic rules when the situation or context is perceived to be more formal, with expectations of standard usage. Not all social markers or non-standard dialect features will disappear from the writing, but many of the more stigmatized forms will. Writers whose oral dialects are largely AAVE or Appalachian, for example, will likely avoid the use of "ain't" or "he be going. . . ." in formal writing or revised drafts but will occasionally delete past tense inflections on "worked" or use a non-traditional verb form like "had went." What this suggests is the linguistic flexibility of speakers/writers and their awareness at some level of different expectations for informal and formal language.

Writing Conventions: Mechanics and Punctuation. Errors in this category exist by virtue of the struggles inexperienced writers have with the conventions of punctuation, capitalization, and spelling. We must understand that they are matters of conventions, common practice, and current usage, suggesting change over time and even from one speech community to another. For example, British English's spelling of "colour" and "metre" and its use of periods and commas outside rather than inside the quotation mark suggest different cultural practices that establish the conventions of that particular system. Even within a given culture variations exist. The use of the comma before the last item in a series is now optional ("apples, pears, and oranges"), as is the use of a comma after a short introductory clause in a sentence ("Despite her efforts the work was delayed."). Though conventions of several decades ago made these uses of punctuation obligatory, they are examples of the rules that change over time.

Despite the usual practice in writing instruction of grouping these items of capitalization, punctuation, and spelling together in the category of writing conventions, Cordeiro cites major differences between capitalization and spelling, on one hand, and punctuation on the other. She cites spelling, handwriting, and capitalization as skills of a closed nature, that can be "routinized and made subliminal . . . learnable in a single, final form" (59–60). Punctuation, by contrast, cannot be made routinized because it is always "open to negotiation" (60) and often subject to the peculiarities of the structure in question. Punctuation, in other words, is an open capacity that is not mastered from a list of rules so much as from continued attention and practice with a variety of sentence structures that are fluid, ever-changing, and contextualized. The ability to use punctuation appropriately increases with reading and writing opportunities and is a developmental process that occurs over time and with experience. Much of this knowledge accumulates slowly, as writers/readers pay attention to the conventions in their writing/reading, but it often takes a more conscious awareness of written form for this learning to take hold.

The Pendulum Swings

As described in Chapter Three, the traditional approach to composition instruction focused heavily on grammar and correctness, based almost exclusively on Standard English. This monolithic approach ignored the true complexity of English usage, both oral and written, privileging Standard English over all other discourses in the belief that skill in this area would lead to better grades, better jobs, and ultimately a better life in the world of mainstream English speakers and writers. Grammar, usage, spelling, and punctuation rules were seen as fixed, and accepted as the only proper way to write regardless of context, reader, or purpose of the discourse. Equipped with classroom sets of grammar and usage workbooks, teachers taught grammar and mechanics in isolated units or even for entire semesters, convinced that these skills would carry over to student writing when they eventually were asked to compose instead of fill in the blanks on worksheets. Often, students were taught and re-taught the same grammatical terms and usage skills yearly. When responding to student writing, teachers focused on errors—deviations from the Standard Edited American English of the grammar text—as if the main reason for writing were to produce mechanically perfect prose. Meanwhile, teachers continued to be frustrated by errors when these skill lessons did not transfer to the actual writing of a paper even though students might do well on grammar and usage tests.

With growing awareness of linguistic diversity and the recognition that all dialects are functioning linguistic systems for their users, educators began to reconsider the traditional approach to grammar and correctness described above. Eradicating students' home dialects in the service of Standard English came under heavy fire. The publication in 1974 of NCTE's *Students' Right to Their Own Language* marked a significant shift in our concept of correctness and what constitutes error. Linguists and educators began to talk about the need to teach students to be flexible language users, able to shift from one dialect or linguistic system to another based on the context of the written or oral discourse. Teaching students to write in Standard English included teaching them to recognize when it was necessary—for example in formal essays or business letters—and when it was not, such as in personal correspondence or early drafts of formal papers. "Correctness" in writing increasingly became a more fluid term, based on appropriateness, leading teachers to question the need for such heavy emphasis on grammar, mechanics, and Standard English usage in their writing program.

Another influence on this shift in dealing with correctness was the growth of the writing process movement in the 1970s and 1980s. Many teachers, newly proselytized to this approach, threw aside all attention to the more mundane mechanical aspects of writing, focusing instead on developing their students' writing fluency, self-expression, creativity, and self-esteem. Armed with good will and a genuine desire to nurture the writer within, teachers sometimes swung the pendulum too far, neglecting all mention of error in favor of uniformly positive support, fearful that attention to grammar and correctness would dampen their students' newly awakened enthusiasm for writing. Armed with knowledge of the multiple studies showing little if any correlation between teaching grammar and improvements in student writing, many teachers opted to ignore it completely.

Partly this was due to an imperfect understanding of how writing conventions and grammatical issues could be taught as part of the writing process. But another contributing factor was the enormous increase in the paper load that enthusiastic writing teachers inevitably found themselves faced with as students began to delight in putting their ideas down on paper. Committed to reading everything just as they had when students were producing far less writing in more traditional classrooms ("They won't write unless I read it all," was a common complaint), teachers focused on content, with little or no attention paid to the sometimes egregious errors that filled their students' papers. In many classrooms Standard English grammar, correctness, mechanics, and usage as the primary goal of writing instruction went to the bottom of the hierarchy of concerns in favor of fluency and self-expression.

An article in *English Journal* by four English educators (Baines et al. 1999), based on observations during six years of more than 300 secondary writing teachers, documents this imbalance. The teachers they observed taught writing using some form of "the process," categorized by the researchers into "classic," "anti-grammarian," and "five-paragraph" approaches. Despite their differences in ways of using "process" methodology, the teachers in this study devoted little if any time to the direct teaching of skills, relying instead on peer response groups to deal with matters of correctness. Creating stress-free writing environments and giving As and Bs to those who did the work, all neglected "error" when evaluating student writing. The researchers concluded that these teachers "seemed more dedicated to 'the process' than to improving the quality of student writing (72)." The "product" of writing—a finished, polished, high quality piece—was neglected in favor of the writing process.

The pendulum is now swinging back to a more medial position on issues of teaching grammar, correctness, and the conventions of Standard English. Nancie Atwell's second edition of her much-acclaimed *In the Middle* (1998) includes much more attention to teaching the conventions of written English than her 1987 edition. Atwell notes her own frustration in earlier years when she found that ten-minute mini-lessons often lasted much longer, adding to her growing realization that developing writers needed more attention to skills. Connie Weaver's text, *Teaching Grammar in Context* (1996), also advocates teaching the elements of grammar that have a direct impact on writing plus the punctuation and mechanics necessary for successful editing. Lisa Delpit, Maria de la Luz Reyes, and other educators of non-mainstream students, decry the process movement's emphasis on fluency, recommending, even demanding, that users of non-mainstream dialects be taught the skills necessary for success in our society, where Standard English is the language of power.

Think/Write #1

How did your own secondary English teachers handle grammar and correctness? Do you remember grammar units, worksheets, heavy marking of papers for errors, or did your teachers use other approaches? Were the strategies your teachers used effective for you? Were they effective for other students in your secondary English classes? What do you think was the biggest influence on your present ability to produce mechanically and grammatically correct writing when necessary?

What Aspects of Grammar, Mechanics, and Usage Should We Teach?

Our position is that grammar and correctness must be an integral component of a rich, varied, well-structured writing program. Students benefit from some knowledge of Grammar II (grammatical structures) and Grammar III (appropriate usage), along with the conventions of written English. We do not advocate isolated six-week grammar units based on lectures and workbooks nor a return to sentence diagramming nor heavy "red-penciling" of student writing. As shown earlier in this chapter, research over the last century presents compelling evidence that these methods do more to alienate student writers than equip them with a set of practical writing skills. We do believe students need a balanced approach to writing that encompasses all aspects of composing from getting initial ideas down on paper to editing a final draft, using the grammatical structures and conventions of writing most appropriate for each piece. We also contend that when students are writing for meaningful purposes, matters of correctness become part of their final objectives.

Grammatical terms and understandings that directly impact writing development are the aspects of grammar that should be taught. The conventions of Standard English usage and punctuation should also become part of every writer's knowledge base. All of this makes practical sense only when it is applied knowledge, information learned not as a set of decontextualized skills, but as a repertoire of strategies and practices that are a natural part of writing growth and development.

So what do students need to know in order to work effectively with written language at the sentence level and produce the Edited American English expected in post-secondary educational institutions and the workplace? We suggest the minimum necessary to achieve maximum benefits over time. These elements fall into two broad categories:

1. Terminology and concepts related to parts of speech and parts of a sentence. (Selected elements of Grammar II)
2. Punctuation, mechanics, and conventions of Edited American English. (Grammar III)

We advocate Weaver's concept of a "scope-not-sequence" approach to teaching these terms and concepts (1998, 23). In other words, grammar, usage, and mechanics should not be codified into a pre-determined sequence of skills to master at each grade level, but should, instead, be dealt with throughout the secondary writing program, with attention to these concerns based on students' developmental needs as writers. We are also indebted to Weaver for her excellent discussion of the grammar and usage skills most useful for writing development (1998, 21–24). Our shared belief that students need minimal grammatical terminology and much writing practice, with grammar and correctness taught "in context," leads to the following list of concepts worth teaching.

Terminology and Concepts: What Should We Teach and Why?

The chart below outlines a minimalist approach to grammar and usage instruction focusing on the terms and concepts most useful for writing development.

What?	Parts of speech: to be able to name, identify, and use appropriately the eight parts of speech—noun, pronoun, verb, adjective, adverb, article, conjunction, interjection.
Why?	For students and teacher to share a common terminology for talking about language.

Objectives? To enable discussion of writing conventions, such as using capital letters with proper nouns, and stylistic elements, such as using adjectives for description or replacing forms of the verb "to be" with active verbs.

Caution: Focus on knowledge that has concrete application to writing, not obscure uses of the parts of speech in complicated sentence structures. The idea here is to equip students with enough understanding to permit use of these terms for fostering writing growth.

What? Development of a "sentence sense," of the way sentence boundaries in writing guide readers.

Why? For students to be able to identify, write, and punctuate complete sentences in their own writing and the writing of others.

Objectives? To avoid run-ons, fragments, and comma faults in formal writing; to be able to manipulate parts of sentences to achieve sentence variety and linguistic complexity; to be able to use varied sentence constructions appropriately for stylistic purposes and to achieve special effects.

Caution: Sentence sense develops slowly and is best nurtured through reading, where students can "see" the sentence boundaries that are so difficult to recognize in oral language and can become familiar with the rhythms, patterns, and sentence constructions of written English.

What? Parts of sentences—subject, verb (predicate), object, clause, phrase, dependent and independent clauses

Kinds of sentences—simple, compound, and complex

Subject-verb agreement with regular and irregular verbs

Parallel structure among parts of a sentence

Why? For students to understand how sentences are constructed in formal and informal writing.

Objectives? To deepen students' comprehension of the internal workings of the English sentence in order to further the development of a "sentence sense"; to provide a common terminology and set of understandings that will enable both stylistic and grammatical discussions; to enable the manipulation of sentence parts for sentence variety and complexity; to help students understand how to use punctuation both within and at the end of sentences to convey meaning; to develop linguistic complexity, fluency, and variety.

Caution: Teaching students to identify and label the various kinds of phrases and clauses is unnecessary. This is the kind of knowledge that disappears after the grammar test and confuses more students than it enlightens, turning language study into isolated memorization of abstractions. Focus on practical knowledge that can be applied directly to produce *varied sentence constructions rather than identifying and labeling them. For example, students do not need to be able to differentiate and label appositive, absolute, and participial phrases. They can, however, learn to write them through the use of models and exercises involving sentence combining and sentence expanding, which will have a direct application to their own writing. Research shows that sentence combining and sentence generating exercises do more to help students develop syntactic maturity than studying abstract grammatical terminology. A later section of this chapter presents multiple methods for helping students learn to produce more varied sentences.*

Punctuation, Mechanics, and Usage: What Should We Teach and Why?

Standard Edited American English has numerous conventions of punctuation, mechanics, and usage that are expected in formal writing situations. Students need to know these rules and be able to apply them in their own writing. They should also understand when it is appropriate to ignore or "bend" these standard practices for informal writing or stylistic purposes.

What? Capitalization

End punctuation—period, question mark, exclamation point

Comma

Semi-colon

Colon

Quotation marks

Apostrophe for possessives and other uses

Dashes, parentheses, brackets, slashes, ellipses

Troublesome homophones such as the following:

their, they're, there
its, it's
then, than
affect, effect
to, two, too
who's, whose
your, you're
a, an

Pronoun reference agreement

Plural versus possessive

Dialect features that are social markers such as "I seen," "he don't," double negatives

Other usage items reflective of Standard Edited American English

Why? For editing/proofreading and stylistic purposes.

Objectives? To enable students to become good editors of their own papers, applying the rules and conventions of Standard English when necessary and appropriate; to give more mature writers the tools and understandings they need to manipulate these rules to convey meaning or achieve special effects.

Caution: When immersed in a rich reading and writing environment, many students unconsciously absorb these conventions of written Standard English and use them correctly with little or no direct teaching, while others need more instruction. By middle school, what students know about punctuation, mechanics, and usage can vary widely, necessitating individualized attention from the teacher. Instead of arbitrarily teaching a lock-step set of punctuation and usage rules to the whole class, the wise teacher observes what mechanical elements students already use effectively and those that need more attention, basing mini-lessons on gaps in knowledge shared by a large percentage of the class and giving individual instruction during conferences or in small groups to those who need it.

Think/Write #2

Part I. Do you agree that all students need to learn the elements of grammar, usage, and mechanics outlined above? If not, what should be added or subtracted? Why? If you agree with all or most of these items, how might you approach teaching them to students? Discuss some methods you would feel comfortable with in teaching correctness. Also consider areas you might need to learn more about before you can help students master them.

Part II. Do you feel you have complete control over all these aspects of language in your own writing or are there areas about which you are still unsure? Discuss your own abilities and concerns with correctness when you write papers for school or other public audiences.

How Can We Teach Grammar, Mechanics, and Usage in the Context of Writing?

Having laid out what we believe to be the minimum basics for the study of grammar, Standard English usage, and the mechanics of writing, we now turn to the question of methodology. Namely, how can English teachers help their students learn the concepts listed above and develop the skills necessary to produce Edited American English?

The following section of this chapter describes many methods for teaching context-appropriate grammatical forms and writing conventions as part of the writing process[1]. The key to success with these methods is a writing environment encouraging multiple drafts, with final attention paid to polishing the paper for

1. Portions of the following material were previously published as "Developing Correctness in Student Writing: Alternatives to the Error Hunt" by Lois Matz Rosen in *Lessons to Share: On Teaching Grammar in Context,* edited by Connie Weaver. Published by Boynton/Cook, a subsidiary of Reed Elsevier Inc., Portsmouth, NH.

readers by attending to matters of correctness. We differentiate revision—attention to content and ideas—from copyediting and proofreading—attention to punctuation, mechanics, grammar, and usage to produce a final draft. When students view early drafts of their work as fluid, rather than fixed, they are free to concentrate on what they wish to say. Aspects of correctness can then be saved for final drafts with specific points of grammar and mechanics taught when necessary as students revise and copyedit their own writing. From the numerous suggestions discussed below, teachers can choose those that best suit their students and their approach to writing, with assurance that these methods guide students toward the mechanically correct writing prized by our culture.

Immerse Students in a Rich and Varied Reading and Writing Environment

As we have stressed throughout this chapter, one of the best ways for students to learn the conventions of Edited American English is through reading. Therefore, our primary recommendation for developing correctness in student writing is constant, even daily, reading in a wide variety of genres and styles, ranging from the standard prose of newspapers and magazines to the essays, non-fiction material, personal writing, and poetry that we assign students to write. Students should not only read widely, they should read models of the kinds of materials they are asked to write. One of the reasons for the awkward, error-ridden, lifeless essays students write in response to school assignments, is that they've never read good models of these forms.

It goes without saying that it is equally important for students to write constantly, even daily, to develop comfort, fluency, and correctness. Mina Shaughnessy (1977) notes that her adult basic writers at the City University of New York brought distressingly little writing experience with them to college: "the basic writing student is . . . likely to have written 350 words a semester. It would not be unusual for him to have written nothing at all" (14).

Provide Classroom Time for All Stages of the Writing Process

The writing process described in Chapter Three is especially well-suited to developing students' skills with grammar and correctness. Students should be encouraged to forget about the mechanics of writing and just get their ideas down on paper for pre-writing activities or early drafts. After the paper has been fully shaped, revised for content, and is satisfactory to both writer and readers, the writer can turn her attention to copyediting in order to achieve a polished final draft. All writers find it easier to concentrate on one aspect of writing at a time instead of trying to get the ideas, the organization, and the grammar and mechanics all correct at the same time. Staging this out, especially for developing writers, makes writing easier, and permits full attention to correctness when it matters most—for producing a final, polished paper.

Use Editing Workshops

We recommend that teachers set aside regular classroom time for attention to grammar, usage, and the mechanics of writing while students are working on their papers. Sending students home to do their final copyediting gives them the wrong message about the importance of this stage of the writing process. It also robs the teacher of a valuable chance to teach grammatical concepts in context, while students have a draft in front of them on which to practice new skills. The four methods below, all useful strategies for editing workshops, engage students in developing new understandings and offer practice in applying this knowledge to their own writing and that of classmates.

Modeling. Many students don't really understand how to review their papers carefully to correct grammatical, mechanical, and usage errors. When directed to "check your paper for errors," they may quickly scan through the piece, perhaps catching a spelling error or adding an additional comma. Most would benefit from in-class sessions in which the whole class works cooperatively on the final editing and proofreading of one paper. This is best done by projecting a paper on the overhead and inviting students on an "error hunt" to produce an error-free final draft in Standard Edited English. The paper should be one that has already been revised for content and is now in need of final correcting. The teacher can ask for volunteers or use papers from previous classes with permission of the writer. The process might go like this: The teacher reads the paper aloud while students follow along on the overhead and then opens the discussion by focusing on content: "What do you like about this paper? What's working well?" Once the class has had a chance to discuss the paper as a whole, the teacher can direct attention to correctness with a neutral question such as "Can anyone find something that needs to be changed?" As students identify and correct errors, the teacher makes corrections on the transparency and asks students to explain why each change needs to be made, elaborating on their answers or clarifying difficult concepts as necessary. The teacher can also point out and explain any errors students don't identify. It is useful to keep a running list on the chalkboard of the kinds of errors found in the paper. The final step in this modeling exercise is for the students to apply this process to their own papers, using the chalkboard list as a guide for kinds of errors to look for.

We recommend the use of this modeling exercise several times throughout the term; it provides an excellent review of basic copyediting skills on real writing in process, and students enjoy doing this. When we modeled this exercise with middle school students in the Flint Community Schools, they kept inching their moveable desks further and further forward to make sure they caught everything and engaged in some good-natured arguing about spelling and whether or not certain features were acceptable in a final draft.

Students can also work on this exercise in pairs or small groups, using a duplicated draft instead of a transparency, but there is much to be gained by a whole-class experience.

Mini-lessons and Extended Mini-lessons. Brief ten-minute lessons on points of grammar, mechanics, and usage can have immediate value when students apply the new skill to their own writing. Many writing teachers like to start daily writing workshop sessions with a mini-lesson based on mechanical and grammatical errors they see on students' papers, things like the difference between *its* and *it's* or the need for a comma after a clause beginning with *if.* Over an entire school year, a great deal of information about grammar, punctuation, and Standard English usage can be conveying in these mini-lessons, with direct application to writing in process. Instead of correcting workbook exercises, students develop their skills by practicing on their own papers and that of fellow classmates, making learning much more practical and personal. They also give the entire class a frame of reference for discussing the mechanical and grammatical elements of their writing. *In the Middle* by Nancie Atwell (1987 and 1998) offers a fuller description of a broad range of mini-lessons on topics in reading and writing, including grammatical and mechanical skills.

Sometimes, mini-lessons need to be longer in order for teachers to offer detailed explanations, give examples, and offer students time to collaborate in applying this information in their own writing. These extended mini-lessons, sometimes twenty minutes or more, allow students to practice a complex skill such as writing compound or complex sentences and share their results. The ten-minute lesson may work well for many of the grammatical and copyediting skills students need to master, but teachers should not hesitate to extend the learning time to allow for more depth and practice. As long as students use the new information to produce their own writing or copyedit their own work, rather than engage in meaningless exercises on text sentences, the class time is well-spent. Figure 4.1 is an example of a grammar mini-lesson.

Think/Write #3
Design a ten-minute mini-lesson on a simple concept. Design an extended mini-lesson on a more complex grammar or usage item. Be sure to have students either apply these ideas to their own drafts or write some examples themselves.

Teacher–Student Conferences on Editing and Proofreading. While students are at work writing, revising, and copyediting their papers, teachers can give individual help with correctness by holding conferences focused solely on this. These can be two- or three-minute conferences at the teacher's desk, or the teacher can move up and down the aisles, leaning over shoulders, and concentrating more attention on students whose writing would benefit from help with mechanics. The dialogue might go something like this. "OK, John, looks like you're ready for a final proofreading and polishing. First I'd like you to circle all the words you think might be misspelled and look them up in the dictionary. Then work on complete sentences. There are several places in your paper where you've got two sentences strung together." The teacher might ask John to work with him in identifying the first few run-ons and correcting them before telling John to do the same throughout the rest of his paper and then let the teacher see it again. There could be a

FIGURE 4.1 ***Example of a Grammar Mini-lesson on There, Their, They're***

1. List *there, their,* and *they're* on the board. Work with each word individually.
2. Ask the class to explain when to use *there.* Write this explanation beside the word. Have every student compose a sentence using *there.* Pairs can share sentences and decide whether or not *there* is used correctly. Ask for volunteers to share their sentences with the whole class. Write one or two examples on the board.
3. Follow the same steps for *their* and *they're:* have students explain when the word is used, compose sentences, share in pairs, share some with the whole class.

To extend this mini-lesson:

4. Have students take a draft of their own writing and circle every *there/they're/their.* Then work with a partner to check that each one is used correctly.

brief lesson on possessives for one student, another on *its, it's* for someone else. Never lingering for more than a few minutes with each writer, the teacher identifies on the student's paper an area for proofreading, illustrates how to correct it, and gets the writer started working independently. The "eavesdroppers" on either side often learn as much as the student being worked with. "Can I help you with anything?" works well as an opening question from the teacher, for it permits an immediate and accurate response to a student's need.

Figure 4.2 shows the mechanical, grammatical, and usage skills Nancie Atwell covered in her editing conferences with middle-school students. Such individualized attention to each writer's needs is quite possibly the very best way to help writers develop competence in this aspect of writing.

Peer Proofreading. Another valuable method for developing students' copyediting skills is to have students work together, proofreading one another's papers. If writing is not seen as a "test" of an individual student's writing ability but as a process that is growing and developing, this method permits learning by both writer and editor. Proofreading thus becomes a collaborative learning experience.

Middle school students enjoy using the editing chart in Figure 4.3. Working from the top down, the writer uses a yellow crayon to fill in each section as he completes the task specified for proofreading his own paper. Then the paper and the chart are given to a reader, who uses a blue crayon to color over each yellow section as he completes the same proofreading tasks. Both writer and reader correct any errors they find. When the triangle is completely green (and a careful copyediting completed by both writer and reader), the student is ready for a final conference with the teacher over the paper.

Another copyediting activity that we have used with students at all levels is to put students in pairs after each has had a chance to proofread his or her own paper. The only rule we impose is that no corrections are to be made on the writer's paper without the knowledge and consent of the author. This means both students must confer over any error on either paper and both must agree on the correction. We also ask that the editor initial all corrections, which gives the teacher some sense of the mechanical skills both the writer and the proofreader bring to

FIGURE 4.2 *Sample Skills Taught in Editing Conferences*

- All right = two words. A lot = two words.
- Put capital letters at the beginnings of sentences.
- Capitalize *Mom* and *Dad* when they're names, but not when they're labels (*I asked Mom for a ride,* vs. *I asked my mom for a ride*).
- Capitalize names of countries and monuments.
- Put capital letters on the first, last, and important words in a title.
- Use *an* (not *a*) before nouns, adjectives, and adverbs that begin with vowels.
- Use brackets when I need parentheses within parentheses: ([ ]).
- Avoid parentheses in narratives.
- When I have to split words between lines, split them between syllables. See a dictionary to find out where a word splits.
- Never split a one-syllable word.
- Keep the voice of my narratives consistent: either *he/she* or *I.*
- Keep my pronouns clear so readers can tell who *he, she, we,* or *they* refers to.
- Keep my verb tense consistent: either *past* (it happened before) or *present* (it's happening now, or in general).
- Use ______ and *I* as a sentence subject (not ______ and *me*).
- Read my pieces softly to myself and put periods where I hear my voice drop and stop.
- Proofread softly to myself out loud and listen for missing words and missing sounds at the ends of words.
- Watch for comma splices, because a comma isn't strong enough to hold two sentences together. Use a period or semicolon, or insert *and* after the comma.
- Use a semicolon between two sentences where I want to show a relationship.
- Use apostrophe *s* to show something belongs to someone.
- Use an apostrophe to show a letter is missing: *let's; that's; don't.*
- Use ellipses to indicate a long, dramatic pause; an ellipsis is just three dots.
- To achieve a dash on the computer, hit *hyphen + option + shift.*
- Use a colon to show a list is coming.
- Use a colon to show an explanation is coming.
- Experiment with — and : to give my writing voice and power.
- On a list, put commas between items and use the serial or Harvard comma before the final *and.*
- Separate mild interjections from the rest of the sentence with a comma: *Wow, that's cool. Hi, how are you?*
- Separate vocatives from the rest of the sentence with a comma: *I told you, Mom, I'm coming. Ethan, wait for me.*
- Use a comma between two independent clauses joined by *and, or, but, nor, so,* or *because.*
- You're = you are. Your = belongs to you.
- It's = it is. Its = belongs to an it.
- There = a place or a sentence starter; their = belongs to them; they're = they are.
- Then = time; than = comparison.
- In a rhymed poem, the rhyming words go at the ends of lines.
- In a rhymed poem, keep one left-hand margin and no indents, except for run-overs that won't fit on the line where I want them: indent these.
- Use line breaks and white space to help punctuate a poem.
- Punctuate a song or poem as prose: no extra commas/comma at the end of each line.
- Use a deliberate, consistent format in an open-form poem, e.g., capitals and punctuation or no capitals and punctuation.
- Delete excess words in open-form poems: cut to the bone, until I can't cut another word.
- Put a comma after the closing of a letter: *Sincerely,*
- If the closing of a letter is more than one word, capitalize the first word only: *Your friend,*
- Don't indent the greeting of a letter.
- On every letter I write, use the same heading:
  my street address
  my town, state, and zip
  today's date
- On a business letter, include an inside address: the recipient's name, title, and address.
- Don't use abbreviations in the heading or inside address of a letter.
- On a business letter, put a colon after the greeting and print my name under my signature.
- Put quotation marks around the words people say out loud.

FIGURE 4.3 ***Peer Editing Guide***

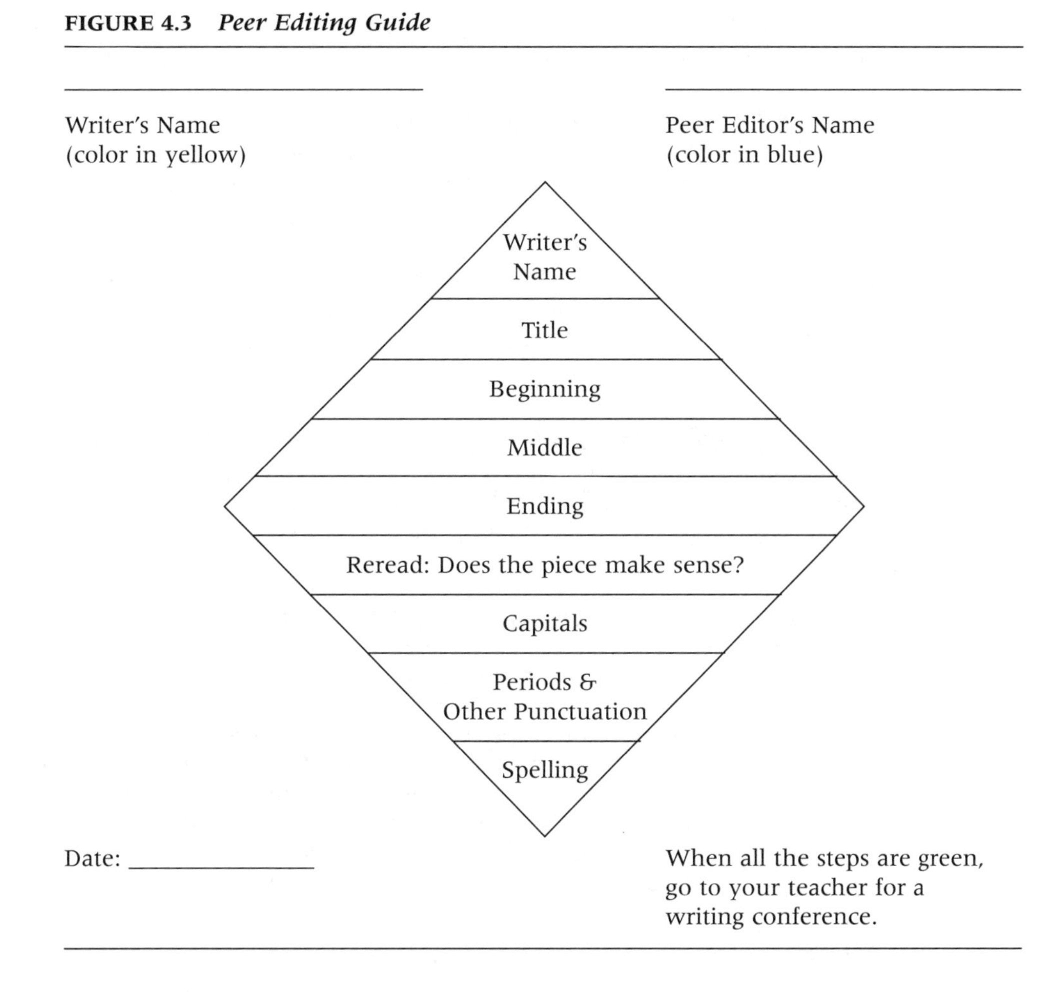

the paper. If the two writers can't agree on an error, the teacher can be called over to resolve the problem and teach a mini-lesson if necessary. Students enjoy being editors for each other, and we find it takes a great deal of pressure off each writer to have this support and corroboration.

Peer proofreading can also be handled in groups of three or four students, who are instructed to pass their papers around the group, each student correcting any errors found. It helps if the groups are structured so that each one has a student good at spelling and mechanics.

Help Students Become Responsible for Their Own Editing and Proofreading

The ultimate goal of any approach to appropriate edited English is to have students become competent self-editors, recognizing, and knowing how to correct any deviations from standard usage in their own writing. Several strategies are aimed at enhancing students' abilities to self-edit. Among the most useful are these.

Provide Editing Checklists. Checklists are lists of common errors that students can use as a guide when proofreading their own papers. Writers can be instructed to check their writing for several surface features such as run-ons and fragments, subject-verb agreement, and possessives. As students learn more of these skills from mini-lessons, these items can be added to their proofreading checklists. Figure 4.4 is an example of a self-editing checklist suitable for a middle school student; Figure 4.5 is a Peer Editing Sheet for the final draft of a senior level formal research paper. The editor is asked to check that the paper meets the minimum requirements for the assignment and to proofread for errors.

Teach Proofreading Strategies. Most students don't understand that proofreading requires an entirely different kind of reading than what one does when reading for meaning. The proofreader can't glance through the material superficially or read through whole sections looking for something to correct. In order

FIGURE 4.4 ***A Self-editing Checklist for Middle School Students***

Proofreading Checklist

Proofreading can improve your paper. As you proofread it helps to concentrate on only one thing at a time. If you answer each question below with a "yes," go on to the next point. If your answer is "no," make your corrections and check the box. By the time you are finished, you should have checked your paper at least *4 times!!!!*

1. *Sentences*
Does each sentence you've used make sense by itself? __________

2. *Punctuation*
Does each sentence have end punctuation? __________

Have you checked each sentence for commas or quotation marks? __________

*Remember: Anything which you copied directly from someone else must be in quotation marks. __________

3. *Capitalization*
Do all sentences begin with a capital? __________

Do other words either begin with a capital or not based on the rules you learned this semester? __________

4. *Spelling*
A good way to check your spelling is to read your paper BACKWARD. This will force you to *see* each word. Circle any word about which you are unsure. Using a dictionary, check and correct all circled words.

Have you checked your spelling with the above method and made corrections? __________

FIGURE 4.5 *Peer Editing Sheet for Final Draft of Research Paper*

Writer ______________________________

Editor ______________________________

I. Please check the following requirements and format of the paper.

1. Are there at least three documented citations from three different sources?
Yes No

2. Does the research paper have a Works Cited page with a minimum of three sources?
Yes No

3. Are there at least two direct quotations?
Yes No

4. Are all facts, statistics, and direct quotations documented correctly?
Yes No

II. Please proofread the paper and make sure that there are

No first or second person personal pronouns (I, me, us, we, our, mine, you, yours)

No spelling errors (circle errors)

No run-on sentences

No sentence fragments

No punctuation errors

No capitalization errors

No pronoun and antecedent agreement errors

No subject/verb agreement errors

(Adapted from a Peer Editing Sheet used by Elaine Porter, Linden H. S., Michigan)

to find errors, the student must slow reading down to focus at the word and sentence level, checking word usage, making sure he has spelled and punctuated correctly, judging grammatical correctness and appropriateness of language. Students can benefit from being shown some specific methods to improve their own proofreading such as the following:

- Read the paper aloud to yourself or a friend, or read into a tape recorder and play it back. Follow along with a pencil as you read, making asterisks at spots where an error is suspected.

- Have someone else—a classmate, parent, or the teacher—read the paper aloud to you, exactly as it appears on the page. Listen for unclear areas, awkward phrasing, repetitive sentence structures, errors in grammar or usage, inappropriate language.

- Run a blank sheet of paper slowly down the composition so you are forced to read one line at a time.

• Read one sentence at a time from the bottom up to take each sentence out of context, thus focusing on errors, not meaning.

• Circle all suspected spelling errors before consulting a dictionary.

• List three of your most frequent errors at the top of the paper, then read the paper three times, each time focusing on one of these errors.

Set Up an Editing Corner. A table or bookshelf heaped with handbooks, dictionaries, and thesauruses can also help students become responsible for their own mechanical/grammatical correctness. The walls around the editing corner can be decorated with a chart on how to proofread, a list of spelling demons, rules of punctuation or capitalization, examples of dialogue punctuated properly. One-page handouts with explanations and examples of common errors and ways to correct them can be filed in this corner along with displays of student writing taken through several drafts, including final proofreading. Students should be allowed free access to these materials as they write and should be encouraged to use the corner to solve mechanical problems themselves.

Teach How to Use Workbooks, Handbooks, Dictionaries, a Thesaurus, Reference Guides, and the Computer's Editing Tools. Students may need guidance in making the best use of these writing tools. A mini-lesson demonstrating how to use each one encourages students to use them independently.

Have Students Keep Their Own Records. Keeping records of their own errors is one way of encouraging students to assume responsibility for identifying and correcting them. Some teachers just have students keep a sheet in their writing folder on which they record errors pointed out by the teacher or peers with the idea that they'll work to eliminate these errors in future papers. Madraso (1993) has students keep a three-column "Proofreading Journal": the first column for the error, the second column for the solution, and the third column for a strategy for spotting the error in the future. Andrasick (1993) uses a system for helping students recognize and learn how to correct their own individual error patterns. When reading student papers, she first responds to content, then goes back and indicates errors using a standard set of proofreading symbols. When students get their paper back, they transfer the list of errors for that paper to a 3 × 5 card; correct them on the paper with help from the teacher, peers, or a handbook; and then make a note on the card of the mechanical/grammatical error they will work on for the next paper. Each student has an ongoing card filed in the class "Goof Box" with this information listed for all their papers. After using this process for several papers, Andrasick asks students to review their "Goof Box" card and write a reflection, noting patterns of change: errors now eliminated and new ones that need attention. She also has them write about and share with each other the strategies they use to identify, learn about, and correct their own errors. With this system, students become consciously aware of their own editing skills, developing a sense of control over proofreading and error correction, and assuming responsibility for their own self-editing competence.

Mark Student Papers Wisely: Abandon the Error Hunt

Another cluster of correctness strategies centers on marking techniques for the teacher, ones which differ significantly from the traditional "red-pencilitis" approach and are always preceded by classroom use of editing workshops and self-editing strategies. Copious marking of each and every individual error is labor-intensive for the teacher and intimidating for the student. In addition, no research study has ever been able to show the effectiveness of this approach. Instead, we recommend the following strategies.

Benign Neglect. Students involved for the first time in the process approach to writing, those newly engaged in journal-writing, pre-writing exercises, multiple drafts, revision, and proofreading, can benefit from a period of teacher inattention to correctness when marking final drafts of papers. Especially if students' previous writing instruction focused heavily on form and correctness, they need time to re-center their attention on what they have to say as writers and to learn the various composing strategies that will make writing more pleasurable for both the writer and the reader. If students are generating a great deal of writing and are frequently engaged in editing workshop strategies, the teacher can safely focus written comments on content for a short time. This benign neglect gives students a chance to internalize writing and proofreading skills and to demonstrate what they *do* know before the teacher begins to identify and work on areas of weakness.

Selectivity. Students are more likely to grow as writers when the teacher's primary purpose in reading student papers is to respond to content. However, if attention to content and correctness are combined when marking papers, it is more helpful to select one or two *kinds* of errors the individual student is making than to point out every error in the paper. The teacher can identify a selected error, point out and correct an example or two on the student's paper, and either explain the correct form or direct the student to a handbook for further explanation. The student might also be asked to identify and correct this particular problem in the rest of the paper and turn it in again for the teacher to review.

Error-Analysis. A marking method that can be especially fruitful for the teacher is to approach it from an analytic perspective. As we pointed out earlier in this chapter, all errors are not equal and shouldn't be addressed in the same way. The composition teacher as error-analyst looks for patterns in the errors of an individual student, tries to discover how the student arrived at the mistake by analyzing the error, and plans strategies accordingly. For example, is the error due to a lack of knowledge about a certain grammatical point? A mis-learned rule? A careless error? Use of a non-mainstream dialect? Overgeneralization of a particular rule?

Kroll and Schafer, Bartholomae, and Shaughnessy have demonstrated the efficacy of error-analysis in helping teachers better understand the source of student error as an aid to planning more effective ways of dealing with it.

When we examine the following piece of first draft student writing, we can be overwhelmed by the total number of surface errors.

> ***The Acident***
>
> It started win I was coming home for school. I was in a happe move. It was so wram and I said to myself noting better than home sweet home. and I eat my dinner and did my home work. and dad came in and he aet dinner and read the newspaper. and It was drak and It was time to pick up mom. Bout on hour way we was waiting at the red light. Then dad was about to trun and. I was looking the other way. and I looked qukely and we crashed. and I boaingd my haed on the dashbo-rad. and the ambulance arrived and I was calling mom mom and dad said she will be here.

The temptation when faced with a piece like this is to overlook the writer's lively voice and grab a red pen. But if we did so, the paper would bleed, and is likely to end up a wadded ball in the wastebasket. Error-analysis provides a better way to respond. Close examination shows only four different kinds of errors: spelling, sentence boundary problems that are often marked by the use of "and" to start a new idea, missing quotation marks for the final dialogue, and one instance of nonstandard dialect—"we was." Selecting one or two of these kinds of errors to discuss at a conference or to comment on at the bottom of the paper is likely to achieve more than circling errors. For example, the student could work on sentences by reading the paper aloud, removing almost all the "ands," and adding capital letters and periods where necessary. He and the teacher or a peer could do this together. Then the student could check all the words he suspects are misspelled and correct them. Focusing on these two kinds of errors would be enough for this paper. If the piece is going to eventually end up in a class publication, a later draft might attend to quotation marks and the shift to Standard English—"we were."

Error analysis of this sort combined with a selective approach when responding to student writing helps both teacher and student understand the student's writing problems and work toward correcting them.

Publish Student Writing for Motivation and Reward

Writers, professionals as well as students, need a reason for laboring over a draft until it is perfect. The urge to see oneself in print can be a powerful drive toward revision and proofreading. Watch what happens when a class publication is handed out. Each writer is likely to flip immediately to his or her own work for a minute of personal pleasure before browsing through the rest of the book. Writing teachers need to take advantage of this human need to be heard, to leave a physical imprint on the world, by offering numerous opportunities for sharing and publishing. See Chapter Three for numerous ideas on ways to publish student writing.

Computers and Correctness

As the use of computers for writing has grown, so has the proliferation of studies examining the effects of computers on writers' processes and final products. Research results are mixed: while most researchers agree that students develop more positive attitudes toward writing and do more revision with computers, the effect on the quality of the papers themselves is contradictory. Numerous studies show computers have no effect on the overall quality of the papers; however, most of these studies were limited to a ten- or twelve-week period of study, perhaps too brief for computer use to impact writing improvement, especially since learning to use the computer often takes up instructional time at first. A 1992 study of eighth graders who were already experienced computer users had more promising results. The researchers found that "papers written on computer were rated significantly higher" than handwritten papers in all the qualities assessed, including mechanics (Owston, Murphy, Wideman). Concerned about the influence of spelling on the higher ratings assigned word-processed texts, the researchers assessed a random sample of papers from both categories, finding no difference in mean spelling errors between the computer-written papers and the handwritten ones, indicating that spelling did not bias the ratings. This study offers evidence that computers might provide yet another strategy for improving students' mechanical/ grammatical skills.

At the present time, it makes sense to involve students in writing on computers as much as possible for ease of revision and the use of such writing aids as a spelling checker, thesaurus, or grammar checker. These computer tools can provide some help with final copyediting, but they can also lull students into superficial sylistic checks. The kinds of syntactic problems raised earlier in this chapter don't lend themselves to mechanical checking systems, and many of the "errors" flagged by the machine are matters for stylistic decisions, such as use of the passive voice. Teachers must remind students that the beautifully typed paper emerging from the printer still needs the same attention to mechanics, grammar, and usage that any piece of writing requires before it is ready for evaluation or publication.

Correctness in the Linguistically Diverse Classroom

Advocates for writing process instruction have been criticized for neglecting form and correctness in favor of fluency by those who don't fully understand the ways in which writing process instruction includes attention to all aspects of writing development. But criticism has also come from teachers of minority students. Delpit (1986, 1988) and Reyes (1992) have been critical of writing process instruction for speakers of non-mainstream dialects, arguing that this method does not give these students explicit instruction in the standard literacy skills they need for access to higher education and the workplace. At first this position seems in direct conflict with the methods advocated throughout this book, and the danger is in misunderstanding their position as calling for a return to isolated instruction in grammar and mechanics. Yet both educators agree that skills must be taught within a context that encourages full development of linguistic skills and "critical and creative thinking" (Delpit 1986).

It is our contention that writing process instruction in the hands of a skilled teacher who fully understands ways to integrate skills instruction into a writing and reading workshop environment would include whatever direct instruction was necessary for students to develop standard literacy skills. Many of the activities described earlier in this chapter give non-mainstream students the instruction necessary for developing Standard English skills, yet also provide a climate supportive of students' individual growth as thinkers and writers: mini-lessons in skills followed by direct application to students' own writing, extended mini-lessons that also include some practice exercises in the skill being taught, individual conferences with the teacher to work at the specific skills each student needs, and an emphasis on preparing writing for publication.

According to Hagemann (2001), users of non-mainstream English need the following in order to develop Standard English literacy skills:

1. Exposure to a great deal of Standard American English in written and spoken form.
2. Aroused awareness of the differences and similarities between their home dialect and the Standard English of school and the wider world.
3. An understanding of the need to shift from one mode of discourse to another depending on the situation, and the motivation and ability to do so.

A classroom rich with a wide variety of linguistic resources—books, magazines, videos, CDs, computers—and a curriculum in which students are immersed in both reading and writing go a long way toward meeting the first of these needs. The second is more complex. Hagemann points out that speakers of non-mainstream dialects may have particular difficulties learning to write in Standard English because their own form of English functions very well to communicate with friends and family, in general business situations such as shopping or travel, and in the normal situations of everyday life. They may not notice the specific differences between their own dialect and that of Standard English users and they may not be motivated to make any changes in their own discourse forms. In fact, she goes so far as to say ". . . it may be easier for non-natives to learn Standard English than it is for natives" (76). To overcome this, students need not only exposure to Standard English but what Hagemann describes as "a pedagogy of overt comparison" (77) in which students are led to compare specific features of their own language with more standard forms. Students must learn to *see* the deviations between their home dialect and Standard English before they can make these changes in their writing. An additional factor here is that formal Standard English forms may feel stiff, stilted, pretentious, uncomfortable, and unfamiliar. For example, a student whose home dialect leads him to write, "I seen that she had went shopping," is likely to find the Standard English form, "I saw that she had gone shopping," both awkward and affected.

Effective methods for helping students move toward Standard English usage in their writing must include both attention to language features and to the concept of appropriateness. Hagemann and Wininger (1999) describe such an approach by a teacher who uses mini-lessons explicitly contrasting "friend talk" and "school talk" based on the work of Mary Berger (1996). Selecting a feature that differs in the students' dialect and Standard English (for example, omission of the verb "to be" in "He my friend" and its presence in the Standard English version, "He is my friend"), the teacher puts both versions of the sentence on the board and explains the rule in each kind of talk. Working with this kind of contrastive analysis, the teacher might have students translate a sentence from "school talk" to "friend talk" or vice versa, or might have students identify which dialect a sentence is written in. A teacher can also ask students to identify the "friend talk" in their own early drafts or informal writing and turn these phrases into "school talk" for a formal final draft. This approach values the language a student brings to the classroom rather than trying to eradicate it, while also teaching elements of Standard English in a manner that recognizes each is appropriate under certain circumstances.

A final factor, the motivation to learn these new forms and make these shifts to Standard English, must come from within the student. Overt discussions of when it is appropriate to use formal versus informal language in writing plus multiple opportunities to shift back and forth between them to perform various writing tasks can help students make this shift. Journals, notes, and rough drafts in the home dialect can be intermingled with formal essays, letters to public figures, editorials, and all manner of published writing projects for anthologies or web pages.

Speakers of non-mainstream dialects and ESL (English as a second language) students may indeed need more instruction in Standard English than students familiar with middle-class academic discourse, but skills instruction for all students is best taught within the context of the writing process and in a classroom that stresses writing as a meaning-making and communicative activity.

Think/Write #4

Part I. Figure 4.6 is a middle-school student's first draft. The assignment was to write about a time when you had fun. Analyze this piece of writing, considering the following questions. What are this student's strengths as a writer? What does he do well? What are the student's weaknesses as a writer? What non-standard dialect features do you see in this piece of writing? What patterns do you find in the kinds of surface errors he makes?

Part II. Plan strategies for working with this student and this piece of writing. How will you respond to it? What feedback will you give the student? What suggestions will you make for revision and proofreading? What do you predict might happen if you asked him to correct his own work in preparation for a class publication? What elements of grammar and usage do you think he needs to learn?

FIGURE 4.6 *Example of Middle School Writing*

The Day I Took Off

On day on Firday everything looking Beautiful
Kids running up and down my street. My
Friend Andy ran past and I call him I said
lets go do something lets have some fun so my
Friend and I went to the park and it was
Fill with people Black White young, old
people. We walked through the parked and we
play a little Basket Ball we won a couple
of games. I wanted something to drink my
Throat was dry Andy ask me did I want
to go to the store I said yes. So we walked
to 7-11 and Bough some of them little juices.
I Bough three apple juice. Andy got three grape.
the juices cost $1.50 for three. we had
five dollar each now we got three dollar and
fifty cent each. We decide to try the Bus
to the mall so we could watch all those pretty
ladys and young lady come out of the stores.
we went to this one Big Mall
it has everything in it. store next to store
then I get tirer walking whose all those store so
I told Andy let's go home I just took off and
no one Knew we will caugh the next Bus home
OK yes.

Sentence Variety

A century of research has failed to show any positive correlation between teaching formal grammar of any kind and writing improvement. Research into sentence combining, however, has demonstrated the effectiveness of this type of exercise in improving the variety and complexity of students' sentences. This does not mean that students who do sentence combining exercises become overall better writers. Content is still more important than the structure of individual sentences. But sentence combining is one way of helping students increase their linguistic fluency and develop a more mature writing style. Sentence combining, sentence expanding, sentence composing, and manipulation of sentence parts to achieve variety, are all useful exercises with more beneficial influence on student writing than traditional grammar study. These exercises work because they are productive uses of language in which students directly manipulate language elements, drawing on their own unconscious linguistic knowledge to produce new sentence constructions.

Sentence Combining

Sentence combining exercises ask students to combine several "kernel" sentences that have only one idea into one longer, more complex sentence. For example, *The girl was late to class* and *She didn't do her homework* could be combined to read *The girl who was late to class didn't do her homework.* Students can be given cues to help them put the sentences together, thus encouraging constructions they might not ordinarily use, or the exercise can be an open one, where students create their own constructions.

Cued Sentence Combining. A cued sentence combining exercise on the two sentences above would look like this:

1. The girl was late to class.
2. She didn't do her homework.
   (use "who")

This could produce two different constructions, depending on what the writer wants to highlight:

The girl who didn't do her homework was late for class.
The girl who was late for class didn't do her homework.

Here are other examples of cued sentence combining:

1. They moved to Detroit.
2. In Detroit he became a carpenter.
   (use "where")

Response: They moved to Detroit, where he became a carpenter.

1. They moved to Detroit.
2. In Detroit he became a carpenter.
   (use "when")

Response: When they moved to Detroit, he became a carpenter.

Open Sentence Combining. Open sentence combining exercises leave students free to draw completely on their own linguistic resources and often produce a wide variety of constructions from a class of students combining the same kernel sentences. The advantage of this kind of activity is the opportunity to evaluate the responses in terms of the effects they achieve. This also leads students to understand that there is no single "right" way to combine sentences, that much depends on the effect the writer wants to achieve or the idea to be highlighted. See what kinds of constructions you can create when you combine the following eight kernel sentences into one sentence. Compare your results with those of others doing the same exercise.

1. There was a storm.
2. The storm was severe.
3. It had lightning.
4. It had thunder.
5. It had high winds.
6. The storm left streets littered with broken tree limbs.
7. The storm caused electrical blackouts.
8. The storm caused serious injuries to many people.

Possible responses:

- A severe storm with lightning, thunder, and high winds left streets littered with broken tree limbs, caused electrical blackouts, and seriously injured many people.
- The lightning, thunder, and high winds of a severe storm caused electrical blackouts and serious injuries to many people, leaving the streets littered with broken tree limbs.

See how many different ways you can combine the sentences below. Compare your responses with others. Discuss the differences among various constructions and consider which combinations are most effective. Evaluate the different effects achieved with various sentence combinations.

1. The party was over.
2. The guests were happy.
3. The guests were tired.
4. The guests spilled out of the house.
5. The guests were laughing.
6. They were talking.
7. The guests got into cars.
8. The cars were theirs.
9. Their cars lined the streets.
10. The streets were quiet.
11. Their cars sped away.
12. Their cars were noisy.

Possible responses:

When the party was over, the happy but tired guests spilled out of the house into the quiet streets, still laughing and talking, got into their cars and sped noisily away.

The streets were quiet when the happy but tired party guests spilled out of the house, laughing and talking, got into their cars and sped noisily away.

Sentence De-combining. It can also be useful to turn complex sentences into a list of the kernel sentences forming the original. This gives students a chance to see the kinds of sentence constructions the author used to transform the list of ideas unpacked in the kernel sentences into the original complex sentence. Here's a short sentence from Annie Dillard's essay "The Fixed" in its original form and then de-combined into a series of kernel sentences:

"I was standing in the driveway, alone, stock-still, but shivering."

1. I was standing.
2. I was in the driveway.
3. I was alone.
4. I was stock-still.
5. I was shivering.

After students have a chance to review the two versions, they can evaluate the stylistic effect Dillard achieved in the way she combines these kernel ideas. For instance, why didn't she say "I was standing alone in the driveway"? What effect did she achieve in choosing to isolate the word "alone" and use it as the first in a list of adverbs describing her physical state?

Here's a longer sentence from Joan Didion's "On Keeping a Notebook," first as it appears in the essay and then as a series of kernel sentences:

"My first notebook was a Big Five tablet, given to me by my mother with the sensible suggestion that I stop whining and learn to amuse myself by writing down my thoughts."

1. My notebook was a Big Five tablet.
2. It was my first notebook.
3. My mother gave it to me.
4. She suggested that I stop whining.
5. Her suggestion was sensible.
6. She suggested that I learn to amuse myself.
7. She suggested that I write down my thoughts.

Classroom discussions can focus on Didion's use of "given to me by my mother" and "with the sensible suggestion" instead of *My mother gave it to me* and *She suggested I stop whining.*

Sentence Expanding

Another way to engage students in working with sentence construction is to have them expand a brief kernel sentence by adding descriptive phrases and clauses. For example, a kernel sentence such as *The cat slept* can lead to *Stretched out on its back, paws dangling in the air, belly exposed to any passerby, the cat slept peacefully on the couch, as safe and secure as an infant dozing on its mother's lap.* The value of this kind of activity is the possibilities it demonstrates for making writing richer, describing more, "showing" more, adding the details that make a piece come alive for the reader. But it also encourages the use of a wide variety of clauses and phrases to create syntactically interesting sentences. No response can be wrong unless it creates an incorrect sentence construction such as a run-on sentence. Expand the kernel sentences below and compare your responses to those of others.

> The wastebasket sat in the corner.
> John made himself a peanut butter and jelly sandwich.
> Susan procrastinated.
> Several students complained.
> The rock singer approached the stage.
> He bought a new pair of jeans.

Sentence Composing and Imitation

Students can be given sentences from professional writers and asked to compose similar sentences, modeled after the examples. Here are two examples of sentences by professional writers and students' imitations.

> The writer, an old man with a white mustache, had some difficulty getting into bed.
> —Sherwood Anderson

> The student, a young girl with rings in both eyebrows and nostrils, had no difficulty getting the attention she demanded.
> —A student writer

> There were black Saturdays now and then when Maria and Miranda sat ready, hats in hand, curly hair plastered down and slicked behind their ears, their stiffly-pleated navy-blue skirts spread out around them, waiting with their hearts going down slowly into their high-topped laced-up black books.
> —Katherine Anne Porter

> There were black Sunday nights now and then when I sat at my computer, textbooks piled up, coffee cup filled from a freshly brewed pot and balanced precariously close to the keyboard, my shabby sweats enveloping me in comforting warmth, waiting with anxiety for inspiration to suddenly emerge from the dregs of the weekend.
> —A student writer

The value of this exercise lies in getting students to use constructions they would not ordinarily consider, either because they are not part of their conscious language use or because they've been unaware of these constructions. At first these constructions may only appear in the assigned exercises, but they will eventually make their way into students' writing, especially if the teacher encourages students to use them and then shares good student examples with the whole class.

In our experience, developing writers are insecure about using new constructions, but with enough practice and praise, they soon develop much more linguistic fluency and are quick to point out interesting sentence constructions in both student and professional writing.

Sentence Manipulation

Exercises in which students rearrange sentence parts to achieve a variety of effects and use varied construction can also be useful in helping students become more flexible and syntactically mature writers. Students can practice this in their own writing or rearrange the sentence elements of professional writers. Here is a student's sentence rearranged in three different ways. Students can continue to rearrange the elements of this sentence and evaluate the effect each arrangement has on meaning.

> I found the hard lenses to be more durable, more comfortable, and less likely to dry out easily although they will crack if too much pressure is applied during the cleaning process.
>
> The hard lenses will crack if too much pressure is applied during the cleaning process, but they are more durable, more comfortable, and less likely to dry out easily.
>
> Durable, comfortable, and less likely to dry out easily, hard lenses will crack if too much pressure is applied during the cleaning process.

Try rearranging the sentence parts in the following sentence by Annie Dillard describing a polyphemous moth emerging from its cocoon in a jar too small to permit full extension of its wings: "Those huge wings stuck on his back in a torture of random pleats and folds, wrinkled as a dirty tissue, rigid as leather." Consider the differences in emphasis and meaning that each change creates.

Recommended Resources for Sentence Combining Exercises

For discussions and examples of exercises to promote sentence variety and syntactic growth at the secondary level, we like several texts by William Strong: *Sentence Combining: A Composing Book,* 3rd edition, *Sentence Combining and Paragraph Building,* and *Creative Approaches to Sentence Combining.* Don Killgallon's *Sentence Composing: The Complete Guide* also offers a thorough discussion of numerous sentence combining and composing activities, based on analyzing, manipulating, and imitating the sentences of professional writers. Teachers will find this a useful classroom resource. Separate sentence composing texts by Killgallon for grades 10 and 11 are also available. Although it is geared for college students, teachers and advanced high school students could expand their understanding of sentence combining with *The Writer's Options: Combining to Composing,* fifth edition, by Donald Daiker, Andrew Kerek, Max Morenberg, and Jeffrey Sommers.

Wordiness and Other Aspects of Style

One of the hallmarks of a more mature writing style is concise use of language. Redundant, wordy, repetitive sentences detract from the clarity of a writer's ideas and reduce the impact of his thinking. Simple activities such as the ones below will make developing writers more aware of the excess and inexact verbiage they often use to express an idea and help them "tighten" their language. Attention to this aspect of writing is best reserved for later in the school year or for advanced writers who are no longer struggling with the more basic elements of the writing process and are ready to work on stylistic matters.

Developing a More Mature Writing Style

Directions: Select one of your past papers or a completed draft of a piece you are now working on. Search for and circle all examples of the structures below. Remove as many as you can, revising sentences, removing wordiness, tightening your language. Goal: delete 15 words per page without altering meaning.

1. Tighten wordy language and language so general it conveys little to the reader. Examples:

   I noticed that . . .
   It may be argued that . . .
   Let me make it perfectly clear that . . .
   I remembered that . . .
   It was an amazing scene.
   This paper is about . . .
   I decided to write this paper about . . .
   As we approached her, I noticed that . . .

2. Remove "there is," "there are," "it is," "it was," and other wordy constructions. Examples:

   There is only one other place in the house that has seen more of me.

   (Only one other place in the house has seen more of me.)

   There are people taking their daily walk or run. There are children that ride their bicycles to their friends' houses.

   (People take their daily walk or run. Children ride their bicycles to their friends' houses.)

3. Avoid "and," "but," and "so" as sentence connectors. Circle each of these words in your paper. Can you re-design these sentences by creating subordinate clauses?
   Example:

   He was my friend and he spent a lot of time at my house so we became even better friends and did a lot together.

4. Avoid the use of qualifiers—*rather, very, little, pretty, quite.* "These are the leeches that infest the pond of prose, sucking the blood of words" (Strunk and White, *The Elements of Style* 65).
   Example:

   I was rather tired, so I decided to take a little nap.

5. Use strong verbs instead of forms of the verb *to be* (*am, is, are, was, were*).
   Examples:

   The Akron game was a disappointment to the fans.
   (The Akron game disappointed the fans.)

6. Vary your sentences, use complex sentences, combine several ideas into one sentence by using modifying clauses and phrases. If you find several sentences in a row constructed exactly the same way with a repetitive opening that is not purposefully planned, work on varying constructions and combining ideas.
   Example:

   One woman is measuring picture frames. *She asks me* my opinion about the frame. *She is looking for* a frame to go with an oil painting she bought at a garage sale. *She also tells me* that her vacuum cleaner quit. *She shows me* the sweeper she plans on buying. *She only has* enough money today for the sweeper and maybe enough for a frame. *She also tells me* that her boyfriend recently bought furniture from the second hand store for his cabin up north.

When a class or group of students is ready for work on this aspect of writing, mini-lessons on each of the areas above can be a productive way to promote tighter, more precise, more stylistically mature writing at the sentence level.

Think/Write #5
Choose a paper of your own and do the tightening exercises demonstrated above. How many words can you remove without altering meaning or style?

Points to Remember

"Grammar" is a term with multiple meanings and associations that range from the unconscious rules of the structure of the language to dialect/usage rules and writing conventions. Within this broad framework, the nature of error suggests that it is a necessary part of learning to write effectively, that children and young adults need opportunities to try out forms before they are in complete control of them. The nature of syntactic development suggests that children and young adults need lots of writing and experimentation with syntactic structures to gain fluency in writing. Differentiating types of errors ranging from developmental to rhetorical, from dialect/usage to writing conventions will help teachers make decisions about when providing guided instruction in aspects of language and grammar will be useful and when that instruction will be more effective.

Grammar, usage, and mechanical correctness are best taught in context as part of the composing process rather than in isolated units of study. Attention to these skills should be saved for the editing/proofreading stages of producing a finished piece when students are preparing their writing for readers who expect Standard English. Students don't need to know much formal grammatical terminology since they already have a great deal of competence in language use; therefore, teachers should focus instruction on what students need to know to produce written Standard English. Many classroom activities promote attention to final editing/proofreading and encourage students to accept responsibility for their own correctness. Speakers and writers of Non-Standard English benefit from specific attention to recognizing the differences between their home dialect and Standard English plus an understanding of the need to shift from their home dialect to more standard forms when formal writing demands this. Research suggests that sentence combining, sentence composing, and sentence manipulation activities lead to more mature writing at the sentence level.

For Further Reading

Atwell, Nancie. *In the Middle.* Portsmouth, NH: Boynton/Cook, 1987 and 2nd ed. 1998.

Berger, Mary. *Teach Standard, Too: Teacher's Manual to School Talk/Friend Talk Scripted Lessons.* Chicago: Orchard Books, 1996.

Delpit, Lisa. "The Silenced Dialogue: Power and Pedagogy in Educating Other People's Children." *Harvard Educational Review 58:* 3 (1988): 280–298.

Hillocks, G., Jr. *Research on Written Composition: New Directions for Teaching.* Urbana, IL: ERIC Clearinghouse on Reading and Communication Skills and the National Conference on Research in English, 1986.

National Council of Teachers of English (NCTE). *Students' Right to Their Own Language.* Urbana, IL: NCTE, 1974.

Weaver, Constance. *Teaching Grammar in Context.* Portsmouth, NH: Boynton/Cook-Heinemann, 1996.

———, ed. *Lessons to Share on Teaching Grammar in Context.* Portsmouth, NH: Boynton/Cook-Heinemann, 1998.

5

The Essay and Other Write-to-Learn Assignments

Students write at their best when they believe the essay paper topic is authentic, interesting, and relevant. We know that much. The assignment has to be embraced by the learner as useful and purposeful. Having said this, we can readily imagine why the formal essay assignment has produced dreadful results over the years, since most paper assignments from the seventeenth century onwards have depended on timeworn, teacher-selected topics. Even today—whether chosen by students or teachers—most essay topics require little investment of their critical thinking or beliefs. The end results, sometimes containing plagiarized passages, are often disjointed. Tackling concepts they little understand, students predictably string together borrowed passages undigested from their reading or clichés from popular opinion. Few students write these papers enthusiastically and almost no teacher grades them with glee. Done dutifully, the grading process is so tedious that seasoned teachers often question the worth of such assignments. To lighten their load, teachers resort to a point system that requires strict conformity to rules for organization, clarity, sentence structure, and grammar. The grader does not care in the end if the research paper actually *says* something so long as the rules are followed to the letter.

Yet, essay writing does have its instructional payoff. When written conscientiously, essays are unparalleled for encouraging students to read perceptively, build new schemata, expand their vocabulary, and experiment with varied forms of text organization. Furthermore, these assignments require higher order thinking—students learn to evaluate the differences between important and lesser information, form connections, draw inferences, apply the information to real situations, analyze, synthesize, and form judgments—all thinking processes at the top of Bloom's taxonomy of critical thinking. We have long understood the educational value of analytic essay writing. In 1986, Judith Langer found that longer essay writing in the content areas was more instrumental in aiding cognitive development—improving students' ability to read, write, and think—than completing study questions or note taking. Because of the nature of the writing process, students are forced to work recursively—thinking, writing, reading, reformulating, and rewriting. More than that, Langer found that essays pushed students to form more complex questions, hypothesize, and evaluate evidence using meta-comments. She concluded, ". . . students seem to step back from the text after reading it—they reconceptualize the ideas in ways that cut across ideas, focusing on larger issues or topics. In doing this, they integrate information and engage in more complex thought" (Langer 406). In essays that combine mastery of new subject matter with composition that demonstrates student thinking, writers learn to solve problems and to synthesize knowledge on a level higher than the mere gathering of information that we find in note taking and other types of report writing.

It is up to the teacher to help students recognize the essay's relevance and value. We can often interest students in the essay by posing questions that require real thinking without the cumbersome apparatus (such as footnotes) of a formal paper. Field notes, case studies, memos, lab reports, research papers, news articles, feature stories, probes, and white papers serve this purpose. Most importantly, it has to be "authentic," that is, writing for a purpose, writing that students can own because it speaks out with ideas they care about. Other directions for authentic writing might include such real life tasks as writing business letters, memos, or web sites. The complaint letter to a company or the letter to the editor are perennial favorites. But the formal paper can also hook a student's attention. Indeed, it is possible to turn a seemingly dull assignment into a piece of writing that a student keeps for years if all parties are willing to invest in the search. If they are open to the process, both students and teachers can even discover surprising enthusiasm for their topics, especially when students are encouraged to conduct a self-directed inquiry on issues relevant to their own lives.

This chapter is divided into four parts. In the first section, we discuss the usefulness of expository writing for teaching students to read closely, to step up their critical thinking, and to learn to write analytically. The idea of writing to learn is the rationale that underlies all essay assignments of one sort or another. In the second section, we offer general advice for guiding students through basic essay writing and we describe approaches for teaching several variants of the essay—the argument paper, the definition paper, the comparison/contrast paper, and the cause and effect paper. In the third section, we wrestle with the research paper, an essay taken to its most complex, most formal level. We pay particular attention to our favorite version of the research paper, the I-Search paper, because it is well suited to the young writer. In the final section, we will offer tips for dealing with assessment and plagiarism.

Chapter Five meets the following NCATE/NCTE Program Standards for the preparation of pre-service teachers in the English Language Arts. Pre-service teachers will be prepared to meet the standards listed below.

3.2.2 Writing, speaking, and observing as major forms of inquiry, reflection, and expression in their coursework;
3.2.4 Writing, visual images, and speaking for a variety of audiences and purposes;
3.3.2 Creation of meaning from texts;

3.4.1 A variety of writing strategies to generate meaning and clarify understanding;
3.4.2 A variety of different forms of written discourse;
3.4.3 The influence of written discourse on thought and action;
3.6.1 The influence of media on culture and on people's actions and communication;
3.6.2 Construction of meaning from media and non-print texts;

Write-to-Learn Assignments: A Definition

Actually, the essay is only one of many longer, write-to-learn assignments. Other types that we will discuss in this chapter include the research paper, the I-search paper, the social action paper, and the summary. What they have in common is some discovery about the self and the world. The term comes from Donald Murray's book by the same name. He says write-to-learn is "to discover meaning in experience" (7). The point is to explore a focal idea through research and writing until something new is understood. For Murray, the write-to-learn exercise begins deep in the writer's "territory," that place that is unique to every individual. It is known and yet mysterious. It is often buried in memory and yet it is at the tip of consciousness. It is familiar and yet surprising. It is teased out by free writing techniques, enriched by memories, and enlarged by experience, thinking, and reading.

Indeed reading is largely the trigger for write-to-learn assignments, since they are often used by teachers to explore the implications of a chapter or article. In this case, student writing serves as a device for extending student comprehension more than a tool for self-expression. One example of write-to-learn is the *summary.* Often called a *précis* or abstract, the summary is a brief readable list of the key points of a given text. The summary is usually a paragraph with transitional phrases that hold the ideas together and place them in some sort of context. The length of the summary can depend on the circumstances in which it is used. Summaries are often used in business to provide quick sources of information on a given issue or policy for an office team or boss. They are used in the sciences to provide a quick look at the results of an experiment. In the humanities they are used as access to large amounts of information. The crucial features are that summaries rarely provide detail or examples and they do not allow for the author's personal opinion. They condense the information to the key arguments or steps in the longer text. (See Fig. 5.1: Writing Abstracts or Summaries for guidelines.) The summary is an excellent assignment for getting students to cut away extra detail, to grasp the core of a reading.

In this chapter, however, we are using the term write-to-learn to refer specifically to papers that originate in the writer's experience and are developed by a need to understand something more about the topic. Although the essay begins in the writer's imagination, it is expanded when he seeks out additional information that helps to construct a deeper meaning. The author may be responding to something he has read, seen, or heard. He may have looked up the answer to a question or learned a new piece of oral history. He may have seen it on TV or on the Internet. The link between the writer's experience and additional information grows out of

FIGURE 5.1 ***Writing Abstracts or Summaries***

The purpose of an abstract or summary is to condense a lengthy report or text for easier and faster reading. It is used in academe, especially in the sciences and social sciences in the introduction to a long study, and it is used in business for efficient circulation of information within the company.

Tips for Writing Abstracts

1. List only the key points, so you pick up main themes, generalizations, and conclusions.
2. Avoid examples, specifics, illustrations, or detailed arguments unless they are central to the original piece.
3. Write only in your own words, so you avoid direct quotations—unless you are picking up some catch phrase like "commie baiting."
4. Use a structure roughly parallel to that of the original piece. If the original, for example, is written in a cause-and-effect pattern, the abstract should reflect that pattern.
5. Proportion the spread of topics equal to that of the original article, so the abstract does not allot undue space to a minor point, or conversely, slight a major point.
6. Avoid adding any material to the original, unless you have to make explicit points that are only implied in the original, and never insert your own opinion; use only the author's material and arguments.
7. Be concise. You rarely write more than a page, regardless of the length of the original material, and most abstracts are only one paragraph long.

Steps for Writing an Abstract

1. Read the material thoroughly to find the main theme.
2. Jot down notes or underline the most salient points.
3. Close your book so you are not tempted by specific passages.
4. Write your paragraph from notes and memory. Connect all the points with transition words like "nevertheless," "however," "and yet," etc., so that you have a smoothly flowing text.
5. Proofread for errors made in haste.

---

the questions that he asks of his experience. The questions that he asks bring meaning and purpose to the paper. His desire to know and his later need to explain all that he has learned are what make this paper authentic writing.

The completed piece may or may not contain the triggers—the original experience and the question—but it always contains the additional information and an elaboration on its significance. The key components to the write-to-learn essay are the following:

- a writer's personal experience;
- the writer's question about that experience;
- additional information;
- a coherent and reader-friendly exposition.

In this chapter we will discuss strategies for teaching the write-to-learn paper—an exercise that usually requires data collection and often some method of documentation such as references to another source, in-text citations, footnotes, or endnotes. Even though the chapter is largely about the essay—how the essay's topics are generated and how the body of the essay is developed—much of the advice can readily apply to any assignment in classes where "write-to-learn" commonly requires students to master a body of new knowledge and write about it.

Invention, or Generating Topics for the Essay

To find a topic, the writer often tries *free writing* or similar alternatives such as *exploratory writings* to find connections. As discussed in Chapter Three, free writing consists of a 10-to-15 minute flow of words without self-consciously correcting for spelling or grammar. The purpose is sheer fluency by listing scattered thoughts and remembrances around a trigger word or phrase. The writing is done associatively, without stopping. One idea should glide into the next like a chain, often without logic to an outside reader. If the writer runs out of things to say, he can always describe the room where he is sitting.

Simple *brainstorming* may also be a means of generating a topic, often by making lists by gathering facts or writing down free associations. Another method of brainstorming is responding to an article from a magazine or newspaper on current issues with a journal entry. A Learning Log or a Double-entry notebook (see also Chapter Six) is another possibility. Reading of any sort is helpful for creating wonder and curiosity and so are films or games. Ideas can grow out of poking around the library or the Internet without doing deliberative research. To make this aimless activity effective, however, students have to be on task or the time is wasted. Other brainstorming can include:

- drawing up a timeline for a given historical event and writing about the turning point or the high point of that timeline;
- composing a letter—real or imaginary—to the author of a book, to the script writer of a television program, or to one of the principal figures in the study;
- listing ideas for changing history and writing about the "moment of pressure," the pivotal moment when things changed into a different future;
- playing 20 questions about a discovery or an historical figure whose biography is not well known;
- debating an issue in class that calls for further research;
- watching a film such as *Glory* that triggers curiosity about a topic such as the role of the African American soldier in the Civil War;
- asking a reporter's questions—who? what? when? where? why?

Another form of free writing is *looping*. In this form, the author stops after five or so minutes, rereads what's been written, circles the most surprising or significant word or phrase and then writes for another few minutes. This cycle can be repeated several times till the process leads somewhere new and interesting. The loop writing process may take many different shapes. What they all have in common is a short, intense piece of writing mined for its language and its insights. The first attempt, usually a story or fragment pulled out of one's memory, lays the groundwork for a further reflection or a second telling. After each five-minute loop, students stop and look for a "center of gravity," a core meaning that is often implied across the series of writings or inside one of the loops. That core idea kicks off the next loop. Peter Elbow and Pat Belanoff suggest that authors try looping five times, "switching tracks" after each loop. They offer the following ways to switch tracks:

- constructing a dialog between conflicting voices;
- relating favorite family stories;
- retelling the same story from a different viewpoint or to a different audience;
- resetting the story in another time or place;
- drawing a quick portrait, then responding in words;
- writing a whole, one-paragraph essay;
- telling bald-faced lies;
- playing with old sayings, folk wisdom, Latin phrases, ad slogans;
- listing failed ideas that almost work;
- producing a collage of words taken from an earlier loop;
- writing about what was almost said.

Even though free writing works well to loosen up a writer's thinking and helps to uncover ideas that are rooted in our thinking, many students grow impatient with the process of pre-writing, particularly writing without producing something they can use almost verbatim in the final draft. To accommodate the student who wants to dig in immediately, we need more than one way to develop topics and ideas. Here are some other forms of invention that are particularly useful for the write-to-learn paper:

Cubing makes an ideal heuristic or discovery stratagem for write-to-learn papers by playing with the topic using categorical ways of thinking about it: writers choose a subject, then describe it; compare it; associate it; analyze it; apply it; argue for or against it. Using "war" as an example, students may be asked to describe the ethos of war, as in World War I: they may compare it to a "police action," associate it with an "incursion," analyze when a victory could be declared in war, apply the term to the brief bombing of a country, and argue for or against war. The class could discuss the topic through these various lenses, looking for questions to pursue in a paper. The statements can also be used to subdivide assignments, so that each student in the group researches a different aspect of the topic.

Chaining questions, as explained by Elizabeth Cowan Neeld, is a question-and-answer exercise that stimulates connections and relationships. Students pair up to ask and answer questions about a specific topic that one of them is considering. The interrogator begins the questioning: "How are the course schedules determined by the school computer system?" The writer tries to answer it: "Students select the courses they want to take." And that answer leads to the next question: "How does the computer sort the list of courses? Answer: "Perhaps it sorts the most popular courses first?" Question: "How would sorting by the largest number be the most efficient method?" and so forth, students asking and answering questions with each other till the writer has some insight into the problem and some notion about where to begin his research.

K-W-L is an old chestnut used largely as a pre-reading device, but it works for generating interest in research topics as well. The teacher marks out three columns on the board—what you ***K***now, what you ***W***ant to know, and what you have ***L***earned. These columns offer an excuse for a student to take stock of everything she knows on a given subject and figure out what she would still like to learn. The last column is filled in after the writing assignment is complete.

Surfing the Internet. This strategy for searching a topic does not require much discussion. Suffice it to say, the Internet has quickly become the most popular vehicle for locating information. The problem is that a substantial number of American families still do not have access to the Internet. Teachers may therefore offer some release time for surfing on an individual basis at school. Students need to make their search a personal quest, so working together during this stage may be counterproductive. Because students can eat up hours and hours doing this, they should probably conduct much of the search at home or during release time from the class if possible.

An *exploratory writing* may be more self-consciously produced and perhaps longer in form, but it can still be an experimental and open investigation of the topic in which the writer explores the subject matter as far as she can. In this paper, the young writer puts down all that she knows—including side arguments—and leaves gaps where more information is needed. Some writers add questions in capital letters when they find a shortfall in their knowledge. The capital letters help them find the holes when they are doing library research later on. Although the probe may serve as a first draft, neither of these exploratory writing exercises should be graded. The best teacher responses are words of encouragement and questions that will guide students toward a narrower and deeper study.

Finally, we should not underestimate the *teacher-student conference* in which the author is encouraged to ruminate on a number of different possibilities for the paper. Some of the best advice for conferencing with students comes from Donald Murray in *A Writer Teaches Writing*, ". . . the content of the writing course comes from the student himself" (152). In short, there is no purpose to the conference if the student is simply waiting for hints and topic advice from the teacher. The student has to come prepared with one or two topics she has explored and sorted out. The teacher's aim is to clarify the student's thought and help her become conscious of her own feelings. Mickey Harris, a veteran Writing Center director and teacher, suggests inviting the student to talk about the topic by using an indirect lead, "Tell me more about . . ." and sometimes a direct lead, "Give me a specific example of . . ." Like Murray, she believes that the teacher responds with some interpretation of what the student is trying to say, "So what you're trying to say is that . . ." and paraphrasing the student's message. Teachers can thus help students discriminate in their choice of words, focus their topics, and fill in missing links, but they cannot set the arguments for students or think for them. In these conferences, teachers should use reassuring phrases and words of approval, but Murray points out that they get nods of unabashed approval from home. What they need from the teacher is something of a "bite," that is "someone who will snap back, who is concerned with what the student has to say, who has standards, whose praise means something"; we need to be more of a motivator than a critic in these conferences (151). Teachers thus guide students toward a more complex way of looking at the issues and to new sources. They should walk away from the meeting with a desire to explain more on paper about their topic.

These invention techniques are meant to help young writers focus their library or Internet time, discover new complexities, and realize the deeper implications of their topics. Because the writing process is recursive, students need time during the writing phase to rethink their topics and their arguments by reemploying periodically many of the pre-writing techniques, even after they've written a draft or two. The hope is that students will eventually recognize an inside track to the topic and write with some ownership of their ideas and that they will focus more on exploring an insight than on the simple mechanics of getting the job done. We assume, of course, that the writer has a will to make meaning—not only to discover a viable topic, but also to push early impressions beyond simple labels or descriptive features towards communicating a message that takes a stand and commits to a position. Lasting writing comes from the personal need to say something, whether writing for oneself, for friends, or for write-to-learn papers. The School Councils of Great Britain underscore the axiom that all writing, even the research paper, begins with idiosyncratic preference, "Impersonal writing . . . needs to be nourished by the continuance of personal writing. At its best, of course (more especially in literature), the impersonal embodies the qualities of personal writing as well; it is both strongly felt and objective, both imaginative and precise" (Murray, *A Writer Teaches Writing,* 152). Personal exploration thus becomes the basis for more public writing.

Think/Write #1

List five different papers where you have used some sort of discovery process for getting started. What kinds of exercises were they? Did you do it only because some teacher forced you to do it? Which invention exercise worked the best for you? Why? Was it because you needed it to get started? If you have never tried any of these exercises, how do you get a lot of ideas for writing a paper?

Collecting Data

Much of the collection in the writing process is determined by topic selection and the type and length of paper that students are writing. The teacher will have to decide, however, what sorts of sources to accept and how many to require. The number and type of sources present a problem of their own. Authorities cited in the paper must be qualified to give an opinion on the subject and they must have sufficient evidence to support their claims. High school writers would produce more insightful papers if they were to discover and analyze the ideological prejudices of their sources. If students were able to situate everyone's (including their own) position in terms of class, gender, religious affiliation, and political views, they would be able to evaluate the readings more perceptively. Short of this, they need to recognize the larger contexts of arguments and decide if the author has a vested interest in the claim. Requiring an evaluation of the sources in the body of the paper or in the footnotes could make students critically aware of the problems of taking information off the Internet. If a discussion of the sources is not appropriate for the paper, then students can be asked to defend their experts' credentials in a separate assignment. Criteria for evaluating websites can be found on the Internet or in Allyn & Bacon's *The New Century Handbook.*

High school students should be discouraged from using encyclopedias or the Internet for most of their material. Fortunately, and unfortunately, these are the sources that students find first. Certainly encyclopedias are useful as quick references and the Internet is a rich source that serves as an electronic encyclopedia, so these options should not be excluded entirely even though they are often abused. To avoid serious problems, teachers are well advised to work with techniques of source evaluation before the paper process begins. Unless teachers prepare students adequately, the disadvantages of the Internet listed below can outweigh its advantages:

- Websites are sometimes difficult to document because authorship is unclear. If they cannot verify the author and establish the source's credentials, then the source should be either discarded or used with caution, perhaps by pitting one expert against another. Students could line up experts on both sides of an issue.

- The quality of information varies considerably from website to website. Sites about current issues often provide reliable information because they're usually up-to-date. Historical matter is hit and miss. Sites developed by support from the National Endowment for the Humanities (i.e., material about the American Civil War) are amazingly useful for American history and literature. But there are big unexplored holes in the coverage and this is likely to remain true because the web can never match the extent of our libraries' holdings. At best, websites are superficial and can only be regarded as an introduction to any topic.

- The best defense against irresponsible and misleading websites is to teach students how to judge information for its reliability. Discussions about the reputation of the publisher or sponsor of a website, the timeliness of the article or page, and whether the information is corroborated by other sources are all places to begin that discussion.

- Some websites are coded to make it impossible to print the pages out.

- Some websites are difficult to relocate at a later date. This is especially problematic for students using writing labs where they cannot bookmark the material.

- Websites disappear overnight and often cannot be revisited, so students must download the material right away, noting the necessary source information for citations and keeping a copy for future use.

- Some websites sell papers to students wholesale, so teachers need to structure paper assignments to anticipate this corruption of the system and make it difficult for students to use prewritten, plagiarized papers. The antidote is to call up the websites designed for teachers who want to search out illegal material and identify the original sources.

While online databases, the Internet, and encyclopedias make research fun and accessible, they also invite students to use information that is undigested and often irrelevant. Some teachers circumvent these problems by disallowing electronic sources altogether. It is one way of forcing students into picking through print material, but such injunctions are impractical and wasteful of the resources that libraries already provide. Requiring a balanced assortment of sources seems to be the strategy that most realistic teachers are taking. Teachers can counter the problems of the Internet with sound advice on how to use it responsibly.

Given the Internet and the ease of downloading material, teachers may have to rethink the role of taking notes on index cards. Although this is a time honored method of data collection, many students are finding it easier to highlight and label printouts and photocopied material. They become impatient copying material by hand. Veteran teachers defend note cards because cards can help students organize vast amounts of material by subtopic. The cards prod students to be more selective about quoted material because they tire of copying. They must read and choose passages carefully to save time and effort. But if we were to be realistic, we would find alternatives to the note cards because they appear to be busy work for students. One solution has been to allow a limited number of printouts from the Internet when students have been directed to make annotations on them and highlight the most important passages with a colored marker. They then have to hand in the printouts with the final draft of the paper.

Think/Write #2
When no one is forcing you to write a research paper using their methods, how do you collect your data and organize it? What works best for you? How do you organize your material from the Internet? Is it different than the way you collect and file information from books? What about information from journals? or interviews? What is your system for keeping the material accessible? Could your system be teachable to a high school class?

The Body of the Paper

Openings for Papers

The goal of the paper's introduction should be to capture reader interest and to suggest the path of the paper. Students can hook their readers with these possibilities:

- relate to the familiar;
- provide background material;
- define a key concept;
- challenge an assumption;
- use a brief quotation;
- review the key positions;
- state the thesis.

For decades, students have been required to form their thesis statements and outlines before beginning to write. So much for the process of discovery through writing. The paper was virtually in the can before the first sentence was written. No wonder students view essay writing as a fill-in-the-blanks exercise. The conventional method of approaching the paper is to begin with thesis statement and outline, but this approach overlooks the very power of language to sort out new ideas. We grow up struggling to make sense of the world around us—our families, our institutions, our culture, the relationships between things, the logic of the natural world—and we use language to understand it. We use language by talking through ideas, by listening to advice, by exploring through reading and writing. In short, we don't know what we want to say until we say it. This is the point of write-to-learn. Ann E. Berthoff explains that we know what we know by using language to bring order out of chaos. One of the best mediums for sorting ideas is composing. She elaborates, "Meanings don't come out of the air; we make them out of a chaos of images, half-truths, remembrances, syntactic fragments, from the mysterious and unformed" (70). Since writing helps us think, shape, organize our thoughts, we use the pre-writing process—not to form the most perfect thesis statement—but to begin to make use of the flood of ideas that come out of the chaos and generate meaning. The process of thinking is by no means complete till the paper is written. We don't entirely know what we mean until we can say it or write it. Berthoff explains, ". . . writing taught as a process of making meanings, can be seen to be like taking in a happening, forming an opinion, deciding what's to be done, construing a text, or reading the significance of a landscape" (69). She is describing something akin to the write-to-learn process: a) observing an event; b) deciding what details are important; c) interpreting the data; and d) drawing conclusions about their significance. In this sense, writing is thinking, perceiving, evaluating, and finding a form. When focused on the write-to-learn paper, students use it as a means of discovery to make sense out of the collection of facts.

So, is forming the thesis statement a superfluous or counterproductive prewriting device? No, it can help some writers understand their focus, but we believe that it is merely a holding place for the central idea that will emerge when the writer has time to discover what she really wants to say. It's a working thesis that can provide a blueprint for some students. For others, muddling through makes more sense. Is a preliminary outline necessary? Probably not. Some students might find a rough outline a handy map for seeing where they are headed—a "game plan" for moving forward. Other students might find it necessary to work out the minute details of their argument in a very thorough outline before writing. For these students, a word processor's outline feature might be helpful. Most students will not draw up an outline until they've seen where they've been, until they've reached the end of the paper. Like the thesis statement, the outline should serve only as a conditional statement, acting as a probationary framework until a stronger one takes hold. Nothing is certain till the end because composing is a discovery and recursive process—write a bit, stop, look back and reflect on what has just been said, resume writing, change one's focus, keep writing, and so on. During this process, we carve out new directions and our arguments take the turns we would never have predicted.

Shaping the Paper's Middle Structure

The placement of the thesis statement is just one decision that the writer must make about the paper's structure. Other decisions—such as which points should come first or how much to say or how to illustrate an idea—are even more complicated than that. The teacher's dilemma is judging how much to help students in the decision-making process by giving them rhetorical forms (such as the Five-Paragraph structure) to follow. In other words, the essay assignment should encourage writers to use a range of genres that more closely mirror "real-world writing." Most secondary students understand the narrative with its beginning, middle, and end very well. Other than the story telling approach, a student might want to be aware of the following structure for presenting an idea or argument backed up by research material:

- introduce the issue with a clear statement of the problem;
- take a position (the thesis) or raise a central question;
- defend or refute that position with evidence, or answer the question in point;
- refute the opposition or alternative positions;
- conclude with an answer to the question, "So what?"

The arrangement of ideas may vary from this order according to what is being argued or asserted. (See Fig. 5.2: The Structure of a Classic Write-to-Learn Paper) The decision about where to place the thesis, for example, should be the writer's to determine and should not be prescribed by the teacher. In an inductive paper, for example, the writer might pile up one piece of evidence after another, leaving the thesis statement to the end of the argument. In this case, the author will open the main idea at the start of the paper without fully taking a stance. To help the reader follow the line of thought, the conclusion must seem fairly obvious. Inductive arguments work best when the evidence is more important than the thesis because the argument is widely agreed upon. An example of this might be the paper that concludes "animals are too often abused." In this paper, the evidence, consisting of a series of examples to illustrate this point, will be more compelling than the conclusion, which is usually a commonly held opinion. *The point is that the content determines the form.* Ann Berthoff is fond of saying, "In composing we make meanings. We find the forms of thought by means of language, and we find the forms of language by taking thought" (69). Berthoff's key contribution to our understanding of composition is that language makes sense out of complex personal perceptions and experiences in an equally complex world that needs to be "composed" to be fully understood, and she is aware of the ways that structure flows out of ordering that language.

What we're arguing against here is the rigidly taught Five-Paragraph essay or any other formula for writing an essay. This is the mechanical process assigned by teachers for years and years to teach the structure of research and argument papers and it is deadly. Paragraph one reviews the problem and ends with a thesis statement that usually has three parts to it. For example, "The French Revolution had three major causes." Paragraphs two, three, and four take up each of the points, one by one. Paragraph five concludes the paper, often by restating the thesis. While

FIGURE 5.2 ***The Structure of a Classic Write-to-Learn Paper***

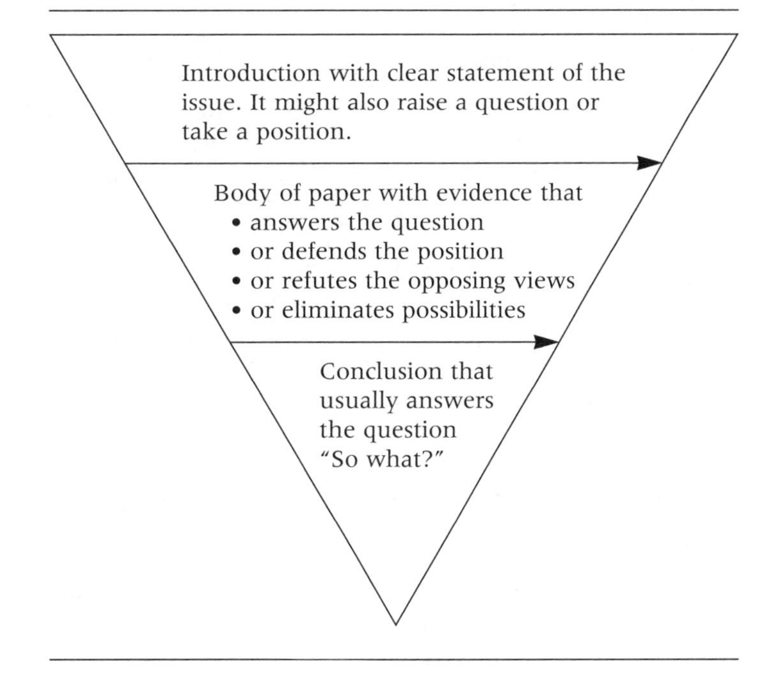

the formula makes it easy to teach the write-to-learn structure and it promotes a clear, logical delivery for ideas, it usually leads to deadly dull, hackneyed papers that oversimplify the issues. The paragraphs are often underdeveloped because the topic is generally too large for short paragraphs. Moreover, the circular strategy for the conclusion crops the paper, cutting off an opportunity for writers to push towards a "so what?" finish. The Five-Paragraph essay so truncates the end of the paper that writers need not make the hard decisions about the content's significance. Furthermore, the one, two, three format is so stultifying that writers become more focussed on the form as they write than the content, also removing any reason for caring about or assuming responsibility for the message.

Although students often need structural guidelines for writing, they should be encouraged to experiment with the rules if the subject matter pushes them away from the standard methods. Teachers who insist on rules to make the writing process easier for students stunt their opportunity to learn how to sort data and formulate arguments on their own. Ann Berthoff says, "We find the forms of thought by means of language, and we find the forms of language by taking thought." She is explaining that effective expression is able to grow with the rhetorical form if the writer is struggling to make meaning through language. Our conclusion is that teachers can and should teach rhetorical forms through direct instruction, but the forms alone should not determine the meaning. Meaning begins with the writer's desire to speak out and communicate. It is further shaped by a constellation of factors that include the demands of the material and the needs of the readers. Organizational plans such as the Five-Paragraph essay are the least important of all.

Writing Conclusions

The end of the paper poses a problem for most writers. It is even more difficult for young writers. Ask them to answer the question "so what?" What is the point of this paper? Why should the reader/writer care? In an argument paper, the "so what?" is answered by driving home the main point—not simply by restating it, but by summing up the main arguments and explaining how or why they are important. In a non-argument or report, a summary of the main points may be useful or there may be no call for a conclusion. Here are some other ideas: end on a quotation that sums up the argument, compare the past to the present, take sides in an argument. But all of this advice is tricky, since the conclusion depends largely on anticipating the readers' need to learn something meaningful.

The Role of the Audience/Reader

The point that we are making again and again is that there are no fixed rules for writing an essay. Neither the teacher nor the student author can fall back on simplistic rules. But both parties can be aware of the factors that shape the unfolding of a paper—the writer's need to express himself and at the same time, his need to guide the reader through the argument. Shifting secondary students from a writer-centered mode of thinking to an awareness of their audience and the role of the reader is very difficult. One reason is that young writers care more about expressing themselves than being understood. They often disavow any interest in what their readers think—"that's their problem," they'll argue. They need to be convinced that readerly considerations are equally crucial, even though they are not obvious to students who write largely for the teacher. Peer editing shifts this dynamic slightly, but most students write for a grade.

Lack of interest in audience is the weakness in the writing process that rhetoricians use to oppose it. In the write-to-learn essay, composition teachers emphasize exploration and quest and skepticism. "Don't worry about your thesis till you know what you are trying to say," we assure our students. "You are writing to discover." And yet, in the final product, the writer must have a firm grip on what's been said. The message has to be stable, not shifting or exploratory. Somewhere in that process, the student has to develop from doubt to confidence in meaning-making. Not only that, but the content has to be organized in a form that is clear to the reader, so the writer needs to find a structure and discourse that is acceptable to both writer and reader. Hence the need for understanding how to use the rhetorical modes of discourse and those other conventions that make information transmittable. We need to invite students to explore, probe, and only after examining themselves in relation to their topic, to begin to work self-consciously with writing conventions. There is a time when the exploratory process has to slow and the writer has to come to terms with restraints that hinder free movement in writing. At that point, they need confidence in their own thoughts to continue along the path of a single argument. At that point, they need to remember the teachers' words of encouragement. In our responses to early drafts, teachers need to remember to help students grasp their message with assurance so they can make the leap from writerly prose ("all about me") to readerly prose ("all about helping you see what I mean"), where audience needs become paramount.

Before writing, students should mull over their readers' backgrounds, even if it's their peers and teacher they are considering.

- Who are my readers likely to be? What range of tastes will they represent?
- How much do they already know about this topic? Do I need more material?
- Will they be bored with the topic? Confused by it?
- Will they share my values? Agree/disagree with my premises?
- Are my ideas too specific? Too general?
- Do I use enough examples and details to convince them?
- What sort of voice do I use to build my audience's trust? Intimate? Cool? Comic?

These questions help students see different ways of developing their argument for public consumption and allow them to forecast how their argument might be received. While trying to suit themselves, writers have to decide what points their readers will swallow and what sorts of information will further persuade them.

They also need to be aware of imbedding readers' guideposts such as transitional phrases and extended explanations that connect points.

The most effective solution is to assign shorter papers that can be directed at real audiences. Teachers should be on the lookout for "publication" possibilities. Students can write for a person in another school or class or they can write for a school publication. Letters to the editor, "My Turn" columns for local publications, complaint letters, websites, and letters to the public work miracles. Students write for real people with more zest and commitment than they ever write for a grade.

The Argument Paper

In elementary and middle school, the most common form of essay writing is the report. Students go out and find information and they describe their findings in a fairly neutral way. It's been described as "and then" writing. Often it is a chronological narrative that shows the problem and then its resolution or it is a series of events leading up to a denouement. Another form of immature writing is the "all about" catalogue of features describing something with an encyclopedia's penchant for overview (Bean 20–24). Both types of essays have their place in the classroom as a way of getting students to explain what they know. They are, in effect, write-to-show-what-I-have-learned essays. A step up in terms of analysis is the question/answer essay in which the student has an open-ended question to answer. Examples might be "Why do we have to go to school?" or "Which is the best fast food restaurant in town?" or "Does TV show too much violence?" On the surface, they appear to be questions that kids could answer without thinking about them, but when attached to issues of education, nutrition, and social behavior, these topics can require research, analysis, and evaluation that are within the scope of a middle schooler's capabilities and they can become vital critical thinking tasks.

Students in middle school are well capable of understanding and pitching their own arguments. It is an ideal time to learn that an argument is not the same as a quarrel nor is there necessarily a winner. It is a way of trying to state one's convictions. Persuasive arguments go one step farther in trying to change the reader's mind, but not all arguments aim to do that. Students will soon realize questions such as: Should we raise the age limit for driving? or Is the average fast food meal nutritious? often have answers that fall into the gray areas and are more complex than they would guess. In addition to teaching analysis, technique and evaluation, arguments dealing with everyday issues such as how to avoid paying too much for clothes can help induct young writers into the world where they are asked to act as members of a community, as responsible citizens, and as consumers of leisure. It can also help them confront the bewildering confusion of voices and prepare them to make decisions in a complex environment. It helps them sort out emotional arguments from fact, true from false, valid claims from invalid, and adjudicate between two valid pieces of evidence. It also gives them a way of drafting a convincing response to those voices.

Rhetorical Modes of Discourse

Writers may know what they want to say, but they may also find it difficult to harness their ideas with a logical and persuasive, readerly framework. The communal medium in which thought is shared is the well-recognized rhetorical form—the definition, the persuasion, the comparison/contrast, or the cause/effect paper. Arguments can usually be organized by one of the classical forms developed centuries ago by rhetoricians who were acutely conscious of audience response. Like the young writers of the past, our students often need some direct instruction that models standard argumentative forms and explains their salient features. Since professional writers rarely adhere strictly to these structures, students should similarly think of them as wise guidance rather than laws set in stone, so teaching them should be done without insistence on following rules to the letter. Listed here are some of the most common rhetorical modes of discourse and the pros and cons of working with each one.

The Definition Paper

The definition paper is generally an underused form in research papers. If a key concept of the argument is confusing or overly simplified in everyday use, the writer's best strategy is to begin with a definition that supports the paper's thesis and its use of specialized terms. Other vocabulary that may need defining are unfamiliar words, technical language, and/or phrases that are key to the argument or discussion. If dictionary definitions are used, they should be stated, then extended to address the paper's issues and tailored to the discussion. Other kinds of definitions may include a history of the word, a personal history association with the word, examples, or a re-definition that stipulates a modified meaning. Sometimes a writer might define a term by explaining what it is not, by attacking myths or misunderstandings about the word(s). This organizational feature is often misused by students who employ the dictionary's definition without questioning or extending it. Dictionaries rarely capture all the nuances of a word's use, so its authority should not be taken at face value. The device is best used when students are willing and sufficiently confident to play with the language.

The Comparison/Contrast Paper

The comparison/contrast paper has two possible outlines. The simplest way to organize the material is this:

- describe A;
- describe B;
- compare (or contrast) B to A with a concluding statement.

With this method of organizing the information, the writer need only supply two key transitions—from the description of A to the description of B, and from the description of B to the final comparison or contrast. The second, more complicated way to organize the comparison/contrast paper is to compare items A and B point by point or to contrast them point by point. These papers tend to be tedious to write and to read because they turn on details and fine points. They also require many more transitions, which often creates awkward decisions for the writer. The conclusion too is difficult because it has to reconcile the convolutions of the argument.

The Cause and Effect Paper

The cause and effect paper has a simpler layout; it generally falls into four parts:

- discussion of the cause or effect;
- an examination of the effects or causes and the reasons for them;
- a rejection of the counter arguments;
- a concluding statement that includes further consideration of the alternatives.

But the order of the arguments may vary with the level of knowledge and attitudes of the audience. Arguing cause is risky because the writer is vulnerable to the following fallacies or failures in argument:

- a doubtful cause, which links two events and makes one the cause of the other, although the proximity of these events might be coincidental. An example is blaming an automobile accident on the full moon.

- an oversimplified cause that may ignore the complexities of the situation. Many examples of this occur in politicians' simplistic solutions to complicated problems; for instance, the use of standardized testing to raise standards in schools.

- effects mistakenly understood as causes, which occur when the cause originated later than the writer supposed. An example of this might be the argument that high consumer debt leads to recessions when high debt usually follows recessions.

- insufficient evidence that establishes the link between the cause and effect. Many causes of cancer have been difficult to verify because of insufficient evidence.

- a straw man argument that rejects alternatives without examining them fairly. In this case, the "straw man" is usually an overly simplified statement of the opposition's argument.

In all of these organizational plans lie traps for mistakes in logic, largely because young writers too often feel they must be forceful to be believable, so they overstate their case. The argument should avoid an extreme or exaggerated claim. Words such as *all, always, never* usually point to hyperbole and should be avoided. They need to realize that the most convincing arguments are those that use qualifiers such as *probably, likely, apparently, seems, largely.* Complex issues require careful deliberation and a reasoned stance that usually falls in the gray area between one pole or the other.

Furthermore, students should take care to avoid false binaries—arguments that are unnecessarily structured with extreme opposites to force the audience to one conclusion or the other. A legitimate thesis statement may reach beyond this false opposition to an alternative position that lies outside the popularly accepted either/or set of arguments. For example, instead of thinking that an act is right or wrong, the writer may argue that there are extenuating circumstances that deem the act acceptable in some instances and not in others. We need to encourage our students to think in the gray areas and outside the box of opposites.

There is a bias in our culture that favors quantifiable facts and discounts anecdotal evidence. The body of the argument paper should use fair-minded factual evidence. It should be current, accurate, sufficient, directly relevant, and typical. Examples, anecdotes, stories, and illustrations enliven a research paper as long as they are accompanied by a discussion that explains their relevance and they are not generalized to the whole. Claiming that they represent the whole is an inductive leap that stretches from a few examples to a whole class of things. Even so, evidence is most effective when it calls on specifics. Ken Macrorie calls them "telling facts," those minutiae that are all around us and "speak powerfully" to the truth (*Telling Writing* 32–33). Macrorie also invokes Emerson with this advice: "fasten words again to visible things" (2). Make the abstract concrete by giving it reality. This is the meat of effective arguments.

Fighting Fairly: Logical Fallacies

If the argument refutes an opposing viewpoint, then it is important to give the opponent a full hearing. Presenting evidence that is contradictory to one's own position, surprisingly, does not undermine the main argument as long as the writer answers the opposing arguments convincingly. Including the opposition's viewpoints in the paper enriches the conclusion and adds a dimension to what may otherwise seem like an obvious proof. In their zeal to contradict an opposing argument, students often misrepresent the opposing view by omission, by skewing the facts, or by overstating their own position. Other fallacious argumentation commonly occurs in papers written by young writers.

- ad hominem statements that savage the opposition based on his or her personality.

- faulty use of authority in which experts are quoted out of context or otherwise misrepresented. An example might be when a celebrity's name is attached to a product or idea that she hasn't endorsed, the Elizabeth Taylor rake for instance.

- false analogies in which two things are compared without proof or without a complete and fair-minded match of the features. A common example of this is calling any strong-handed leader a Hitler or a fascist.

- false dilemmas arise when the writer suggests that there are only two alternatives. Example: if you're not part of the solution, you're part of the problem.

- slippery slope, which suggests falsely that one step will lead inevitably to a second, less desirable outcome. An example of this often arises when compromises between strongly opposing sides are on the table.

- emotional appeals that are usually irrelevant or that mask other purposes. Many examples of this can be found in advertising and "feel good" political promotions.

- begging the question, which assumes that the very question being argued has already been proved. Circular reasoning sometimes works like this: because of x, y is true, proving that y is true. These fallacies occur when the writer uses the very point in question as the reason for his defense. For example, he might say that the film is immoral because it has risqué scenes.

If the teacher reads an early draft monitoring largely for the logic, the flow of the arguments, for coherence, and for clarity, most of the grammar problems will take care of themselves in the revision. The students' use of language usually becomes unclear or ungrammatical when they are still trying to work out what they want to say. Once they've cleared up their thinking and find the most focused way of saying it, most of the mechanical difficulties surprisingly take care of themselves. Looking for problems of logic and unity should be the primary aim of the first reading.

The Research Paper

When educators speak of the research paper, they usually mean an argument paper of some length (more than three pages) and one that synthesizes the information from several sources. It usually draws on the essay for the infrastructure and the argument for tone and tenor. It is often based on textual research with print materials found in the library or Internet, but it may also be based on data gathered in interviews, case studies, films, or television shows where print matter is at a minimum. For evidence, students can employ primary sources—usually raw or uninterpreted material—or secondary sources—usually experts' arguments. Rather than assign one long paper that takes weeks to write and grade, high school teachers often assign several short papers (3–4 pp.) that use citations and a bibliography.

The Role of Multigenre Writing

Research papers need not be limited to one medium. Michael Ondaatje's *The Collected Works of Billy the Kid* tells his story in a mixture of straight narration, verse, monologue, newspaper style, songs, thumbnail sketches, photographs, drawings, and more, using "crots." In *Writing With Passion,* Tom Romano describes crots as short passages that are able to stand as a discrete whole with "certain integrity," but they also create a tension between a coherent concept and a fragmented structure. Bruce Olds' *Raising Holy Hell,* a biography of John Brown who fought Union soldiers at Harper's Ferry, is another example of writing with crots. Olds' book combines newspaper clippings, statements by such statesmen as Abraham Lincoln, John Adams, Thomas Jefferson, slave narratives, poetry, diaries, interviews, letters, documents, and historical fiction to produce a rich reading for high school students in English studying the American Civil War. Students might enjoy imitating this assortment of styles by assembling a document of crots. They might also combine a shorter version of their papers with the creation of a website, a video, or play. Research papers that accompany a creative component may chronicle the student's methods for exploration—how they decided what to collect and how they went about their research. The final paper could include a journal on their methods for working, the problems they had to solve, and what they want their audiences to understand about the meaning of their work. Although the paper might be less formal than the conventional term paper, it is a crucial supplement to the creative project for encouraging a reflective process and for articulating the process of the creative experience. The final paper helps students see that the steps for developing a visual text are very similar to those needed for producing a print text.

Citations

Styles for footnotes, endnotes, and intext citations employed by the humanities are spelled out on many websites, in the *MLA* (the Modern Language Association is at MLA.org) *Handbook for Writers of Research Papers* or the *Chicago Manual of Style,* for people in business and publishing. Both formats are commonly used by college professors and professional writers, so they serve high school students for years to come. Whether students use the MLA intext style for the humanities, the APA (American Psychological Association) style for the social sciences, or CBE (Council of Biology Editors) for the sciences, or any other reference style is unimportant, so it is not important to be picky about the details. Most professors, teachers, and publishers are tolerant of variations as long, as the writer maintains internal consistency and observes the obvious conventions, especially since there is no one right way to format all citations. The easiest strategy to keep up with the most recent style sheets for electronic sources in particular is to consult the websites for that organization.

The most important lesson for young research writers is to gain an ethical understanding about how and when to use quoted material and citations. They must realize, first of all, that they have to credit the originators of language and ideas. All directly quoted material must be enclosed by quotation marks and end with a citation. All paraphrased material ends with a citation without the quotation marks. Few students fully understand how much material they can borrow without attributing the work to another author, and so they become confused about whether to cite paraphrased ideas, a sequence of arguments, or paraphrased material. Even when they know they have to cite most facts and quotations that they have read, they are sometimes confused about whether they must cite paraphrased ideas and concepts that they have gathered through their reading. The answer is yes. Yes, *most* of the ideas in a research paper must be credited to another source. If students are unsure whether a fact or idea is common knowledge, they should footnote it anyway to be on the safe side.

This practice may seem like overkill, but many students have become cavalier about the music that they have downloaded from the Internet, so they are extending that defiant attitude to other areas online as well. Words and ideas are property—whatever their source—so they should not be taken without permission and without acknowledging their owners. Citations should not only tell readers who owns the property, but also act as a courtesy tip of the hat to the original author for allowing use of that property. Citations should meticulously note the source's details, so that readers can locate the larger work for themselves and read further about the subject. Having said this, we have to concede that illegal borrowing will continue and we need to address the varying degrees of student opinion on this by discussing it openly in class.

Teachers should pay more attention to the spirit of using citations than to the intricacies of commas and colons because questions of plagiarism are at stake. To look for the latest rulings on the fair use of citations and materials, teachers might consult one of the reference guides mentioned above or *The New Century Handbook* by Christine Hult and Thomas Huckin, a text that is updated regularly to keep abreast of changes in citations for the Internet and other hard-to-document sources. Or they can check the NCTE (National Council of Teachers of English at NCTE.org) website. This is an invaluable source for information on copyrights and other concerns for English teachers.

The I-Search Paper

Since ownership of the material is at the heart of the project's success, a substantial commitment to topic development can reward students in ways they would not expect. Ken Macrorie's "I-Search" paper has long been the paradigm for some of the best research-type papers being written today. He defines the I-Search paper as one that "comes out of a student's life and answers a need in it" (Preface). It begins with the author's personal need to know and it ends with a telling of what the author has learned. The features of the final version of the I-Search paper follow.

- The I-Search paper combines the personal expression of an individual quest with the materiality of gathered facts and opinions. Topics grow out of students' thinking about their central concerns and turning these interests into an inquiry. They begin by asking questions they care about answering. Macrorie illustrates the continuity between the self and the investigation by pointing to the moebius strip, which has an inside wall that turns to the outside and eventually flows back into the inside. Like the moebius strip, our attentions can fix on a body of information long enough that it turns back into some part of ourselves. His I-Search is an ideal model for secondary research papers because it helps bridge the gap between personal and structured writing. This is the biggest leap that students have to make from their own narcissistic interests to the needs of the audience/reader. Keeping the research model in mind, students are more likely to see the need for that leap.

- Information for the I-Search is often gathered through a variety of experts or authorities. Print resources may be only one of several types of expertise that students consult. Sometimes they watch or interview on-the-job practitioners. They may conduct formal and informal interviews, often asking friends or family members for information. The experts may explain where to find useful books, magazines, newspapers, films, and websites, or experts may provide their own information. Inquiry should be conducted in stages—read a little, talk to sources, read a little more, then consult new sources, and so forth—so that the most informed and professional advisors are consulted when the investigator has substantial knowledge about the topic and can ask useful questions. Clear prose indicates comprehension of the material. The information of the experts is tested and evaluated against information found elsewhere.

- The final paper often takes the form of a *story telling* in which the account of the investigation is combined with the findings. An I-Search paper might begin like this: "This summer I want to build a kayak/canoe to float the Michigan rivers. I want to design a boat that is as stable as a canoe, but as light and maneuverable as a kayak. I wanted to find out the features of the best canoes and the best kayaks . . ." Macrorie divides the I-Search into four parts—a) what the student knew when starting out and what she wanted to learn; b) why she wanted to write the paper and how the paper will make a difference in her life; c) the story of the I-Search—where she looked, where she ran into dead ends and where she was successful; d) what she learned or could not find out.

- Periodically during the writing process, a teacher may prod students who are losing their way through the argument with exercises that help them refocus. (See Fig. 5.3: Ideas for Exploring Essay Topics During Drafting.)

The I-Search process follows the general procedures of the writing process with its own specialized variants for invention, discovery, and narrative. The greatest advantage to this Expressivist method is that the student is involved in the topic and in every step of its development. The I-Search paper reinforces student responsibility, generates personal interest, and sidesteps the potential for plagiarism.

The Social Issues or Problem-solving Paper

Another paper that engages students because it places a high premium on content and a committed point of view is the social issues paper. Like the I-Search paper, students go beyond the mere assemblage of facts in that they begin by questioning the world around them and they write for social change. It is most similar to the argument paper in that students have a point to make—a solution, a recommendation, or a plan of action. Although there is a legitimate use for neutral research or report writing, those are papers that students have been producing since

FIGURE 5.3 ***Ideas for Exploring Essay Topics During Drafting***

After research papers are in full swing, writers sometimes need to step back and honestly assess their own progress. This may be a time to gain a renewed interest in the topic, to sharpen the focus, or to rethink the thesis. Here are some exercises for stimulating and deepening an interest in the long writing project.

E-mail correspondence
Although you cannot count on everyone in your class having e-mail, you can ask students to take some time out each week to go to the school library or writing lab to send the rest of the class an e-mail. You can set up your LAN (local area network) in your lab to store all the sent mail in your own folder, so you can read what students have written and respond to it. Teachers that have tried this successfully have often posed an open-ended question each week to start the writing. Students may respond to the teacher or to each other. They too can keep folders on the LAN network.

A low tech version of this exercise is an index file box that contains the kickoff question for the week on an index card taped to the lid. Students respond on index cards of their own and file them after scanning the cards that others have written.

Website
Two or three people can plan a website featuring the subject of their research. In it, they can include graphics and several links to already established sites. Most important is their own newly generated material. Students usually do a page apiece, linking them to a home page. Since the information is compact and underdeveloped, they need to accompany the website with a short hard copy explanation for the teacher that includes: a) the point of the website as a whole, b) their criteria for material selection, and c) how the pages speak to the whole.

Another possibility is to use frames to annotate text with pop up windows and/or footnotes to a given text. For example, they can explain the reasoning behind parts of the Declaration of Independence with pop-up windows or footnotes. Both of these projects could be done just as easily on poster board or newsprint as a low tech exercise and both could be expanded to serve as an alternative to the paper.

Writing at the Beginning of Class
Class time may be used to report an update on the research project. It could feature a log of how the time outside of class has been spent, but it is better used for a true exploration of the ideas that the student is wrestling with. A teacher could ask

- What new information has surprised you?
- Where are you stuck?
- What more do you need to know?
- What concerns you most at this point?
- What do you like best about the project?
- How might you refocus your project?

Writing Dialogues
Ask students to imagine a conversation between the two or more people who hold opposing views on the topic. This strategy is handy for breaking writer's block, for prioritizing the issues, and for preventing the one-sided argument in the paper. It can also be used in a group project with several people writing the dialog together.

third grade. By the time they reach the upper levels of high school, students should be writing papers that go beyond perfunctory data collection to an assignment that will make a difference to them. They need to know that *what* they say counts more than how they say it.

This paper, suggested by Ira Shor, is usually assigned as an all-class project built around a commonly held economic or political interest. Such a paper may be written collaboratively by dividing the topic into as many subtopics as there are students in the class and each one writes from an individual perspective. For example, if the class decides to investigate the way trash is recycled in the community, then subtopics might be the extent of the trash problem, the problem of chemicals and aerosol cans, city council resolutions, who makes money from recycling, places to send second-hand clothing, etc. The possibilities are endless. If students are encouraged to disagree as well as agree with mainstream thinking, to explore all sides of the issues, to feature less obvious positions, and to propose alternative solutions, they begin to recognize how richly we can interpret the facts and how binary opposites—pro and con—are too simplistic for most social issues.

At the core of this project is an investigation of issues that students care the most about—for example, a proposal for a new skate boarding park, the design for a new school addition, a foster care program in that student's community, the advantages of attending a prestigious university, if any, and the curfew law that keeps them off the streets at night. Topics work best if they grow out of the students' culture and desire to know (Shor 204). Teacher-generated suggestions will produce predictably little enthusiasm if students are steered towards a mainstream inquiry for which there is just enough controversy to offer two safe choices for a selecting a final position. Teachers need to talk to and listen to students' concerns to help the class make a viable choice, but they also need to be aware of the community's tolerance. It is equally important that teachers and students are sufficiently aware of community sensitivities to avoid topics that are too complex or controversial for students to handle wisely. Here are some areas that might help a class decide their issue.

- What do students talk about, read about, and write about?
- When do they read and write, and for what purposes?
- What do they watch on TV, read about in newspapers, and listen to on the radio? Do they trust the media to give them an accurate picture? What news are they not getting?
- What images do they have at home on their walls?
- What do they say are the most important problems in their lives?
- What are the social relationships like in their community?
- What are the community conditions—housing, health care, mass transit, crime, playgrounds, sanitation, commercial, and government services?

Selecting a topic with local interest is only the first step in a project such as this. They must then test it for its audience appeal. The subject must also be debatable with credible arguments on at least two sides. Students next raise crucial questions concerning the issue after identifying its problems and sharpening the focus of their inquiry. Their questions need to dig beneath the surface to interrogate contradictions and to reveal what lies behind the glaring facts.

After they've collected a reasonable body of knowledge, the class discusses possible solutions or answers to the question "so what?" If the paper is to be meaningful, the writers need to grapple with the point of the investigation and think about possible solutions. The conclusion to this paper built around social issues should suggest possible actions, next steps that make sense given the facts of the research. Or students may predict what could happen. Many of the problems will have no clear or easy solution, so students should not be encouraged to produce simplistic or "happy face" answers to complex issues, but they can be pushed to identify the tensions that are at play in this issue and what might be done next. If nothing else, they can speak in the conclusion about the significance of the issue and list possible actions from the ideal to the practical that might resolve it.

The value of Shor's project lies in the way it seizes students' imagination and participation and in its ability to turn students from passive learners in their education to active agents. It is also a powerful tool for building a participatory democracy in which knowledge, shared purpose, and shared ideas empower its members. It develops methods for critical inquiry, scientific thinking, cooperative relations, and social habits. It establishes a community of learning and offers students a manual for contributing to their democracy.

Think/Write #3

List five different issues in your community that would interest students in middle school and high school. Under each item, briefly list a few implications of these issues for young students. For example, if there were a new community center, who has access to it? Will there be a enough for kids their age to do? What sorts of rules govern the meeting rooms? Will the kids have a voice in how the center will be run? If not, how can they make it more of a place that they can enjoy? What sort of research assignment can you make to help kids understand the way the city is run and what their role is in the local government?

Assessment of the Essay

The connection between reading and writing is never more apparent than in the results of write-to-learn activities because the quality of written work depends heavily on the reader's ability to comprehend the text. Readers must grasp key concepts of the material before paraphrasing, summarizing, or transferring the ideas. For the reader to complete any of these tasks, he has to penetrate the core of the text and focus on the crucial detail. Teachers can informally assess which students have been successful in their reading because the writing of readers with high comprehension will be presented in a digested form supported by the telling facts. Efficient readers are likely to produce the clearest writings. Students with low comprehension will tend to borrow too many words from the original text or they will refer to the original in vague generalities without the specifics that indicate a mastery of the material. Furthermore, they will not be able to apply the new ideas to build blocks of knowledge or to gather more information. Their writing samples will reflect many of their reading difficulties.

A more formal assessment of essay writing generally follows the guidelines for evaluating the kinds of writing that we have set out in other chapters. Since logic, clarity, organization, and coherence are central considerations, points for content should outweigh those given for following directions, footnote accuracy, mechanics, or paragraphing. Teachers can evaluate logic, clarity, organization, and coherence by a quick, holistic reading of the student paper, and this overall impression should guide most of the remarks the successive drafts—whether evaluating the second or the final drafts. (See boxed Sample Rubrics in Chapter Seven) Early drafts may not receive a grade as such, but they should nevertheless be at the forefront of the peer editor or teacher's considerations.

When distributing points, students should be rewarded handsomely for participating in the process of research and writing. Many teachers underscore the importance of invention and exploration by awarding points for experimenting with invention strategies without grading them, and points could be awarded for multiple drafting, so students can earn the bulk of their grade before the final draft is handed in. When pre-writing and rough drafts earn a generous number of points and the teacher emphasizes process over product, students are taught the value of the exploration and experimentation and the value of writing as a tool for learning. It also discourages students who are inclined to put all their energies into a last-minute push. Moreover, they are less likely to plagiarize when the grade cannot be saved by a last ditch effort.

On the final draft, teachers usually reward students for attending to the details of citations with capitals and spacing, etc., but they should also recognize students who abide by the spirit of documentation by supplying sufficient information, even if the structure is found wanting. The final draft should be polished so that it shines. It should contain very few problems with spelling, grammar, and the mechanics of punctuation and capitalization. Points might either be awarded for a clean draft or deducted for careless work. Some teachers also award additional credit to a sensitive use of language, imagination, style, and creativity. Although the final rubric is the prerogative of the teacher, she should give students her rubric before they begin writing so they know where to place their greatest energies. Suggestions for assessment on various types of essays appear in Chapter Seven.

Plagiarism

Students often resort to plagiarism when they are forced to read and write about material they cannot fully understand, when they are short of time, and when they feel that more of the paper's points are awarded for following instructions than for content. Because we have already hinted at some of the problems with plagiarism, particularly our students' inclination to "borrow" material from ready sources such as encyclopedias and the Internet, we would like to suggest some ways of thinking about a problem that seems to be growing worse:

1. Students need to understand the concept of intellectual property rights. In the future, teachers will be expected to follow the new developments in the law that will occur as many copyright battles are fought in the courts. High school students will not understand the illegalities or the gravity of lifting material from other sources if their teachers don't stay apprised of the issues.

2. The deeper their understanding of the topic, the less students will be tempted to plagiarize. Trouble can often be sidestepped if teachers require students to work with locally important issues and with topics specific to the class that students care about and understand. Ongoing class discussions on current events and issues can help students broach difficult reading. The more they know about a given topic, the easier they will find the reading. Assigning magazine or newspaper articles each week can contribute to their prior knowledge. Once they have received close guidance in reading unfamiliar texts, they will begin to build schemas for these topics. Many local newspapers may be bought with discounted classroom subscriptions.

3. Teachers can avoid other problems by requiring work that has to be submitted for scrutiny every three or four days. These assignments might be free writes, note cards, a weekly journal documenting progress, summaries, photocopied material with annotations, etc. None of it has to be graded, but all of it helps teachers monitor their students' thinking as well as their writing ability. The trouble is that keeping up with it is tremendously time consuming.

4. Students need plenty of practice learning how to paraphrase and summarize material. Few cases of plagiarism involve material that is lifted wholesale from electronic or print sources. Most students plagiarize when they try to change a few words in the original passage, then call it their own. The trouble is, they often do not think of borrowed short phrases as plagiarism. We can recognize it as copying because the plagiarized passages contain sophisticated vocabulary and subtle reasoning and they leap out at the teacher. We can help students avoid plagiarism by giving them practice paraphrasing difficult passages. Regularly assigned summary writing, bi-monthly for instance, and the paraphrase of hard-to-understand paragraphs show students the difference between an honest paraphrase and mosaic plagiarism, which is a paraphrase that leans too heavily on the original wording. (See Fig. 5.1: Writing Abstracts or Summaries above.) Regular work with this problem in class sends an important message to students about the importance of doing their own thinking and writing.

5. The safest route is to require photocopies of all the sources. This procedure will help teachers catch students who genuinely misunderstand the fair use of material. It will also slow down students who hope to copy someone else's work or hand in papers they have bought. A teacher need not read all these sources, but they are a good preventative measure.

6. Above all, we need to be very careful of accusing students of plagiarism. Even mediocre students can do brilliant work when they are excited about the topic. If you have found absolute proof of plagiarism, you can confront the student. If you only suspect plagiarism, then you should question the student about her methods for summary or paraphrase and her understanding about citing material. Do more to coach these students than dun them, even when you suspect laziness. Like the rest of us, they are usually trying to finish their work with the least time and effort.

7. Punishment for students who plagiarize should run the range from a re-write of the offensive passages to a rewrite of the whole paper, depending on the extent of the plagiarized material. The student who deliberately hands in someone else's paper or wholesale passages taken from other sources should be dealt with most severely. Teachers should find out the school's policy regarding these matters and make certain their school administration will back up their punishment. In any case, they should be certain to photocopy all suspicious work and keep a log of their transactions with the student and her parents. These incidents can become very serious matters, even leading to court action. Having said that, we want to assure teachers that a large proportion of plagiarism is likely to be inadvertent, occurring largely when students honestly believe they are doing enough to paraphrase or summarize the original text. Our recommendation is that teachers treat most first-time offenders as though they only need additional instruction in paraphrase and/or summary as well as a chance to rewrite the paper. Harsh measures should be reserved for the most egregious cases of borrowing or cheating.

Points to Remember

This chapter features essay writing in many of its variants. As we have known it for several hundred years, the essay has traditionally followed the outline of an introduction to the issues and the point of the essay, a body of evidence to support the argument or reporting, and a conclusion that often answers the question "so what?" This sequence has been a given in western writing since Aristotle.

In its simplest form, the essay is a write-to-learn assignment, an exercise to discover what one has learned while reading. In its most complex form, the essay is a research paper that is thoroughly explored and well documented. In between are various specialty essays—reporting, argumentative, definition, cause and effect, and comparison/contrast—that are information based and are largely expository in tone and style. Although we often consider the essay the bread and butter of writing in the English classroom, we soon realize that it is only one of many forms of written expression, and not necessarily the best assignment for teaching writing.

For Further Reading

Bean, John C. *Engaging Ideas: The Professor's Guide to Integrating Writing, Critical Thinking, and Active Learning in the Classroom.* San Francisco: Jossey-Bass, 1996.

Elbow, Peter and Pat Belanoff. *A Community of Writers: A Workshop Course in Writing.* 2nd ed. New York: McGraw-Hill, 1989.

———. *Sharing and Responding.* 2nd ed. McGraw-Hill, 1995.
Goodman, Ken. *What's Whole in Whole Language?* Portsmouth, NH: Heinemann, 1986.
Harris, Mickey. *Teaching One-to-One: The Writing Conference.* Urbana, IL: National Council of Teachers of English, 1986.
Hult, Christine and Thomas Huckin. *The New Century Handbook.* Allyn & Bacon, 1999.
King, Laurie and Dennis Stovall. *Classroom Publishing: A Practical Guide to Enhancing Student Literacy.* Hillsboro, OR: Blue Heron Publishing, 1992.
Macrorie, Ken. *The I-Search Paper: Revised Edition of Research Writing.* Portsmouth, NH: Heinemann, 1984.
———. *Telling Writing.* New York: Hayden Book Company, 1970.
Murray, Donald M. *Write to Learn.* 5th ed. Fort Worth, TX: Harcourt Brace, 1984.
———. *A Writer Teaches Writing: A Practical Method of Teaching Composition.* New York: Houghton Mifflin, 1968.
Ondaatje, Michael. *The Collected Works of Billy the Kid.* New York: Vintage Books, 1996.
Powell, David. *What Can I Write About? 7000 Topics For High School Students.* Urbana, IL: National Council of Teachers of English, 1981.
Romano, Tom. "The Multigenre Research Paper." *Writing With Passion: Life Stories, Multiple Genres.* Portsmouth, NH: Heinemann/Boynton Cook, 1995.
Rottenberg, Annette T. *The Structure of Argument.* Boston: Bedford Books, 1997.
Slack, Delane. "Fusing Social Justice with Multigenre Writing." *English Journal* 90.6 (2001): 62–66.

6

Responses to Literature and Nonprint Media

Most teachers of English love stories and love to read. Nothing is more pleasurable to most of us than taking a book to the beach or curling up before the fireplace with an apple and a cracking good novel. We read newspapers at breakfast and poems before falling asleep. We join drama reading circles and book discussion groups. We take travel narratives on long trips and medical journals to doctors' offices. Many of us therefore wonder why we can't infect our students with the thrill of reading. Despite our best intentions, we fail to convince even adult friends about the rewards of reading fiction. They too often remember English classes that killed the pleasures of reading. Most of our friends hated school reading because the book choices were forced on them and because they did not like analyzing the readings and writing about them. Plagued by the fear that they never could "get" what they were supposed to grasp in a poem or film, they hated book reports, chapter questions, and the tedious essays that seemed to dissect books, films, poems, and plays to the last word.

Examining complaints such as these, we English teachers have to admit that we're so busy teaching the elements of a story or some other academic approach that we forget to encourage reading for its own sake. Too often we allow the Table of Contents in our anthologies to set the syllabus at the expense of free reading. Or we feel pressured to teach to the measurable aspects of literature, such as finding the main idea or examples of irony, hoping that our students might score higher on the standardized tests. No wonder students get the twisted message that literature and film in English classes are consumable materials and of little value for personal pleasure. Believing that they must read texts primarily for the sake of being graded, too many feel that most fiction reading is a pointless academic exercise.

Students lose sight of literature—both light reading and the "classics"—as a source of lifelong enjoyment or enlargement of their understanding of life. We can send them another message, if we would first emphasize the importance of literature for addressing the key questions they have about living. After students have made sense out of it for themselves, they can learn about a critical awareness of "texts." Only then should they have to learn about the literary significance of the texts. After they understand patterns of meaning that are familiar to them, they can search out the not so obvious messages often embedded in texts. After they have read and digested the text on literal and personal levels, they can study how texts are constructed by authors and how they point to other meanings both intentionally and unintentionally beyond the text.

One way to enhance a student's enjoyment of films and poetry, short stories and novels is through writing about them in journals, letters, quizzes, formal essays, and/or creative writing. Writing in response to literature helps students figure out more about themselves and the world around them, lending the literary texts real importance in their lives. Journals, for example, are helpful for sorting out what we think about the world of the text. Compositions using argument and analysis are excellent for developing critical reading and thinking skills, and they are invaluable for enriching a sense of the language, particularly when they direct student attention to the special turn of phrase, forms of dialect or grammatical patterns. As we have seen in Chapter 5, these are often called *write-to-learn assignments* and they are used for many other reasons as well. They may teach students to read closely and carefully. Note taking, outlines, and summaries—even with literature—help students understand their reading on a literal level and responses in the form of creative writing may help them understand the original works on a deeper level. Short answer quizzes and essay tests inform teachers about what students have prepared and digested. Problem-posing assignments that have no definitive answers prod students to make connections they might have otherwise missed. All of these writing exercises improve our students' ability to express themselves clearly on paper, to discover what they think, and figure out how to articulate it. Given the richness of the interplay between writing and reading, it is little wonder that teachers naturally lean toward written responses to literature and it is clear that such assignments will continue to be a mainstay of the English classroom. But wait! Aren't these same writing assignments the reason students say they hate high school reading and critical analysis? Possibly. Writing in response to literature has the potential of either souring students on a critical examination of texts or helping them become lifelong readers of high quality literature. The outcome depends on how and when we make the assignments.

The purpose of this chapter is to discuss how assignments can effectively enhance the reader's understanding and pleasure in both print and and nonprint media. It begins with a discussion of the reading process to demonstrate the interplay between writing and reading literature. It also covers writing about film. We will then describe a wide variety of potential writing assignments that could be used as responses to literature. We will discuss not only conventional writing assignments, but also the more experimental and creative writing assignments that can enhance the reading experience. Although our emphasis will be on print texts, much of what we discuss can be applied to the nonprint media (such as films) as well. In this chapter we will discuss the following topics:

- the need to identify various purposes for assigning reading and writing;
- the nature of the aesthetic response and strategies for eliciting it;
- examples of journal writing and other assignments that could enlarge the aesthetic experience of texts rather than destroy it;
- Reader Response criticism, Formalism, and an historical approach—critical approaches that elicit and validate diverse student response;
- creative writing as an alternative to nonfiction for opening up classic literature;
- assessment of responses to literature.

Each section will emphasize the teacher's opportunities to promote the pleasures of the text through meaning making and to suggest multiple strategies for using composition as a response to the "texts," a term which here refers broadly to any material work of art—the film, photograph, novel, poem, advertisement, television program, or play. In this chapter we will meet the following standards for teaching literature drawn up by National Council of Teachers of English (the numbers in parentheses refer to NCATE/NCTE's program standards).

2.2 An understanding of how the English language arts can help students become familiar with their own and others' cultures;
2.4 Designs for assisting students to develop habits of critical thinking and judgment;
2.7 Promotion of the arts and humanities in the daily lives of students;
3.1.2 Some knowledge and understanding of how reading, writing, speaking, listening, and viewing are interrelated;
3.1.3 Recognition of the impact of cultural, economic, political, and social environments upon language;
3.1.4 Respect for and an understanding of diversity in language use, patterns,dialects across cultures, ethnic groups, geographic regions, and social roles;
3.2.1 The influence of language and visual images on thinking and composing;
3.2.2 The use of writing as a major form of inquiry, reflection, and expression in coursework;
3.2.5 Knowledge of language structure and conventions to create and critique print and non-print texts;
3.3.1 Different ways to respond to and interpret what is read;
3.3.2 Writing strategies that may be used to discover and construct meaning from print and non-print texts;
3.3.3 Writing strategies that may be used to comprehend, interpret, evaluate, and appreciate texts;
3.4.1 Writing strategies that can be used to generate meaning and to clarify understanding;
3.4.2 Different forms of written discourse;
3.4.3 An understanding of how written discourse can influence thought and action;

4.8 Suggestions for responding critically to different media and communications technologies;

4.10 Ideas for engaging students in making meaning of texts through a personal connection to the reading;

4.12 A variety of assessment tools for evaluating student response to literature, i.e., journals, formal essays, individual projects, creative writing.

Instructional Purposes for Reading and Writing about Literature

There are many reasons for teaching literature and our best writing assignments usually reinforce these agendas. Given the huge range of writing assignments that we teachers can devise for students, we need to clarify our key purposes as the first step. In setting the lesson's objectives, we need to understand for ourselves why we are assigning the reading and what we hope to achieve in the writing. Again, our choices as teachers are numerous.

Think/Write #1
Brainstorm a quick list of all the reasons we ask students to write about literature. Your list may range from the practical and mundane to the theoretical. After you have a half dozen items or more, star one or two goals that seem most important to you, while acknowledging that our teaching objectives will change with the difficulty and style of the literature. Be prepared to defend your answers.

The goal most important to many of us is probably "literature-as-preparation-for-life." More than anything, English teachers hope *to engender a lifetime of reading and interest in the literature that reflects our communal values and our cultural heritage.* For example, we might teach American literature to cultivate such attitudes as Franklin's Puritan ethic, Emersonian beliefs in the goodness of humankind, Leslie Marmon Silko's faith in nature, individualism in Hemingway's Nick Adams stories, or the dangers of conformity in Shirley Jackson's "Lottery." Teachers hope that through an exposure to the liberal arts education and reading, we will encourage a complex understanding of freedom, the public good, humanitarian behavior, and any number of other commonly held American virtues. We teach stories that reflect our values. We rarely articulate these values directly when we design our class exercises, however; instead, we pass them on indirectly as a part of the subtext in the canonical literature that endorses them. For example, a love of the land is implied in the descriptions by Washington Irving in his stories of New York state. The life and times of the authors also add to these values and help to create our national myths—the stories about Henry David Thoreau at Walden Pond, for instance. Somewhere in the discussion of these national myths lies an acknowledgment that we are addressing fundamental ethical and moral issues in our classes. They become the stuff of essay competitions and they are the subject matter of many literary essays that students must write. While it is a high priority among English teachers to advance literature for its emphasis on its ethical or moral perspectives, there is some evidence that we endorse these reasons for instructional purposes often at the expense of personal enjoyment. If reading is truly "literature-as-preparation-for-life," it should not risk sacrificing one goal for another.

A second set of reasons for teaching literature is to *enrich other classroom activities.* English teachers will often choose a piece of literature because it fits into plans for a thematic unit—a short story about the Civil War, for example, to accompany a team-taught course in American History. The reading thereby supports a body of knowledge acquired for extra-literary reasons. Indeed, much of it reproduces mainstream ideologies that validate power structures and exclude many groups whose literatures are not privileged. For example, we avoid teaching literature that glorifies the South's position in the Civil War. Much of what appears in standard anthologies is selected for its cultural capital, its promotion of power structures such as successful enterprises and commonly held political positions. Students are often exposed to the titles of works, famous literary lines, or characters for the sake of "cultural literacy," a commonly shared knowledge of facts and references. This is the E. D. Hirsch approach to education—lists of information that children of the elementary grades "need to know." Parents, school boards, and employers often take pride in their "well educated" students who can identify such names as Shakespeare, Edgar Allan Poe, Langston Hughes, or Lewis Carroll. Although this type of information has a payoff in public relations, it serves little in terms of developing literary appreciation, critical acumen, or reading ability unless it also allows students to grapple critically with the language or ideas of these authors. Otherwise, the references merely become the basis of quiz shows and tests that rely on such trivia as tools of assessment.

Because literature is a handy tool of reference for language, it is also used *to teach dialect or linguistic structure or style.* A poem may be selected for its ability to illustrate a particular literary tradition (e.g., the pastoral) or for its rhetorical devices such as irony and metaphor. Through textual analysis, students might learn about such composition devices as rhythm, cohesion, story grammars, and discourse patterns. Literature is also a handy source for examples of punctuation, dialog, elision, idiomatic expressions, palindromes, or any syntactic structure that we can name. While literature is one of the best ways to explore language or grammar, students may unintentionally get the message that its *only* value is material for teaching other subjects.

Fourth, literature is often used as a tool *to teach critical thinking.* Through literary analysis, students may apply literary terms such as dramatic monolog, metaphor, or iambic pentamenter. Through the study of character motivation, students may learn inferential thinking and reading between the lines. Through cultural criticism they may learn to recognize the values that lie embedded in the texts and yet remain neatly hidden behind suggestion and innuendo. When students learn to read the nuances of literature, to question authors, and to interpret texts, they can also dissect the underlying assumptions and discourse of newspaper stories, letters, editorials, speeches, political cartoons, or advertisements. These critical skills are indeed transferable. Through reason and argumentation, students are able to develop the analytical moves. The literary paper is therefore one of the best assignments in a teacher's bag of tricks to teach abstract thinking, logical reasoning, evidentiary support, and organization of ideas. Unfortunately, in the rush to teach these valuable skills, the potential pleasure of reading is often overlooked or ignored for the sake of teaching higher order thinking and composition.

A fifth purpose for teaching literature is *to help readers learn something about themselves and the world around them.* Much of what we give them to read relates to their world—their complex of emotions, their families and social relationships, and their needs for sorting out the issues of emerging adulthood. Furthermore, it expands their horizons so they can learn about people in other cultural and social worlds. Not only can our students develop open mindedness for the customs and truths of other cultures, but they can also glimpse some of life's sorrows from a safe berth—the war torn mother who considers revenge for her soldier son, the child of an alcoholic parent who must forge a future for herself, the teen who has to live with his own bad decision. Through science fiction and mysteries, young readers can investigate the worlds of "what if . . ." These new worlds of the lives of others may be explored through Reader Response criticism (described below), in the form of journals and letters, and through creative writing in poetry and drama scripts.

However worthy, most of these reasons for teaching literature are likely to force us to make choices about time and resources. The decisions we make often limit our students' opportunities to respond at some aesthetic level to the literature. Fortunately, this is not simply an either/or issue: we do not need to choose between an appreciation of literature and the uses of it for other purposes. With a careful sequencing of the writing assignments that accompany the reading, we can plan for more than one outcome. Indeed, one set of purposes can often reinforce another, especially when the teacher understands clearly how to time the assignments. When instructional purposes are clear, composition may be used effectively to support these purposes—reading for the sheer pleasure of it and reading for information—particularly if an aesthetic response is encouraged *before* other outcomes are pursued. Students will have a chance to engage in the reading if given that opportunity early in the reading process. They are also likely to show a greater understanding and appreciation of the literature if they are able to set their own goals for reading. If teachers are willing to defer interpretative/analytical/summative assignments until *after* students have had opportunities to try their open-ended responses and if teachers choose the type of writing assignment wisely, any of these goals may be realized.

What may be concluded, above all, is that a teacher's purposes for instruction inevitably channel the potentially diverse array of students' responses toward a single goal. Teachers should therefore be cautious about the type of assignment that is made at the early stages of the reading. Initial assignments are more effective if they call for a personal response. Later assignments may ask for information and analysis. Since pleasure reading is so easily overridden by more analytical goals, focus on a work's genre, its structure, style, and other formal elements should wait until after the whole text is read and appreciated in more informal discussions. Assignments demanding formal criticism predictably require students to treat the text as a source of information, distancing themselves from the text. Teachers must resist pushing students prematurely into this kind of analysis. They can dissect these formal elements later. A teacher's lesson plans should include a wide variety of writing forms and compositional activities sequenced to invite a range of responses. A number of these possible assignments are listed in Figure 6.1 Ideas for Writing in Response to Literature.

FIGURE 6.1 ***Ideas for Writing in Response to Literature***

Personal Writing
Journals
Diaries
Dream accounts
Descriptive observations
Two-column journals
Unsent letters
Process logs
E-mail exchanges

Popular Forms
Ads
Commercials
Propaganda
Posters or flyers
Satire
Web pages

Imaginative Writing
Fiction
Poetry
Dialogues
Epitaphs
Songs
Copy Change

Drama/Oral Responses
Mime
Charades
Debate
Interviews
Puppetry
Choral reading
Readers theatre

Informative/Persuasive Writing
Expository essays
Editorials
Reports
Booklets
Telegrams
Bulletin boards
Book reviews
Newspaper articles
Magazine essays

Media Composition
TV scripts
Radio programs
Soundtape
Montage or collage
Film
Videos or CDs
Storyboards

Other Write-to-Learn Exercises
Summaries
Problem-posing exercises
Metacognitive observations
Outlines
Character sketches
Timelines
Essay exams
In-class writings
Frame assignments
Freewriting
Probes

Based on a list drawn up by Stephen Tchudi and Diana Mitchell in *Explorations in the Teaching of English.*

Each student experiences the text in unique ways and her individualized moments of surprise and frustration while reading are not easily predicted by the teacher. Initial writing assignments—journals, quizzes, or other early assignments—should allow space and opportunity for students to express their own experiences of the reading and to talk about what they envisioned while reading the text. Initial questions on the reading should therefore be open ended to allow for a range of responses, and prompts for writing should often encourage students to examine and recall some of their experiences while reading. For example, a teacher could ask about character motivation or about off-stage action that the text has not explained. Speculation about the text and its meanings offers rich opportunities for multiple readings.

Given a greater chance to develop aesthetic sensibilities, students may develop a taste for reading. A larger store of reading experiences does increase an appetite for and appreciation of literature. Indeed, research tells us that students learn to read by reading widely and they increase their ability to read critically by reading large amounts of different genres. For that reason, teachers find that assigning a number of Young Adult novels in a semester is more successful at promoting lifelong readers than one, large classic novel. Students need exposure to many different books and they need the opportunity to write openly about them. If students are afforded multiple opportunities to generate ideas about various literatures for themselves, they should eventually be ready to write expository prose with a critical approach. Whatever the goals for teaching a piece of literature, teachers should avoid insisting that the text has *one* theme as the definitive reading of a text. Teachers should therefore delay a heavy emphasis on criticism or a discussion of their own interpretation of the material until after students have had a chance to discover first what they know and think about it.

What follows is a discussion of three critical approaches to literature that teachers may take when assigning the "response to literature" essay. Because no one critical approach is appropriate to all literary genres, literature teachers should experiment with these and other approaches. In addition to adding variety to the class, multiple critical approaches also suggest that unusual interpretations of the literature are possible, even desirable. Each of these approaches has its advantages and disadvantages for producing solid student writing.

Reader Response Criticism

Teachers have long known that a single text may elicit a variety of readings and any interpretation that the teacher proposes in the classroom must negotiate these multiple responses. The most active readers hold a personal and idiosyncratic identification with the text, so they are loathe to give up their own peculiar views of it. Looking at a car grill and seeing a smiley face, cartoonist Scott McCloud in his witty book *Understanding Comics* explains it this way: "We see ourselves in everything. We assign identities and emotions where none exist. And we make the world over in our image" (33). He is describing a relationship with everyday objects that is very similar to our interaction with literature. As we "read" print and nonprint texts, we invest something of ourselves in the written material. Realizing that everything points to some other meaning, we make the words an extension of ourselves in order to construct new meaning.

Reader Response criticism recognizes this close identification between self and object as something that naturally occurs as part of the active and creative reading process and validates it. It recognizes that reading is subjective and relative and so it grants every reader permission to determine for himself what the text means. Neither the text nor the reader, however, holds all the meaning. The reader must bring her own experiences and filters to bear on the text. Given the many experiences of readers constructing it, most texts are resistant to a closed construction, one that elicits only a fixed, single response from all readers. On the contrary, most texts offer conditions that enable multiple interpretations, associations, and critical judgments. Furthermore, the text's meaning does not rest solely in the mind of the reader, but beyond his own personal response as well. There is always some part of the text that remains for further interpretation by others. The result is a process that Louise Rosenblatt calls *transactional reading,* a construction of the text that exists *between* the text and the reader. It demands active meaning making in which the reader determines how the text is to be understood and appreciated. Depending on the readers' knowledge and understanding of the images and concepts suggested by the text, their guesses will guide and prioritize choices as they activate critical judgment. The text signals the options and the reader decides which aspects are most important to attend to, based on her prior experiences with that information. For example, reading a jingle about Lizzie Borden's "forty whacks" makes sense only when the reader knows that Lizzie Borden was a young woman accused of killing her parents with an ax and that the doggerel was meant to ridicule a murderer who was never convicted. A reader lacking that background may believe that the rhymes were making light of murder and violence. And the text remains to be read in still other ways by future readers. If research reveals that Lizzie did not kill her parents, for example, then other interpretations could open up.

Reader Response criticism acknowledges the transactional process and encourages an awareness of the reader's involvement in a way that the text shapes the reader and the reader shapes the text. Because most readers engage in the transactional process without even thinking about it, we can help students become consciously aware of their natural reading processes by encouraging Reader Response journals or other writings that give them a chance to explore these inner responses. In the Reader Response form of criticism, the writer shuttles back and forth between a "reader-based" engagement with the text that draws on the reader's own response and a "text-based" analysis that analyzes the text from a greater distance. The reader is always building a "third text," one that is constructed out of a combination of associations and the words that are on the page. A more complete explanation of the reading process appears in *Multiple Voices, Multiple Texts: Reading in the Secondary Content Areas* (Dornan, Rosen, and Wilson).

A Reader Response Journal or Essay

A Reader Response journal or essay usually asks students to connect the reading to their own personal experience. The best results are often guided by questions that the teacher poses, which concentrate on the intersection between reader and text. For example, when reading *The Great Gatsby,* a teacher might ask students to write about someone in their lives who is richer than they are and is callous about the less fortunate. When posing these questions, a teacher might draw on some of Richard Beach's strategies for readers/writers in which they

- connect text with an autobiographical experience or with other texts that have similar situations or that find some other way to identify with the characters;
- pick out significant turning points in the narration that point to the writer's interpretation of the text;
- develop character profiles to make a list of their traits, knowledge, plans, goals;
- read between the lines to determine character motivation and beliefs;
- become aware of the cultural norms and conventions of the text's world to explore alternative cultural perspectives and patterns of behavior suggested in the text.

Think/Write #2

1. Select a passage, character, theme, or topic that most interests you in a favorite poem.
2. Explore that passage, character, theme, or topic with a little brainstorming. Let your interests or associations bring some flash of insight you might have had as you read the poem. You may have connected part of the text with something that happened to you, something you have heard, or something you read in the newspaper or another book. Or you may be reminded of someone you know who has had a similar experience.
3. Start writing. Make connections between the text and your association. Use your past knowledge to say something original about the text. Avoid focusing primarily on yourself and your own experience. Remember that this connection is supposed to help us (your readers) see something new in the text, to understand what connections to beliefs or attitudes you have made.

Other Reader Response Writing Assignments

Some students find the Reader Response invitation to self-expression openly liberating and their subsequent writings are articulate and insightful. They will write volumes in response to the text. Many teachers, however, work with reluctant readers who read the words without assigning to them any real significance and they hate the response journals. Jeffrey Wilhelm understands how to encourage the most resistant students to reach out and form the most productive transactions during their reading.

In *You Gotta BE the Book,* Jeffrey Wilhelm observed what his most enthusiastic readers were doing to become engaged in their reading and how they were able to articulate a wide array of responses to the literature. They seemed to construct richer meanings out of the text and lust for more. Engaged readers more fully evoked the text. That is, they were able to relate more completely to the characters, to picture them in their heads, and to associate them with people in their own lives. Engaged readers filled in plot and setting that the author left unexplained. These readers moreover developed a "relationship with the author" and were able to live in the story world of the text as a vicarious experience. Using their formulas for successful reading experiences, Wilhelm sought ways to help his less enthusiastic readers to find a way into the world of the reading. He settled on ten different dimensions that were important for students who were able to respond successfully to the literary world:

- preparing for the story world by thinking about what it might be like;
- comprehending the story on the most fundamental level;
- asking questions about the pending action;
- relating to the characters;
- picturing the story world in their heads;
- filling in the story gaps by inferring details that go beyond the text;
- associating the events to their own knowledge of the world;
- reflecting back on the story to interpret what it meant;
- noticing literary devices and other story-making conventions;
- understanding their own reading processes;
- evaluating the author as an agent of story telling and relating to the author (46–47).

To reading experts, there is nothing surprising in Wilhelm's findings, but his list is invaluable for teachers who are designing writing assignments because it points to a sequencing of crucial moments in the reading process that could trigger meaningful responses. Teachers planning a lesson could select one or more of these opportunities for students to envision the text and plan a writing assignment to reinforce it. Wilhelm's success lies in how he helps his reluctant readers build images of characters and setting with pictures from magazines and other cutouts. He also uses drama effectively for building plot and deeper comprehension.

For composition classes, we suggest Reader Response journals and *Two-Column Protocols,* which Wilhelm used as one approach to his classroom research. For the Two-Column Protocols, Wilhelm lists key points of the story on one half of a lengthwise sheet of paper. On the other half, he asks for written comments that record a reader's reactions to the story and reflect on his own reading behaviors. *Double-Entry* or *Dialog Journals* are a variation on this idea.Students select passages while they are reading and they record on the left side of the page parts of the passage, key words or images, and/or descriptions of the scene, and the page numbers. On the right, they write reflective commentary. See Figure 6.2 Double-entry Log for *Rules of the Road* by Joan Bauer for an idea of how this can be done in response

FIGURE 6.2 *Double-entry Log for* **Rules of the Road** *by Joan Bauer*

Writing Prompt: As you read Chapters 10–15, think about the strategies that Jenna uses to cope with difficult people. In your Double-entry log, list some of the moments that jump out at you and comment on what you think about Jenna's tactics.

The Book	*Me*
p. 83–84 Her dad says that he can take care of himself and that he doesn't need her help.	Jenna is sad because she has to help her father or try to avoid him. She mostly avoids him.
p. 83 Jenna tells off Mrs. Gladstone and tells her to get help from a doctor.	This is not very realistic. I wouldn't tell a lady like Mrs. Gladstone what to do. I could tell off my father, but not an old lady who never did anything to me.

to a writing prompt. Teachers often need to guide students on how to do this efficiently because it can be very time consuming, but it is effective for helping students to think metacognitively, to make connections in the story, and to demonstrate that they are keeping up with the reading.

Wilhelm's assignments are useful examples of Reader Response criticism. He uses Reader Response as a supplement to talking and role playing. Symbolic story representations using picture cutouts are Wilhelm's way of helping students picture the storyline in their heads. Rather than work on the literal level by simply retelling the story, he prods students to read between the lines and beyond the text when they can in order to establish a connection to the work. Most of all, he asks students to imagine themselves both as a part of the text and yet still see themselves as separate from it.

Process Logs. Kathleen Dudden Andrasick has also developed a number of journal exercises that help students engage with the text. The process log asks students to read the text (in her example she is working with a poem) a couple of times—the first time without annotations, the second time with marginal notes. The journal describes the process of the reading. Here are the questions she uses.

- What did you understand, think, feel after your first reading?
- What questions did you have?
- What words/phrases were confusing?
- What words/phrases helped your understanding?
- What words/phrases seemed to have particular importance? Can you tell why?
- As you read the [text] a second time, marking it, what insights did you still have?
- What areas are still confusing to you?

- What feelings does the [text] evoke for you?
- What meanings do you feel the poem is expressing? (60)

Rather than ask for answers to all the questions, Andrasick calls for a free write to describe both HOW they read and WHAT they read and understand. Notice how this type of journal recognizes the various stances that a reader might take during reading and asks the reader to focus on them. Andrasick explains, "Our reading and our teaching become clumsy if we plunge into literary analysis before first allowing students (or ourselves) full opportunity to recognize highly personal, often emotional, experiences with texts" (72).

The Disadvantages of Reader Response Criticism

We have given you the ideas of Wilhelm and Andrasick to illustrate just a couple of the many ways that Reader Response criticism can be employed to encourage the aesthetic response in reading through composition. But this approach also has its drawbacks. One theoretical danger of Reader Response criticism is that so many potential readings may compete for understanding that no shared meaning may be found. Occasionally an author will deliberately tease the reader by including contradictory material or leaving so many gaps in the text that a commonly held reading cannot be found. David Mamet's play *Oleanna* about a student who accuses her professor of sexual harassment frustrates audiences with that idea. It is so cleverly written that audiences will literally split along gender lines in response to it, and both sides can find evidence in the play to support their opposing positions. But such examples are rare. In response to most pieces of fiction, students will identify a fairly acceptable range of meanings.

A greater danger for secondary classrooms is the wild card reading in which the reader feels the freedom to impose any meaning at all on the text. An "anything goes" attitude by the teacher may invite many unconventional meanings that spill out of the bounds of the discipline. While in theory the reader should be able to consider any text a Rorschach test for her ideas, Louise Rosenblatt argues that this way of reading is abusive of the process. She offers these rules for a valid reading: "The reader's interpretation should not be contradicted by any element of the text, and . . . nothing [should] be projected for which there is no verbal basis" in the text (1978, 115). In other words, the reader must read closely and account for all that is in the text. The reader must also avoid adding meaning that is not somehow supportable by evidence in the text. These rules seem to serve as a corrective to most aberrant readings.

A third disadvantage to Reader Response criticism often arises when young readers are asked to explore personal associations with the text. They begin by writing about the text, but they often become so absorbed in their own story that they forget to discuss the original text. Questions such as those developed by Wilhelm or Andrasick help guide students towards commenting on their perceptions and reflections on patterns in the text. It is perfectly feasible with the right questions to move students from the emotive and experiential response to more formal, analytical papers. The end product usually results in an exploratory paper that emphasizes ideas discovered early on. The next few sections of this chapter discuss critical approaches that may complement, supplement, or substitute for the Reader Response approach. A lively program in English should experiment with all of these approaches at one time or another during the school year.

Viewing Nonprint Media as Texts

Common sense tells us that the images of nonprint media are as powerful as the impact of the word in their potential for shaping the young. John Dewey recognized long ago that the world of art, which includes imagery, expands our horizons in lasting and meaningful ways. Indeed, art influences our perception of the world. Anyone who has seen the Charles Knight murals of dinosaurs at the Museum of Natural History in New York City and elsewhere is forever impressed by his images of prehistoric life. Even though Knight painted these murals decades ago, years before we had today's grasp of paleontology, his images continue to influence science and the public's perceptions of these extinct animals. Such is the lasting power of art and the image. Sensing how enduring the artistic image can potentially be, Dewey argued that art may change us irrevocably. He wrote, "The world we have experienced becomes an integral part of the self that acts and is acted upon in further experience. In their physical occurrence, things and events experienced pass and are gone. But something of their meaning and value is retained as an integral part of the self" (*Later Works* 10, 109). Something of their meaning and value is retained as an integral part of the self. These words not only account for the way images nourish children, but also why they should write about what they see.

Not surprisingly, most of the principles that we have discussed concerning the Reader Response approach to print texts may also apply to viewing and appreciating films, advertisements, cartoons, and photographs. Although images are more readily accessible to the viewer in a nonprint text than in a conventional print text, they still require a viewer to establish connections among them for coherence and meaning. Like readers, viewers of nonprint texts call on memory and experience to create meanings between scenes and characters and to grasp the text as a whole.

The film goer, for example, watches the film selectively based on her prior knowledge and her ability to gather together the fragments that are most useful for making meaning out of such film conventions as montages, flashbacks, and dissolves. Like the reader of print texts, the film viewer decides where to set her attention. She looks at the screen, replete with images and incomplete explanations, and she fills in the gaps by filling in details that are not depicted on the screen. She constructs the meaning out of her imagination and experience. The more abstract or stylized the image as a film convention, the more the viewer works to make sense of it out of her own experience. In viewing a film that represents a world close to her own experience, the viewer may have little trouble identifying with the characters or explaining the film's themes. She may also fill in the gaps created by cuts in the film. In the detective film, for example, she might invent a picture of the violence that occurs off stage or imagine a whole host of dangers about to assault the protagonist. She is also able to make judgments about the "good guys" and the "bad guys" of the story. As in reading, the aesthetic moments occur for the viewer in the interplay between living in the moment of the film and experiencing it at a distance.

The major difference between the film and the print text lies in the weight that the image carries in the visual texts. Students have to understand that *every image stands for something else.* Although this is also true of print texts, the relationship between the sign and the thing that it points to (the signified) seems to be less apparent with the visual image. The image seems to stand for itself and nothing more. What students soon learn, nevertheless, is that the film takes on an even livelier function when they realize that every tiny detail immediately stands for something other than what it actually is. The car's make and model probably suggest something about the class of the driver or they might carry other social meanings. For example, an audience that is culturally tuned in knows the difference between a gangster who drives a Corvette and the one who drives a Ford Escort. Moreover, gestures, clothing, landscapes, food, language—all carry cultural baggage that suggest coded meanings that are fluid and variable. A detective who wears an old, crumpled raincoat conveys something about his relaxed, unpretentious personality.

Some images function as *icons,* which closely resemble what they stand for. The number five or a photograph is an example of an icon. The connection between a symbol and its meaning for the film director, however, is arbitrarily set by convention and cultural acceptance, so there is no fixed meaning. The image does not bear a substantial meaning on its own, but carries significance only by virtue of its difference from something else portrayed in the film and/or the ways it fits into a network of relations set up by that film and any other film. For example, the image of King Kong climbing the Empire State Building becomes an icon that may be carried from monster film to monster film. The figure of King Kong bears no real symbolic meaning of its own, but after it is used again and again, that huge gorilla carrying the tiny Fay Wray begins to take on a beauty and the beast significance, so that it can be parodied and imitated by later films. An association with the "Beauty and the Beast" fairy tale is cultural and so are the many other uses of the King Kong figure. The more a movie goer is educated to film conventions, the easier it is for the viewer to attach popular meaning to the thousands of images that play off other films and cultural experiences.

To begin to understand the significance of what they see, students should look at the recurring images. When they begin to notice patterns in the film—visual images that are repeated, for example—they will be able to relate them to remarks that the characters make as well as other indicators such as race, class, gender, and nationality. Although these images are often carefully chosen by directors, set and costume designers, and writers to represent larger meanings, they also communicate secondary, unintended meanings that the viewer will be able to see for himself. He should look toward a larger understanding of what these images might suggest to him.

The goal of the teacher should be to nudge students toward a larger understanding of what these images might suggest and encourage them to locate their texts as well as themselves as viewers within their own social contexts. They need to be able to critique and understand the inner connectedness of the cultural contexts that give rise to these images. But a teacher has to take care—just as she does when teaching a print text—that the pressure to do cultural criticism does not flood the students' own personal responses to the film, suppressing their initial appreciation of it.

Alan B. Teasley and Ann Wilder in their book *Reel Conversations* emphasize an open-ended approach to film criticism. When they are teaching the film, they select "meaningful chunks" and stop the action periodically to discuss what the students have noticed. During each chunk of the film, students take notes on what they see and hear. Teasley and Wilder offer work sheets that solicit these questions:

- What vivid sounds or interesting use of music did you notice?
- What details about the landscape in the scene stood out?
- What vivid visual images struck you as interesting?
- What did you observe about the daily life of the people?
- What have you learned about [any given character] in this part of the film?
- What conflict(s) seem to be developing?
- What is the mood of the film so far?
- What themes seem to be emerging in this film? (53–55)

Teasley and Wilder then ask "What did you notice?" and they rouse class discussion by encouraging students to talk to each other using their notes on interesting shots, sequences, or dialog. At the end of the film, they go back over the parts and consider the whole using the following points of reference:

- changes in their own feelings or opinions;
- emerging patterns in visual images and sounds;
- all the things that the film could be about;
- all the conflicts in the film;
- associations they made with the characters, the incidents, or the objects in the film;
- the film's position—if any—on the issues raised in it;
- what the film says about the culture of the people depicted in that particular time and place. This is particularly important when they ask what students have learned about the American experience from the film. (65)

Teasley and Wilder use the students' notes as a form of brainstorming that leads to longer writing assignments. Out of the viewing guides that they prepare using the eight questions above, students may write personal essays, analytical essays, and/or writing that goes beyond the film such as poetry, legends, myths, film scripts, and storyboards. Their personal essays may take the form of letters that reflect on one striking aspect of the film or about how the film changed or affected them, or about a way in which the film connects to something else in their lives. Their approach is a Reader Response form of criticism, which offers a model for responses to film or literature that is particularly effective for use with adolescents. What is important about all of these approaches to writing assignments is that they first demand student involvement and they are subsequently combined with a hardcore analysis that follows the personal response.

Understanding the impact of popular culture on high school readers, Jeanne Larvick of Lansing (Michigan) Catholic Central High School has developed a "Poetry Video Unit" in which she asks students to compare the lifestyle and language of contemporary rock musicians to the nineteenth century Romantic poets of Britain. Early in the unit, she raises words such as "sensuous," "mystical," "corrupt," and "tyranny" to point readers to the counterculture lifestyles of both groups. The class also discusses the criticism of established authority and specific beliefs and philosophical values that both groups hold in common. She encourages discussions about violence in their personal lives and problems with abuse of drugs and alcohol and they read a few representative examples of Romantic poetry. Larvick ends her unit with this assignment:

> Select a poem from the unit we have studied. Work with a group of three or four students. Create a video to accompany the poem. Being aware of the theme depicted by the poet, use symbolism to express that theme. You may use music to accompany your video. The video should include a reading of the poem. The group should also write an interpretation of their symbols and how these symbols express the theme of the poem. The group shall give an oral explanation of the video at its conclusion.

This sort of assignment combines composition with nonprint media—in this case, film and music—to help students unpack print texts and write responses that they will never forget composing. It teaches them the power of the iconic symbol and many of the ways that texts function. It also offers a composition opportunity with the lasting value that Dewey talks about, both for them and the audience of their films.

Formalism, or New Criticism

Reader Response criticism of the 1960s was historically an answer to Formalism, or New Criticism, a popular approach that came into its own in the 1940s and 1950s and is still widely used as a way to stimulate a closed reading of the text. New Criticism grew out of a movement in the 1920s and 1930s that regarded the text as a system of formal elements that point to a fixed meaning in the text. It is based on the assumption that the text was a unified expression of the author's inner thought. The author posits a theme for a given poem or short story and selects any number of literary devices—tone, plot, metaphor, setting, metrical rhythm—as support of that specific theme. It functions on the premise that we may read a poem, for example, about the struggle between good and evil, then look for metaphors or other devices to support that theme. The reader's goal is to demonstrate textual unity, to prove that one particular interpretation is correct because it is reflected consistently in all parts of the work. Formalists today still look closely at the interplay of formal elements in a piece of fiction, but they are now willing to concede that there is no definitive reading of the piece.

Since many of the anthologies used in secondary schools are organized by such Formalist elements as tone, metaphors, irony, characters, and setting, this critical approach has persisted over the years as a popular approach in secondary English classes. It is easy to teach because it appears to be objective and testable, but students often dislike it because "correct" interpretations are often more obvious to the teacher than the students, and teachers often abuse this approach by claiming absolute authority over the text's interpretation. Our suspicion is that it is this critical approach that we remember about the bad ole days of high school English.

Even so, some students have "discovered" literature through New Criticism and have become excited by its substance. Reading beyond the surface features of a story, students begin to understand more about the world behind the appearances, and they begin to grasp the complexities of a text. They realize for the first time that there is more to producing a film or a book or a poem than they thought. Looking at recurring images of a text, probing the author's selection of a color or suddenly seeing the story within a story in the narrative structure can lead to exciting new readings and a realization that appearances in the world are not what they seem.

Nevertheless, we should be aware that this form of criticism is often given short shrift on the college level. At best, it is regarded as appropriate for a critical response to American literature written at the middle of the twentieth century, so it is not considered useful as a response to all literatures in all periods. It does not work well with post-modern literature, for example. In college classes, it is largely a method reserved for introducing literary conventions and it is not the only approach used in literature classes. Because we teach literature for more than one purpose, we should not fall back on textual analysis as the most important form of response to literature. Students are equally enriched by investigating other approaches. An example of an equally effective approach is the cultural aspect of literature, investigating where the work is situated in the historical tradition and what its contributions are to our understanding about ourselves as a nation and as a people.

High school teachers might find greatest success with New Criticism by combining a few of the literary conventions and close textual reading with Reader Response. They might assign Reader Response journals up to the closing chapters of a book, for example, then bring in discussions of the Formalist elements that support the text when students appear ready to make evaluative remarks and lay out interpretive responses. An examination of these elements provides a viable excuse for going back and reviewing the text as a whole and for insisting that students support their interpretive claims with textual evidence. Some ideas for this sort of assignment at the close of *The Great Gatsby* might be the following journal prompts that ask students to think about symbol, tone, and character respectively:

- Now that you have finished the book, look back and think about the symbolism behind the names of East Egg and West Egg. In your journal, list six references to each place (twelve in all) and the page numbers where you found them. Next to each listing, write a quick interpretation of what Fitzgerald might have meant by the reference. Finally, look through everything you have written about each location and summarize what East Egg and West Egg seem to represent in the book.

- Beginning with the paragraph on p. 179 "One afternoon late in October I saw Tom Buchanan . . ." to the end of the book, describe Nick's mood and attitude toward Tom Buchanan. Contrast it to the tone of voice that he used when he first met Tom. What has changed? Why? Write about this in your journal, giving page numbers where necessary.

- What does it mean when a man like Jay Gatsby "invents himself"? Go back through the book and list all the major passages where Nick talks about this and write a paragraph that explains how Nick seems to characterize Jay Gatsby's conception of himself.

Group work and class discussions around these Formalist elements may lay the groundwork for expository essays such as those described in Chapter Five. The best essays grow out of a need to explain oneself. Students will find they have a great deal to say if they take time to construct the text transactionally and find a balance between their personal experience of the text and the constraints that the text makes on their reading. The transactional experience requires that the reader persists in a search for meaning and continues to question that meaning based on the content and form of the work. Formalism could become one more tool in that quest. Since young critics often cannot distinguish between judgment that requires a self-conscious articulation of the meanings and personal preference, they may employ the Formalist elements as a way of proving that their response is more than a matter of taste.

The Historical Approach

An underemployed form of criticism on the secondary level is one that combines literature and/or film and history. The approach largely considers the impact on texts of historical movements, cultural trends, and political forces that shaped the piece then and now. Much of historical criticism is concerned with the role of power, ideology, status, and resources that influence the themes, the characters, the production, and publication of the works. The idea is that our view of historical events and literary texts changes over time and those changes account for multiple perspectives among the readership. The student using the historical approach will often compare the literary text to an original document from that period or will use some historical research to expose some little understood aspect of the period. Some New Historical scholars, for example, have examined the role of the working classes in Shakespeare's plays. Such investigations can allow fresh insights into Shakespeare and an understanding of political trends (Elizabethan and contemporary) that were not readily apparent to us. English teachers find these approaches new and interesting for secondary students because they offer opportunities for interdisciplinary research topics that tie together ideas from their economics, history, and literature classes. The possibilities are endless. The sheer variety of new topic possibilities also helps to prevent plagiarism, since teachers can insist that paper topics be linked solely to class discussion and class interests. The more we can avoid impersonal topics, the more we can avoid marking papers downloaded from websites.

In the New Historicism, a specialized form of the historical approach, the reader attempts to situate the text in its historical and cultural context—either in the period of the work's setting or in the period of the author. There are many ways to assign papers using history. Here are a few.

- If the author lived at the time of the setting in the artistic work, find an historical or contemporary document that amplifies an historical event in the work and compare the two texts using a close textual reading. An example might be to look at Greek burial practices at the time of *Antigone* to compare the way that royal family members and ordinary citizens were buried and compare that material to Kreon's commands for the burial of Polyneices and Antigone.

- Look for biographical material in the artist's life that might find its parallels in the text. For example, Truman Capote's life growing up in the racially divided South might be contrasted to the life of the southern boy that he depicts in his stories, where race plays little or no role. One has to be careful with this approach not to assume that the author is a character or narrator's voice in the play, short story, or novel. To do so is called an Intentional Fallacy. It assumes that the author has made a statement of intention in the work that fixes its meaning. It also assumes that sentiments expressed in the work are a faithful reflection of the author's thinking. Although a biographical comparison might reveal some interesting parallels, it is dangerous to read too much into the text. There will nevertheless be some slippage between the fictional and non-fictional characters and it is at the point of these differences that the study may become most interesting.

- Look for historical material that is at variance with the life and times depicted by the author. Authors very often write about earlier periods and it is interesting to compare their representation of the earlier period to the one that is represented in an historical document of that time. Finding a Roman historian's description of the succession to Caesar, for example, might be interesting to compare to Shakespeare's conception of it in *Julius Caesar.*

- Similarly, it is interesting to compare some part of the earlier history to the times of the author. Looking at a document on royal succession in Elizabethan times and comparing it to Shakespeare's concerns about succession in his history plays could also be revealing. Even *Hamlet* or *King Lear* lends itself to this sort of examination. If one were to take a New Historical approach to *The Great Gatsby,* one could read about the consolidation in banking and industry that made some people in the 1920s very rich and concentrated the wealth in the hands of a few. The consequence was the domination of American industry, transportation, and finance by giant magnates. The process assured the power of people such as Jay Gatsby and it pitted new money against old money in the Northeast. In this critical approach, a student might compare the life of one of these magnates who were known for their destructive tactics to the lives of Gatsby or Tom Buchanan. Another possibility is to look at the middle classes of the 1920s and to speculate on how the middle class or working class survived the pressures of industry.

The difference between New Historicism and the old historical approach is that an assignment under the old approach might have focused on the more entertaining aspects of the 1920s—speakeasies, Al Capone, and the rise of the moving pictures. Under New Historicism, the critic is more interested in the underrepresented persons in the text, such as Nick Carraway—and the role of power and money. New Historicism often challenges old interpretations of favorite texts by exploring new perspectives, not to reinforce received notions about those times, but to see them anew by defamiliarizing the texts. The point is to find out more about the text through historical research in order to challenge traditional views. They can often detach the text from the weight of previous literary scholarship, for example, by focusing on issues of state power and on how it is maintained by gender and class relations and on how the language often creates a reality of its own. We can similarly help students compare historical and literary texts by asking such questions as:

What is missing from either text?

Where are the contradictions between them?

What has been omitted from either text? Why?

What has been added to either text? Why?

What has been forgotten? Revived? Renewed?

What has been transformed? Distorted? Emphasized differently?

How are large institutions such as law, education, government represented?

How are the people who are most powerless represented?

Like Formalism, the historical approach offers an opportunity to read texts closely and to search out meanings that are suggested, but not explicitly stated in the text. Even so, many texts do not lend themselves to this form of criticism and finding suitable materials for making the comparisons can be time consuming. Fortunately, an increasing number of primary sources is being made available on the Internet, so secondary schools are not necessarily bound by the meager references in their own local libraries. The key to all of these approaches is an acknowledgment that since readers cannot assume a fixed unity in the text, they may construct meaning transactionally with the text. Given the plurality of meaning among readers, we need to offer a variety of approaches to help student tease out their multifarious responses. Some of these approaches will lend themselves to a more aesthetic response and some will test expository writing skills. All approaches have their place in the classroom.

Creative Writing as a Response to Literature

Another approach that is too often overlooked as a response to literature is the creative writing assignment. Writing in the style of a particular author, for example, can require a close examination of the author's mode of discourse, punctuation, and theme. Our favorite assignments come from suggestions made by contemporary poets.

Kenneth Koch offers invaluable advice to teachers in *Rose, Where Did You Get That Red?* He shows children how to "find perceptions, ideas, feelings, and new ways of saying things" in traditional poetry. Then he asks them to write poems in which "they have to talk about the same thing in different ways." For instance, he draws on William Blake's idea of asking an animal how he got that way in "The Tyger." He asks young poets to think about Blake's language and syntax and to ask similar questions of other natural phenomena—how did clouds or sky or apples get the way they are? Koch and his students also play around with notions of a secret language. How would the Tyger answer him? What is the secret language of an apple or a cloud or an animal like? What do these things imagine and feel that makes them different? After teasing out the central ideas of the poem and kicking them around the classroom, Koch asks students to write one in the same spirit as the original. One student asked where the dog got his bark and another asked the monkey where he learned to climb.

Think/Write #3
Find a short poem that you might teach in a secondary classroom. Think about the ideas and feelings suggested in the poem. Make a list of questions for the students to think about and discuss before writing a very similar poem. If you are stuck, look up Kenneth Koch's many books and read further on his hints for teaching responses to poetry through writing.

Stephen Dunning and William Stafford are poets with concrete advice for teaching an understanding of literature through creative writing. Dunning and Stafford suggest Copy Change as a way of helping students imitate the work of a well known author. The writing strategy is somewhat similar to Kenneth Koch's exercises. The student may use a passage from a story or novel or a poem and rewrite parts of it while remaining as faithful as possible to the original style. For example, he might use Blake's poem, changing the word "Tyger" to "Fire Fly."

Then the rest of the poem is changed to make sense of the new word, but the student should try to follow the original rhythm and rhyme scheme. Since the poem is no longer about a powerful beast, but one equally mysterious, the exercise should be one of finding new vocabulary to reflect the new topic. Meanwhile, the student is forced to count syllables, rhyme words, and grapple with Blake's meanings on an intimate scale before solving all the problems of the Copy Change. A modified form of this exercise appears in Figure 6.3 Copying Steps.

An example of copy change might be this one based on Jack and Jill:

Bat and ball flew up the hill
when Bobby lost his temper.
His mom came down
gave him a frown
and sent Bob to bed thereafter.

FIGURE 6.3 ***Copying Steps***

1. Choose one of your favorite poems.
2. On a blank sheet of paper copy the text **exactly.** Use the same words, same spellings, punctuation, and the layout. Copy it by hand. Put the poet's name on your copy.
3. Carefully check your copy against the original. Read it aloud to someone with all the punctuation to see if you got it right.
4. Now work with your copy and note the specific things you admire and would like to imitate. Here is Dunning and Stafford's partial list of possibilities:
   - beginnings
   - repetitions of language and/or sounds
   - strong, vivid, exact images
   - comparisons, especially similes and metaphors
   - places where the poem sounds especially musical or rhythmically interesting
   - "moves" or "turns," catapulting the poem forward
   - patterns of images; echoes of images and sounds
   - line breaks that create surprises, interest you
5. Write down three or four elements you're interested in trying.
6. Still working with your copy of the model poem, copy-change the parts you would like to work with. Choose at least three variations for each change. For example, copy-change the beginning by substituting words for the topic and make at least three other changes.
7. Select the version that seems most exciting to you and develop it fully. When you want to or need to, leave the original poem behind, especially when you need to make sense of your changes.
8. When you're content with your imitation, stop and credit the author's model—whether or not you have exact use of language and style.

Based on Stephen Dunning and William Stafford's *Getting the Knack* (197–198).

Other creative forms of response could include extending a story with new endings, experimenting with prequels and sequels, rewriting a part of the story from someone else's point of view, drafting a letter or a speech in character, writing missing scenes or scripts for videos, composing and illustrating collages. Teachers could also assign projects in other media—short videos for the Internet, for example. We do not have time to explore all the possibilities here. The point is that creative writing and allied media in the arts—when done well—may require critical thinking and student organization that are equal to the effort and rigor that goes into a formal expository essay. So often the formal paper falls short of what we hope to inspire in our students. We want them to digest the reading, to find some way of their own into it, and to formulate a response that is fresh and yet legitimately in line with other readings in the class. Too often, however, the formal paper has forced our students to borrow ideas from the Internet or other ready sources and submit them as their own. Too often the formal assignments push students into responding on an analytical level of criticism that they little understand or care about. We know that most students are able to respond to their reading with personal responses and we rightfully hope to nudge them beyond that subjective point to a more distanced understanding of what they have read. They should be able, for example, to apply student-developed criteria to their readings. They should also be able to appreciate a reading for its historical significance, even if it does not speak to them personally. But teachers must scaffold these assignments, assisting students' movement from one kind of response to another. A steady diet of formal papers laid out in the standard five-paragraph essay pattern inevitably falls short of leading these students to a more nuanced understanding of the works and destroys their appreciation for reading some of our beloved literature. Given the different backgrounds, tastes, learning styles, and reading practices among students in the class, a teacher would best serve them by assigning a wide assortment of ways to respond to literature. Earlier in this chapter is a sample assignment from one high school unit on the Romantic poets that demonstrates the potential of creative responses in a traditional class.

Aesthetic and Efferent Readings

Teaching critical responses to literature has its rewards in opening students' eyes to meanings that were not obvious to them. When many students discover criticism for the first time, they are amazed by what one can see in a book or a film beyond its surface meaning. But there are dangers in an overemphasis on criticism, as we have already noted in the discussions of each approach. One of these drawbacks is that students might be turned off from an enjoyment of the film or poem because the act of critique naturally distances the viewer/reader from the work. Keeping a certain amount of ironic distance from the work is necessary. To critique a play, for example, one cannot indulge in a total immersion in the experience because a conscious awareness of the actors and the playwright's devices are forgotten. Indeed if the audience forgets that it is a play, they may lose perspective. This was the case when listeners took Orson Welles' radio play *War of the Worlds* too seriously and thought America really was being invaded. A viewer who cannot maintain some distance when watching *Othello* might leap up on the stage and try to prevent Desdemona from being strangled. Similarly, the viewer can ruin the play for himself if he maintains too much distance. He might see Iago's ploys as too obvious to be believed by Othello and the plant of the handkerchief as too unrealistic to be taken seriously. In short, to gain maximum pleasure from a work of art, the viewer has to maintain a distance between consciously seeking information and suspending disbelief in a simple aesthetic stance.

In *The Reader, the Text, the Poem,* Louise Rosenblatt explains that readers' responses may range from the *aesthetic* stance, which occurs at one end of a continuum, to the nonaesthetic (or *efferent*) reading, which stands at the opposite end. In the nonaesthetic reading, the perceiver approaches the text primarily as a source of information that can be carried away from it. She gives the example of reading the directions on a fire extinguisher after a fire has broken out. The reader is combing the text for meaningful information. Rosenblatt explains that the reader is not focused on the aesthetic qualities of the text because he is attending to the cognitive impact of the text (Rosenblatt 45). By contrast, the aesthetic reading is one in which "the reader's attention is centered directly on what he is living through during his relationship with that particular text" (Rosenblatt 25). An aesthetic response is one in which the reader is focused primarily on her own experience of the text. The key difference between the efferent and aesthetic responses is determined largely by the reader's initial attitude toward the text and the selective attention she brings to it. When seeking information from the text, the reader will invariably concentrate on finding, classifying, remembering, and determining the significance of information instead of savoring the experience of the text, as he might have otherwise done in an aesthetic reading. The reader may also decide what is important by combining her prior knowledge with cues in the text. If cues such as numbers and formulas signal mathematics information, for example, then she will probably approach it with the anticipation of an efferent, nonaesthetic experience.

Thus, the verbal cues may signal a specific stance that the reader should take—aesthetic or efferent. But the nature of the genre may also fill that role. If the text is set to look like a poem or play, for example, the reader will usually assume an aesthetic stance in which he will focus on the reading event rather than plying the text for information. If the text contains literary allusions or other stylistic devices, the reader may be alerted to the text's literary values and enjoy a more distanced experience of trying to decode the symbols. Or he may focus more on the emotional experience of the symbols. When the reader chooses to engage aesthetically in a literary piece, according to Rosenblatt, he experiences various "strands of response," often concurrently. He first imagines the "world of the work" with its language and plot and characters; then he will respond to it with emotion and with some reasoning, perhaps aware of the formal structures that constitute the text. His primary purpose, however, is to enter that world and "to participate as fully as possible in the potentialities of the text" (69). At the crossroads of this evocation of the text with its words and the reader's grasp of them through his own schemata and intentions lies the potential of the aesthetic experience.

Rosenblatt echoes John Dewey's *Art as Experience* as she writes about the "lived through" experience of the text. Dewey writes, "To see, to perceive, is more than to recognize. It does not identify something present in terms of a past disconnected from it. The past is carried into the present so as to expand and deepen the content of the latter" (24). The perceiver becomes consciously aware of the art form and his own "living through enjoyment" of it (27). Thus an aesthetic appreciation of art exists on a continuum with past personal experience and it occurs when the focus is on the object as an artistic and lived through experience. Elsewhere, Rosenblatt emphasizes the experiential and the personal as that which feeds the aesthetic experience and this occurs when "instead of thinking of the text as either literary or informational, efferent or aesthetic, [the reader] should think of it as written for a particular predominant attitude or stance, efferent or aesthetic, on the part of the reader" ("Literature–SOS!" 446–7).

When does the aesthetic moment occur according to Rosenblatt? Periodically. Every time the reader is aware of experiencing the moment of the text. As the reader moves mentally into the text and begins to lose himself, he can experience those "lived through" moments. But he will cycle in and out of the text—sometimes being aware of himself or the information that the text offers and sometimes losing himself in the content of the text. It is in the process of identifying with the text and being immersed in it that the aesthetic moments occur, as long as the reader does not become frustrated with his understanding of the text. When there is an agreement between the reader's anticipation of the textual signs and their significance and he is able to form a consistent picture, then illusion takes over. The reader is able to project a consistent understanding of the text based on his own "theory of the world in his head." But in the process of building a consistent picture of what the text is saying, the reader will also begin to accumulate "alien associations," pieces that do not fit with his schemata, and he will be forced to give up his sense of coherence. While forming the consistent picture, the reader is comfortably participating in the text, but as soon as the illusion breaks off, he will experience a tension that will leave him "suspended, as it were, between total entanglement and latent detachment" (Iser 127). This breech begins a period of a more distanced perspective on the text. The reader continues to oscillate between illusion forming and illusion breaking. He will watch himself reading and consciously noting the changes when his expectations are frustrated. It is in these moments of tension that the reader experiences the text as a "living event" (128). It takes a balance of consistency-building and a disturbance in the reader's involvement to create reading pleasure.

Judith Langer has another way of describing this cycling in and out of the text as a series of "envisionments" (40) and she imagines four phases in the reading process:

- Being Out and Stepping Into an Envisionment–this is the pre-reading phase in which the reader taps into prior knowledge about literary conventions and/or the subject matter of the text;

- Being In and Moving Through an Envisionment–this is the point at which the reader is totally immersed in the text and is only marginally aware of himself;

- Stepping Back and Rethinking What One Knows–this is the point at which the reader reflects on the text using metalanguage. For example, he might ask how much he understands or whether he needs to review earlier information or whether he generally understands the text;

- Stepping Out and Objectifying the Experience–this is an evaluative stance in which the reader responds to the content, the author's style, or to the reader's own experience. (1992, 40)

Langer is quick to add that the reader will vary the process by moving back and forth through all four stances as the reading experience requires. Although Langer does not speak of the aesthetic moment, we can speculate that it has the potential of occurring at any point throughout this process. A great deal about the aesthetic experience depends on the reader's prior knowledge and comprehension. Much about the relationship between reader and text is personal and it is also governed by generic assumptions, textual necessity, and idiosyncratic choice.

Aesthetician Michael J. Parsons maintains that there is a sequence of insights that the child will experience as he learns more and more about objectifying his experience with the aesthetic. While Parsons is concerned mostly with a response to painting, we can apply much of what he says to the child's ability to appreciate literature as well. Parsons' assumptions about the function of painting are based on the mainstream views within the "expressionist" school of aesthetics, which includes philosophers such as John Dewey and Susanne Langer whose views connect to our work in composition and English education. Parsons believes that "art is not just a series of pretty objects; it is rather a way we have of articulating our interior life," a view long held by teachers who would simply substitute the word *literature* for *art.*

In the first stage of Parsons' taxonomy, the *Favoritism Stage,* the child shows largely an unguided delight in response to art (we co-authors supplied the names for these stages). Few children show a preference for the style or subject of art—whether it is representational or abstract, for example—but they have an open acceptance of whatever they see. In the second stage, the *Beauty and Realism Stage,* they are more likely to respond on a gut level to the art object. Beauty is largely associated with their own associations with the represented object. They may like pictures of puppies, for example, because they love dogs and they measure a picture by how faithfully it represents the dogs. Most of our secondary students are beyond these two stages.

In Stage Three, the *Expressiveness Stage,* the viewer is looking for an intense experience with the work of art, and she can usually separate the topic of the piece from her intuitive response. She may also be able to accept that she does not share the views of the artist and yet appreciate the artist's perspective for the sake of a new experience. For instance, students at this stage may be fascinated by Picasso's painting *Guernica* about the German bombing of a Spanish village or Kurt Vonnegut's book *Slaughterhouse-Five* about the American bombing of Dresden, even though their imagining of these events horrifies them. Mainly what they like to read at this stage is something that grabs them. Anything else is "boring."

In Stage Four, the *Style and Form Stage,* students learn to respect a new style or form, even though the genre is not representative or familiar to them. For example, students might show a fascination for Cubism in painting or satire in literature, even though they might be new art forms for the student experience. To make the leap to this stage, students have to accept the piece of art or literature as an historical and social achievement, existing in a respected tradition. They need to be responsive to discussions on style, technique, form in an attempt to understand works that seem foreign to their own experience. They have to accept the critical analysis of others and they must be willing to allow the critical opinions of others to influence their tastes and appreciation of the work. It takes some sophistication and open mindedness to take this step.

In Stage Five, the *Autonomy Stage,* students are able to make independent judgments of their own based on informed criteria. More than simply view the work as part of an historical tradition, they need to recognize that traditions change over time, demanding newer and newer artistic expression. They need to be able to re-examine accepted views and question their own experience. Finally, they need to be able to articulate their own personal views on behalf of others, much the way that a professional critic may pass judgment.

Although Parsons insists that these stages are not necessarily age related, we can assume that most of our students fall within the stages three through five and that with any given piece of art or literature they will respond at one critical level or another. They are likely to waver between being simply appreciative and analytical in their responses to most works, but the level at which they respond will not be the same for all works. Even though they might be ready to respond at the Appreciation Stage after reading Faulkner's "A Rose for Emily," for example, they might not be able to grasp T. S. Eliot's "Gerontian" in the same way. In the aesthetic, as in the efferent response, much depends on the reader's prior knowledge, her stance before reading, and her associations while reading. Multi-genre writing experiences help students' range of response grow as they mature in their ability to read an assortment of literary works and to accept the critical views of others.

The most important point here is that teachers should show considerable caution when insisting on activities that push students toward the highest analytical stages of writing about a work if their students are not ready for them. Students who are still in the stages of searching for meaning are not prepared to analyze style or perform a critic's review. Teachers can kill an appreciation for the reading altogether with discussions about such technicalities as meter, tone, and poetic devices if students are not willing to go beyond the Stage of Expressiveness. This will be particularly true when they understand little about a given work. Of course, as they are exposed to the arts in all their forms—music, literature, and visual arts—they will become flexible in their responses and will find themselves more in a position to form open-minded, independent judgments.

Assessment of Writing As a Response to Literature

Many written responses to literature should not be assessed. Teachers should not attempt to assess first impressions, for example, the writing that students do after reading moving passages and surprising turns of events. Journal or in-class writes that make an exploratory attempt to articulate themes, character profiles, the cultural climate of the text, and what ifs should not be assessed either. At the most, a teacher might award points for participation and effort.

For the rest, a teacher should link his rubrics to his instructional purposes for the reading. His thinking might be something like this: Is the purpose of this assignment to help students learn something about themselves and the world around them? Should it also encourage critical thinking? Or should it help students examine the alternative worlds and unfamiliar experience in the story? Perhaps it should help students recognize textual conventions—underlying patterns in the story. Although all of these potential purposes are valid, he must focus his attentions on one or two key objectives. The decision for the final paper assignment should grow out of his class' emphasis, the discussions and fragments gathered from the shorter writing exercises.

Teachers need also to think about how they can help students to grow in their interpretation of literature. Effective formal paper assignments should help students examine their own responses and their ways of thinking more fully about the cultural context of the literature and its meanings. A teacher's aim should be to help students move from an understanding of "What I Like, and Why" to "What Makes Good Literature, and Why." This is that difficult movement from the relativistic Expressiveness Stage to the more analytical Style and Form Stage, which acknowledges conventions. To make that move, students need to develop a respect for the author's cultural and historical context and an awareness of the reasons that other readers have for prizing this literature. Too often students do not understand that some interpretations are richer than others. Without an effort to take into account the unfamiliar territories of the author and other readers, students often distort the meanings of the text to reflect their own personal circumstance and needs. Students will arbitrarily assign meaning to a work by ignoring portions of the story or its context, and they justify their own interpretation with the argument that any one reader's opinion is as good as another. Although multiple readings are built into any text, two considerations are important to remember—valid interpretations should address *all* sections of the literary work and they should reflect the internal *consistency* of the text. No part of the reader's view of the book should contradict the text; nor should any part of the book be ignored. If a reading is not supported by all parts of the text, the reader must learn to adjust her interpretation to reflect the work and its cultural context. Awareness of the unified nature of a text—its internal logic—is necessary for reaching beyond a simple appreciation of it to an analysis of it. Composition is invaluable for helping students to run the length of that process, to stretch into new levels of aesthetic response. So a teacher's rubric for a response to the literature should evaluate the student's ability to grasp the whole of the process. Since every text has gaps that allow for multiple interpretations of theme, motivations of characters, and significance of plot, students should be encouraged to develop a broad assortment of interpretations as long as they are consistent with the text and the conditions under which it was written.

Quizzes that follow chapter assignments, for example, are assessed based on the key focus of the reading, and discussion may often follow about how students may recognize the key focus. Assessments of more formal assignments are likewise linked to the specifics of the instructional purpose(s) and the critical approach. For example, a paper assignment for an historical approach might suggest the following:

> Write a paper that discusses the impact of the impending war on Finney and Gene in *A Separate Peace.* Assuming that they will go into the U.S. Army, speculate where they are likely to fight. What conditions might they have to face on the home front? What might scare them the most? Where in the plot, tone, or setting does Knowles hint at these fears? To answer some of these questions you will have to do some reading about World War II. Look for a first-hand account of what it was like to fight that war (hint: there are many of these accounts on the Internet). As best you can, tie the information into a discussion of the book.

There are several things to notice about this assignment. One, that it is genre specific. It takes one aspect of the critical approach and offers guidance for writing the paper. Two, that it suggests criteria for assessment. Three, that it offers ways of thinking about the topic and multiple strategies for tackling a particular type of analysis. Here is a rubric for student use that grows out of that assignment. Note that points are awarded at the end of each stage of the process:

> *Topic Exploration*–speculate on the conditions of WWII and how the characters might have behaved as soldiers. You will be awarded points on effort and a willingness to try new methods for generating ideas (looping, journaling, diary writing, clustering, letters from the home front, etc.). Hand these paragraphs in before you start your research. Below each exploratory paragraph,

make a list of the things you would like to look up when you go to the library or the Internet.

Research–you need two or three historical documents that might help you write your paper. Points will be awarded on the effort that you put into looking for these documents, their appropriateness for the assignment, and punctuality. If you cannot find the information, write a description of your methods, where you have looked, and why you think you have not found anything.

First draft–you need a reasonably coherent minimum number of pages and at least three critiques by other readers (family members and classmates). Points will be awarded on the effort you put into making it a readable piece, the number of readers you have asked to critique your draft, and punctuality.

Final draft–you need a polished paper that is considered ready for a final grade. The paper will be judged on the following: a well-developed idea that grows out of your research and its meaning for understanding the characters, organization, clarity, and polished mechanics. Additional points will be awarded for the appropriateness of your source material and accurate citations. Please include photocopies of your sources.

This is just a sample. Of course, more drafts could be included and other criteria could be added or substituted. To develop an adequate tool for assessment, the teacher has to know what she wants to accomplish with the assignment, and her rubric should reward students for the tasks that meet those instructional goals. Furthermore, the rubric should be genre specific, tailored to meet the specific reading and writing tasks.

Points to Remember

In this chapter we have discussed the potential for writing assignments to enhance the student's reading experience or to kill it. We have seen that a productive assignment begins with clear teaching objectives and an awareness of the reading process. Working with those givens, the teacher has a variety of critical approaches; each one may be undergirded by writing assignments. For example, it is an effective strategy to subdivide longer texts into "meaningful chunks" and to assign writing that supports those subsections. Teachers have a variety of writing strategies and critical approaches for making assignments. Crucial, however, is an understanding of how the timing for the writing assignments, the selection for the appropriate critical approach and the choices for writing activities can determine a great deal about how the students understand a piece of literature and how much they appreciate it. As for developing composition skills, it is an axiom that the more one writes, the more one is able to write well, so frequent and steady writing assignments that accompany reading will hone our students' ability to write clearly and meaningfully. A quick list of tips for writing effective writing assignments in response to literature appears in Figure 6.4 Guidelines for Assigning Writing.

FIGURE 6.4 *Guidelines for Assigning Writing*

1. WRITE CLEAR INSTRUCTIONS

   Focus the objectives.

   Tie them to the concepts and ideas at hand.

   Base criteria on rhetorical genre and style (e.g. newspaper writing, argument essays, comparison, cause/effect, persuasion, journal, etc.).

   Suggest sometimes how to structure the essay.

   Specify length range.

   Complete them with suggestions about how it will be assessed.

2. LAY OUT CLEAR RUBRICS

   Explain where the emphasis is placed.

   Tell how points may be assigned.

3. PROVIDE SCAFFOLDING FOR WRITING ASSIGNMENTS SUCH AS
   - creative writing of any sort—but especially poetry, short stories, plays
   - newspaper writing—editorials, features, news writing, columns
   - research papers—citations, logical argument, rhetorical structure, note taking, advice for avoiding plagiarism

4. ALLOW MULTIPLE DRAFTING FOR LONGER ASSIGNMENTS INCLUDING
   - opportunities for brainstorming, multiple drafting, peer critiquing, and polishing with grammar instruction
   - clear instructions for criteria for peer critiquing

For Further Reading

Andrasick, Kathleen Dudden. *Opening Texts: Using Writing to Teach Literature.* Portsmouth, NH: Heinemann, 1990.

Dornan, Reade, Lois Matz Rosen, and Marilyn Wilson. *Multiple Voices, Multiple Texts: Reading in the Secondary Content Areas.* Portsmouth, NH: Heinemann Boynton/Cook, 1997.

Dunning, Stephen and Stafford William, *Getting the Knack.* Urbana, IL: National Council of Teachers of English, 1992.

Fagin, Larry. *The List Poem: A Guide to Teaching and Writing Catalog Verse.* New York: Teachers and Writers Collaborative, 1992.

Koch, Kenneth. *Rose, Where Did You Get That Red?* New York: Vintage Books, 1993.

Padgett, Ron. *The Teachers and Writers Handbook of Poetic Forms.* New York: Teachers and Writers Collaborative, 1992.

Tchudi, Stephen N. and Diana Mitchell. *Explorations in the Teaching of English.* 3rd ed. New York: Harper/Collins, 1989.

Teasley, Alan B. and Ann Wilder. *Reel Conversations: Reading Films With Young Adults.* Portsmouth, NH: Heinemann Boynton/Cook, 1978.

7

Assessing, Evaluating, Grading, and Responding to Student Writing

Writing teachers carry student papers with them wherever they go. We three authors have marked student writing in doctors' and dentists' waiting rooms, airports, conference hotel rooms, coffee shops, automobile service centers, and deck chairs around the pool. We identify fellow National Council of Teachers of English conference-goers waiting for airport taxis by their book bags bulging with student papers. We commiserate with one another over marathon marking sessions into the early hours of the morning. We spend Thanksgiving or Memorial Day haunted by the papers waiting for us once the holiday celebration ends.

For most of us, grading is the part of teaching we like the least. It is labor-intensive work without much of a payoff other than one more grade in a gradebook. Giving Joe yet another C for a paper he labored over while Amos gets another A for a paper he barely had to revise does little to help either student become a better writer. In fact, it probably does more harm by stifling creativity in those who are afraid to jeopardize the high grades they need to please parents or get into college, while instilling hopelessness in struggling writers whose efforts result in a low grade. Grading also conflicts with the role of supportive, constructive writing coach we assume in the classroom. Having nurtured rough drafts with conferences, suggestions, peer group critiques, and editing workshops, we now find ourselves in the role of judge and evaluator, putting a grade on the very paper we helped coach to completion.

Peter Elbow points out other "contraries" in evaluating writing:

- The profession has no accepted definitions or criteria for what "good writing" really consists of.
- The process of grading and commenting is necessarily subjective since our individual tastes, our moods, and our feelings about the individual personalities of our students cannot help but play a role in our judgments.

• Even apart from accuracy of judgment, it's not clear what kind of commenting actually helps the student to write better next time. Recent research throws doubt on the efficacy of much teacher commentary (161).

Evaluating and grading student papers is a problematic issue for all these reasons. Teachers often tell us, "I really like to read and respond to my students' writing, if only I didn't have to grade it." Yet our observations of the grading phenomenon in writing classes echo those of researcher Paul Diederich, who says that the classes he visits are "fantastically over-evaluated," with teachers "piling [grades] up like squirrels gathering nuts" (2).

Although we admit that we have no magical means for eradicating grading or resolving its many dilemmas, we've learned methods for minimizing its stress for both our students and ourselves. School districts, administrators, parents, even students require grades on report cards in addition to scores on external assessments. But good writing classrooms can downplay the emphasis on grades, focusing instead on response and evaluation strategies that support writing growth. These strategies will be the focus of much of this chapter. After defining several terms that are often confused and conflated, we will discuss methods for responding to student writing, various approaches to writing evaluation, including alternatives to grading every piece students write, rubrics, grading scales, and portfolios. The chapter will conclude with a section on the politics of high-stakes writing assessment and issues of equity in evaluating writing from speakers of non-standard dialects and English as a Second Language.

This chapter addresses the following NCATE/NCTE standards. Candidates will be prepared to meet the following standards after reading this chapter.

2.4 Integrate into their teaching and student assessment, practices designed to assist students in developing habits of critical thinking and judgment;

3.1.4 Demonstrate a respect for and a deep understanding of diversity in language use, patterns, and dialects across cultures, ethnic groups, geographic regions and social roles and show consistent attention to accommodating such diversity;

3.2.5 Demonstrate knowledge of language structure and conventions in creating and critiquing print and non-print texts of their own and their students;

3.7.1 Use major sources of research and theory related to English language arts consistently to support their teaching decisions;

4.7 Engage students often in meaningful discussions for the purposes of interpreting and evaluating ideas presented through oral, written, and/or visual forms;

4.12 Integrate assessment consistently into instruction:

- Use a variety of formal and informal assessment activities and instruments to evaluate processes and products;
- Create regular opportunities to employ a variety of means to interpret and report assessment methods and results to students, administrators, parents, and other audiences.

Terminology Defined: Responding, Assessing, Evaluating, Grading

In his introduction to *Alternatives to Grading Student Writing,* Stephen Tchudi makes a useful distinction among the many terms used when one talks about writing assessment. Moving down a scale of four descriptors—*Response, Assessment, Evaluation, Grading*—he characterizes these according to "decreasing degrees of freedom in reacting to and evaluating student work" (xii).

Responding to writing, commenting on papers at any stage of the writing process during conferences or on the papers themselves, is the most open of these terms. With no necessity for formal evaluation, the teacher is free to comment as reader ("Your story reminded me of my own experiences learning to drive a car"), as responder ("I like the way you described your cranky boss"), or as constructive critic ("Can you give me an example of what you mean here?"). As we've shown in earlier chapters of this book, positive response, good questions, and constructive suggestions can be extremely helpful to the writer. Responding to writing puts teachers in the roles they like best: responsive readers, supportive coaches, editors, collaborators, fellow-writers. Evaluation is implicit as we make unavoidably subjective decisions about what to say, how to say it, and where to focus our questions and suggestions; but our primary concern tends to be on communication with the writer, not evaluation. Much of the paper-marking described in the opening paragraph of this chapter is response-centered.

Assessment is the broadest of the next three terms. When we assess, we collect data with the purpose of describing what's going on. Thus we assess the success of our writing program or of an individual assignment we made to the class by asking, "Is it working?" and seeking demonstrable evidence that it is or is not. We include all types of data-gathering under the broad term assessment: essay tests, papers, informal observations, portfolios, etc. Assessment may start with criteria to guide data-collection, such as the goals a teacher sets for eighth grade writing workshop; or criteria may evolve as the data-gatherer asks questions such as "How did this writing assignment turn out?" Collecting and organizing this information may make it possible for others—parents, teachers, administrators, or students—to use it for evaluation purposes. According to Tchudi, however, assessment tends to be descriptive rather than judgmental (xiv), although we have seen the term used to subsume both concepts and even to include evaluation and grading.

Evaluation narrows the field to making judgments based on explicit or implicit criteria. Evaluating writing does not necessarily mean grading it, but it does mean comparing the piece to standards and making judgments on its effectiveness. Readers of student writing can act on these judgments in the constructive ways recommended throughout this book or render negative judgments ("Your paper is disorganized and your arguments are weak"). We differentiate two types of evaluation—formative and summative. *Formative evaluation* is for the purpose of giving feedback to help the learner/writer improve. Peer response groups and conferences over drafts give formative evaluation. They apply criteria for the assignment or for good writing in general and offer feedback and suggestions to the writer. We like to think of formative writing evaluation as "forming," influencing, and shaping the piece at hand as well as future writing. *Summative evaluation,* on the other hand, "sums up" what the writer has done and gives a grade. It usually finalizes work on the paper, presenting the student with a comparative judgment on the quality of the finished product. Successful writing classrooms provide students with as much formative evaluation as possible, reserving summative evaluation for a few selected pieces or for the entire output of a student's work presented in a portfolio.

Grading is the narrowest form of responding to student writing. Its goal is entirely judgmental and summative, reducing the teacher's freedom to a limited number of alternatives: A, B, C, D, E or F with their accompanying pluses and minuses. To quote one very frustrated young writer: "What does a D+ mean?" Teachers who rely too much on grades to convey their evaluation of students' writing are not communicating much that's of value to a developing writer. Grades may be a required part of teaching, but we must once again repeat that successful teachers of writing keep them to a minimum. Future sections of this chapter will present several alternatives to grading writing.

Varieties of Evaluation and Response

Teachers can use three different kinds of response and formative evaluation in the writing classroom: self-evaluation, peer response, and teacher response.

Self-Evaluation

If students are to become self-reliant revisers and editors of their own writing, self-evaluations are a good way to invite a more objective look at their own writing. When students have completed first drafts, a few minutes spent on self-evaluation can be extremely beneficial before working with peer groups or holding a conference with the teacher. A general self-evaluation form like the one below guides their thinking, preparing students to discuss their paper with readers.

Writer Self-Evaluation Form

1. My purpose in writing about this subject is to

2. I want my reader to

3. I feel this way about my paper now

   This is what I like about it:

   This is what I think still needs more work:

   These are the questions I want to ask a reader about my paper:

For more specific, detailed, self-analysis of a work-in-progress, teachers can use a self-evaluation guide based on criteria for the paper and writing skills taught in mini-lessons. The following example of a self-evaluation guide focuses the student on analyzing the paper for a central thesis, development, organization, and language.

Self-Evaluation Guide for Rough Draft

		YES	NO
*	Is the thesis (purpose) of this essay clear to my audience?	____	____
**	Do I develop my thesis adequately?	____	____
	Is each of my ideas illustrated with several details or examples?	____	____
	Do all points relate to my thesis?	____	____
	Does each paragraph build upon the preceding one?	____	____
	Is there a beginning, middle, and end?	____	____
	Does the introduction arouse interest?	____	____
	Is my language appropriate to the audience?	____	____
	Have I accomplished what I set out to do in this essay?	____	____

* What is the thesis of my paper? It is:

** How do I develop my thesis? Here are the examples or points I cover in developing my topic:

What reservations do I have about this paper, if any? Are there areas I am unsure about? What questions do I want to ask a reader? Here are my questions:

What do I like best about my own paper?

Another useful self-evaluation guide is a list of multiple questions students can ask themselves as they re-read and evaluate their own drafts. Teachers can tailor these to cover general features of good writing or reinforce concepts taught as part of the writer's craft. Nancie Atwell uses a handout entitled "Having a Writing Conference with Yourself" in which students ask themselves fifty-eight questions grouped under the following six categories. One example is included from each category.

- Questions about purpose: "Does the writing answer the question, 'So what?' "
- Questions about information: "Have I told enough? Have I explained each part well enough that a reader will know what I mean, every step of the way?"
- Questions about leads: "Does the lead engage readers and bring them right into the theme, purpose, tone, action, or the mind of the main character?"
- Questions about conclusions: "How do I want my reader to feel and think at the end? Will this conclusion do it?"
- Questions about titles: "Is the title a 'grabber'?"
- Questions about style: "Have I used strong, precise verbs?" (247–249)

Teachers can design similar sets of questions for students to use in conferences with themselves, perhaps starting with general questions early in the semester, then adding new categories as students are taught additional writing skills throughout the term.

Peer Response

Earlier chapters have given guidelines and methods for using peer evaluation in the classroom. We might only add here that once students learn to work effectively together over drafts, peer response can dramatically reduce the teacher's paper-marking load while giving students a great deal of helpful reader feedback. In addition, the papers teachers read tend to be better because they've gone through a peer review process, which makes commenting easier, more pleasurable, and faster. Research also suggests that the peer reader benefits as much as the writer receiving the feedback. Over time, readers begin to internalize the characteristics of writing they discuss in peer response groups, applying these to their own self-evaluations and subsequent revisions (Resh). The combination of self-evaluation and peer response can be a powerful means for helping young writers develop independent revising skills.

Think/Write #1
What has your experience been with peer response groups in this class or other writing classes you have taken? Were these groups helpful or not? Why? What worked? What didn't? Were you able to be helpful to the other writers in your group? Write about what you learned from participating in peer response groups.

With Pen in Hand: Commenting on Student Papers

One-on-one conferences are certainly the best way to respond to students' writing, but this isn't always possible. Secondary teachers, who may have from 125 to 180 students in five or six classes, may find that an individual conference with every student over every draft, desirable as it may be, is unrealistic. Even with many in-class conferences over papers, teachers usually need to take some papers home to read more closely, to comment on final products, or to grade.

Some Mechanics of Responding. We do not recommend a red pen under any circumstances simply because of its negative connotations. In fact, a pencil works best because a comment can be erased if the teacher changes her mind or wishes to re-phrase what she's already written (even teacher comments sometimes need revision!). Copious commenting on every single item a teacher notices does more to frustrate a student than enlighten. Research has never been able to prove that numerous responses are more effective than a few well-chosen responses and specific questions or constructive suggestions (Rosen 1983, 60–65). Some teachers prefer to make comments in the margins or at the end of the paper or both. Some teachers write comments on a separate sheet of paper, viewing writing, especially final products, as a piece of art that must not be desecrated. Others like to comment orally on a cassette tape. If the school is well endowed with computers and students have ready access to e-mail, teachers can type a response to each paper on the computer to print out and attach to the paper or send on e-mail. These choices are purely a matter of preference. Teachers might try them all to see what works best for them and their students.

Higher Order Concerns and Lower Order Concerns. Responding to first draft writing is considerably different from commenting on revised work or final, finished pieces. Initial drafts benefit most from comments on what we consider Higher Order Concerns (HOCs): ideas, information, focus, organization, transitions, coherence, logic, examples, details, leads, conclusions, purpose, audience, and the answer to the question "So what?" Attention to these elements of good writing must come first before the writer or the teacher begins to deal with what we consider Lower Order Concerns (LOCs): punctuation, spelling, grammatical and mechanical correctness, word usage, sentence construction, and style. Although equally important to the success of the final product, LOCs are not worth commenting on until the content is fully revised. We would caution teachers not to do both at the same time with works-in-progress because it gives students the false message that everything is of equal importance and must be worked on simultaneously. Because writing is such a complex process, developing writers learn best when they focus on one stage of writing at a time. Teacher comments should do the same. The list of questions in Chapter Three for conferences over first drafts can be equally useful for written comments. Also see the section in Chapter Four entitled "Mark Student Papers Wisely: Abandon the Error-Hunt" for further suggestions on responding to mechanical and grammatical errors on student papers.

If grades are given on final drafts and the paper has received adequate response while in process, the teacher can comment on improvements from earlier drafts, progress the student is making, or give additional praise for work well done. When further revision is permitted, even though a grade was given, the teacher can continue to make suggestions. Some teachers consider all work open to continued revision, gearing their comments in that direction.

The Value of Praise. Students are more likely to remember what teachers praise (and do it again in future papers) than they are to value comments on problems in the paper. "I like the way you. . . ." or "Good word here" or even just a star in the margin at good spots in a paper can go a long way toward encouraging better writing and committed writers. The implication of praise is that the writer's ideas have value, making the paper worth working on. Praise for the good parts interspersed with questions, suggestions, and reader response comments, guide revision so the student doesn't feel at a loss for what else to do with the paper.

Think/Write #2
Examine the comments teachers have written on several of your own papers. If possible, select papers written for more than one teacher. Are there differences in the comments written by different teachers? What kinds of comments predominate for each teacher? What is your response to these comments in light of the information given in the sections above? Write a description of the kinds of comments you see on these papers and then consider what each teacher's purpose might have been in commenting as he or she did.

Respond More, Grade Less: Guidelines for Evaluating Writing

Not all pieces of writing need to be read or graded by the teacher. Much of the writing students do can be thought of as practice just as musicians and athletes practice many hours for special performances. Students should be doing roughly two to three times more writing than the teacher reads and grades, including prewriting, jottings, rough drafts, unfinished pieces, journal writing, and informal writing-to-learn activities. If a teacher has time to read and respond to everything students write, the students are not writing enough (or the teacher is headed for burnout!). Teachers sometimes complain, "Students won't write unless I read it all," but that's because the teacher has set up the expectation that writing is only worth doing if it's marked and that the teacher's response is the only one of value. Students especially need to understand that grades are not the only reward for writing; satisfaction should come from many sources, including an increasing sense of writing competence and a growing body of one's own writing.

Here are some guidelines to consider when setting up an evaluation system for a classroom writing program.

- The central goal of every writing program should be to help students become better writers. The more a teacher focuses students on writing development rather than grades, the more likely students are to achieve this goal.

- Most of the time, grading finalizes work on a piece of writing; therefore, if grades are to be given for individual papers, this should be reserved for selected pieces that have undergone extensive work on revision and final proofreading and polishing.

- Evaluation and grading should take into account not just the final product—the paper or papers the student has written—but also the student's writing process, growth as a writer, and commitment to his own writing development. For this reason, many writing teachers work with their students to set goals for the writing course in addition to individual goals for each writer. Grading then takes into account the progress the student has made toward course and individual goals.

• Use check-plus, check, check-minus for informal writing. A check-plus indicates especially good work, a check equals competent work that meets the requirements for the assignment, and a check-minus indicates poor or incomplete work. When report card grades must be given, a string of these can be averaged: so many check-pluses for an A, so many for a B, etc.

• Give participation credit or points for completed work such as free writing, journal entries, and reading responses. If students use these in class for small or whole group sharing or for further work on the topic, they can be stored in the student's writing portfolio without any further evaluation.

• Involve students in the evaluation process as much as possible by setting criteria with the class for papers and assignments and having students do individual goal-setting, self-evaluations, reflections on papers, and reports on progress toward goals. Whenever possible, let students choose the papers to revise and the ones to be graded.

• Use rubrics and grading guides to make criteria clear, speed up the grading process, and give students specific feedback on their writing. Rubrics will be discussed in fuller detail later in this chapter.

Alternatives to Grading Every Paper

Selective Grading. Kari Molter's writing workshop class at Kearsley High School in Michigan required students to complete one paper each week. Sometimes topics were assigned and other times students were free to choose their own topics. The room was full of student writing anthologies from previous classes that students could use for inspiration. Class sessions began with a daily mini-lesson and included all the other elements of a writing workshop. Kari held conferences with students over topics, read drafts in class, provided opportunities for peer response groups, frequent sharing sessions, and classroom publication. Every fourth week, students selected one piece from the previous three weeks to revise, edit, proofread, and polish for grading. Fifty percent of the student's grade for the class was based on the graded papers, fifty percent on the completion of all the other writing collected in a portfolio. Kari read and responded to everything her students wrote, but she only graded the piece completed every fourth week.

Point System. To de-emphasize grading and focus on productivity, writing teachers can use a point system in which students get points for the satisfactory completion of various writing tasks. For example, Figure 7.1 is the point system for one marking period's work in a middle school writing workshop. The maximum points possible for each item are specified and the left column leaves spaces for the actual number of points the student received. Students receive full credit for such items as setting weekly goals and keeping their folder well organized if this is done regularly as required. Other items, such as the descriptive paper and two writing workshop pieces selected for revision and editing, may receive points based

FIGURE 7.1 ***Writing Folder Requirements Based on a Point System***

Points Received	*Points Possible*	
______	(10 pts)	Weekly Writing Goals
______	(10 pts)	Weekly Writing Folder Well-Organized
______	(30 pts)	School Publication Entry, Final Copy
______	(50 pts)	Five Writer's Journal Entries, One Page Each
		List Topic on the Line:
		1. ______________________
		2. ______________________
		3. ______________________
		4. ______________________
		5. ______________________
______	(20 pts)	List of Writing Skills I Can Do
______	(100 pts)	Descriptive Paper
______	(80 pts)	Poetry Book Using Eight Different Styles
		Title of Book: ________________
______	(80 pts)	First Revised and Edited Writing Workshop Piece
		Title: ________________
______	(20 pts)	Peer Conference Over Draft
		Reader's Name: ________________
______	(80 pts)	Second Revised and Edited Writing Workshop Piece
		Title: ________________
______	(20 pts)	Peer Conference Over Draft
		Reader's Name: ________________

This Workshop Folder is worth 500 points! Work very hard!
Extra Credit/Or Any Additional Work

1. ____________________	4. ____________________
2. ____________________	5. ____________________
3. ____________________	6. ____________________

(Based on writing folder requirements used by Laurie Lee, Imlay City Middle School, Michigan.)

on a rubric. Any work not completed satisfactorily or not done at all receives few or no points. The final grade for the marking period depends on the number of points the student has earned.

Contract Grading. This is another system teachers can use to avoid grading everything students write and also to give students some control over their grades.

Students are given a list of all the work they must do for an A, B, C, or below. Students "contract" to do the work required for the grade each would like to receive. Quality control can be a problem with this system (as well as with a point system) unless the teacher makes criteria for satisfactory work explicit. Undermotivated students can also take advantage of the system by contracting for less than they are capable of.

Achievement Grading. Adkison and Tchudi advocate what they call "achievement grading," in which both quality and quantity are taken into account. Students who produce a wider range of work with greater depth receive higher final grades although all work is graded credit/no credit. Unacceptable work can be redone until it is deemed "creditable." They describe it this way:

> The requirements for credit are stated in terms of *tasks* or *assignments* to be completed. The criteria for credit usually specify both the amount of work to be done (quantity) and the kind of thoroughness and polish required for acceptance (quality). The teacher may be the sole determiner of tasks and criteria, but usually students are involved in the negotiation of both (194–195).

Rooted in both the point system and contract grading, achievement grading seems to recognize and reward exceptional work while avoiding the necessity for grading individual assignments.

The Not-So-Simple Act of Putting Grades on Papers

The act of giving students grades for finished work begins long before they hand in their papers. The teacher must think about how to grade those papers at the time she is initially designing her assignment because most of the grade will hinge on how well the student has met the lesson's objectives. She must decide, is the goal of the assignment to demonstrate knowledge? Then most of the points will be awarded to content. Is the goal of the assignment student self-expression or personal exploration? Then she may simply award points for completing the writing. Is the assignment's primary objective to develop a student's writing skills? Then she has to decide how much emphasis to place on each phase of the writing process or on metacognition, that is, the student's ability to think about the choices he is making while writing. Here are suggestions for getting started on grading that pile of papers that is bound to feel heavy and oppressive once it is sitting on the desk:

1. List learning objectives for the lesson in descending order of importance.

2. Write out the assignment for students, especially if it will take them several days to complete.

3. Draw up a rubric, that is, a grading scale based on the particulars of the assignment as you have described it. Pay most attention to whether you are grading the process or the product. If you are grading only the final product, meaning the student has only one chance to write it, then completion of the assignment, punctuality, and judgment of a specific body of knowledge or skill will figure into the rubric. The best rubrics are specific to the assignment and the particulars of the content might be listed as well. If grading for process, then you will have to decide how to award points for various parts of the writing process—particularly the student's use of invention, the drafting, and the final, polished paper. More on setting rubrics below.

4. Add the rubric to the written description of the assignment and hand it out.

5. Keep reminding students what is most important in this paper.

6. After collecting the papers, read about half of them. Carefully keeping your rubric in mind, sort the papers into piles as you read. Avoid setting grades on the papers at first. Instead, write reflective comments and ask questions. You will begin to see emerging patterns in the ways that your students have interpreted the assignment—what constitutes an "A" paper and the trends that the average students are setting. After establishing a performance profile for that particular set of papers, you can begin to assign grades and finish the rest of them rather quickly. This part of the process will go even more quickly the next time you make the same assignment, but it is our experience that every class will respond somewhat differently to an assignment depending on the group's psychology, their prior knowledge, aptitude, and enthusiasm for the class.

The student's grade thus rides on the teacher's emphasis in the lesson plans, the teacher's rubric, as well as the student's relative standing in the class' understanding of that particular assignment.

Writing Rubrics

When evaluating student papers for classroom use, teachers may choose between two common approaches used for diagnostic purposes. The first is *analytic scoring,* which measures the ability of the writer to meet certain established criteria such as mechanics, focus, organization, and elaboration on a given writing assignment. The criteria are usually laid out in a rubric, or rating scale. The second is *primary trait scoring,* which rates the writer's ability to perform a given compositional task in relation to the abilities of other writers accomplishing the same task (Applebee 11). We will offer examples of both kinds of assignments and scoring approaches here.

A typical assignment in an English class might be to ask students to argue for or against dieting. The teacher might plan to emphasize the writing process for developing the writer's point of view on the topic. She will then set her rubric, or grading scale, so that it emphasizes the various phases of the writing process. She might also wait until the student finds his own focus and has an opportunity to write all the drafts necessary to say what he hopes to say before she finally evaluates the process. Following Donald Murray's advice, "Each new draft, of course, is counted as equal to a new paper" (6), she will wait till the final draft to award any points. At that time she might allot additional points for other completed work and student effort made along the way. The emphasis for the assignment is thus on meaning making and personal quest as well as the writer's process. The generic rubric for the process of writing a research paper, for example, could look something like the one below. Note how nearly one-third of the points are awarded to the process of discovery and research; roughly another third of the points are based on getting the basic argument down and clear and only a little more than a third of the total points are awarded to the polished paper. Items are weighted for their importance to the process. The rubric is based on a 100-point scale, which makes the final grade easy to convert to a percentage.

Sample Rubric for the Research Paper Using the Writing Process (100-Point Maximum)

Invention exploration using various methods for topic discovery (5 points for each method explored)	10	5			
Research (5 points for each type of source explored in detail—library, interview, Internet, experiment, etc.)	10	5			
Minimum number of note cards	5	4	3	2	1
Extra research effort	5	4	3	2	1
Exploratory Draft(s)					
Strong Focus	5	4	3	2	1
Clear, well reasoned argument	5	4	3	2	1
Minimum number of pages	5	4	3	2	1
Critiqued by class member	5	4	3	2	1
Handed in on time	5	4	3	2	1
Final draft					
Well developed idea	5	4	3	2	1
Logical argument	5	4	3	2	1
Organized	5	4	3	2	1
Supporting evidence	5	4	3	2	1
Effective use of language	5	4	3	2	1
Polished mechanics	5	4	3	2	1
Conclusion that pulls ideas together	5	4	3	2	1
Neatness	5	4	3	2	1
Complete and accurate bibliography and citations	5	4	3	2	1

This is a rubric that employs analytic scoring. The purpose of this rubric is to allot points for the key aspects of the composition—soundness of content and thinking, development of argument, attention to style and conventions, voice, and audience. It lays open the grading process for students and it sends them the message that these are the most important features of writing. Final distribution of points may vary from assignment to assignment, according to the lesson's objectives, of course, but many of the rubric's criteria—clarity of focus, style, use of conventions, effort in the writing process, etc.—will be repeated for all sorts of papers. There will, of course, be plenty of variation as well. If the rubric is written for a short story, for example, points will be awarded to creativity, plot development, and description, instead of formal organization. Many categories will remain in the rubric; for example, attention to supporting detail, common sense logic in the piece, care about language conventions, and evidence of the writing process.

The Generic Rubric. As important as the writing process is for promoting discovery and the intellectual rewards of language play, teachers often have other, equally legitimate purposes for assigning writing. For example, students taking quizzes may have only one chance to write about what they know. Practically speaking, *most* of their everyday assignments are likely to depend on a one-shot attempt to say what they need to say. Regardless of the nature of the assignment, rubrics are needed for grading most of their writings. The spread of points for the assignment will, of course, shift from process to form and/or content. The sample rubric below demonstrates how an expository essay might be graded:

Final Piece Evaluation (25 points)

Ideas and Content (Total 7 points)

______ Focus—clear, central idea, makes sense to reader (2)

______ Logic—argument sound, without contradiction (2)

______ Details—supportive and accurate (3)

Organization (Total 5 points)

______ Piece has clear beginning, middle, and end (2)

______ Flows from beginning to end—transitions are effective for reader (2)

______ Conclusion does more than simply summarize the arguments (1)

Style (Total 5 points)

______ Good lead—draws reader in (1)

______ Title—fits, makes sense (1)

______ The voice of the writer shows in word choices and sentence structure (3)

Conventions (Total 8 points)

______ Punctuation and capitalization (2)

______ Spelling (2)

______ Grammar (2)

______ Neatness (2)

Note how many points this rubric shares in common with the one above for the research paper. After students have used rubrics for a few weeks, they should begin to recognize how many of these elements are repeated from assignment to assignment and how they should allocate their time and energies to the most emphasized elements in future assignments. Eventually, students should also be able to design rubrics of their own that score for the typical features of writing. Before they begin each new assignment, the class might talk about the categories that should be included in evaluating it and how to distribute the assignment's points with the appropriate emphases. In the discussions, they will learn more about how to describe the best papers and how to write to those standards.

Example of How an Essay Might be Graded. In Figures 7.2 and 7.3, we have given you a sample student essay and a scoring guide from the State of Michigan Revised

FIGURE 7.2 ***A Model of Assessment: A Student Writing with Scoring Guide***

The Test's Writing Prompt for Session #2
In dealing with people who have wronged others, some choose justice; some, revenge; some, mercy. Write a paper in which you examine how this choice affects the people involved in the dispute.

Student Sample
Individuals. Single beings. Seperate entities. All these words are words I use to describe the people of this planet. No two people have the exact same experiences in the world; therefore we are all different. I ask you, the reader, "Am I wrong?" No? Well then how can we have a standardized justice system or let disputes fall into the hands of other people? We can't because it's unfair. Justice for one person isn't the same for another person. Your principles aren't the same as mine, therefore my idea of justice is most likely nothing like yours and thus we would be hard-pressed for a solution if a dispute came up.

I was born in Michigan, ten pounds and seven ounces, at exactly 6:28 in the PM. I've had many different haircuts, pets, houses, clothes, and I am not 5'9" tall, weigh 135 pounds and have a 3.5% fat to overall body weight ratio. How many people can say the exact same thing? None. I am a completely seperate entity from all life that has ever existed before. No one has the exact same philosophies I do and I am proud of that.

If you read the other essay I wrote about my definition of justice, you'd know I believe that you get what is deserved of you. If you are in a competition and you finish first you should get the prize fair and square because you are better than the rest. If someone cheated and won then they would be denied the prize. Why? Because to cheat you have to break the rules. The rules of what? The rules of the contest, not the rules of justice. The "justice" is the actual winner receiving the award, not a cheater. The winner worked harder overall to win, therefore the justice is the winner receiving it.

Chances are your (the reader) definition is a more classical definition and you believe that this a rather silly venture of your time without much merit. But then again, thats just your opinion.

By permission of the Michigan Educational Assessment Program (MEAP) High School Test, April 1998, accessed on-line January 2002.

FIGURE 7.3 ***Scoring Guide for Communication Arts: Writing***

SESSION 2

4 The writing is engaging, original, clear, and focused; ideas and content are richly supported by details and examples where appropriate. Control of organization and transitions move the reader easily through the text. The voice and tone are authentic and compelling. Control of language and skillful use of writing conventions contribute to the effect of the presentation.

3 The writing is generally clear, focused, and well developed; examples and details support ideas and content where appropriate. The presentation is generally coherent, and its organizational structure is functional. The voice, tone, diction, and sentence structure support meaning. Use of writing conventions is not distracting.

2 The writing has some focus and support; ideas and content may be developed with limited details and examples. The presentation shows some evidence of structure, but it may be artificial or only partially successful. The tone may be inappropriate or the voice uneven. Sentence structure and diction are generally correct but rudimentary. Limited control of writing conventions may interfere with meaning some of the time.

1 The writing has little focus and development; ideas and content are supported by few, if any, details and examples. There is little discernible shape or direction. The writing demonstrates no control over voice and tone. Faulty sentence structure and limited vocabulary interfere with understanding. Limited control of writing conventions (such as spelling, grammar/usage, capitalization, punctuation, and/or indentation) makes the writing difficult to read.

From Michigan Educational Assessment Program (MEAP) High School Test Revised Model of Assessment, 1998.

Model of the Assessment for Writing in 1998. The state readers correctly assigned it a score of #3. Reading the criteria in the Scoring Guide for each of the categories (#4 is the highest score) in Session 2, we can see how the student earned that score. The writing is clearly engaging and has a strong voice. The young author has a very clear sense of him or herself and of the reader. The author speaks out to us readers and draws us in by challenging us to think about our own definitions of individualism and the term "justice for all." The author's details of what constitutes an individual are compelling. They make us take the argument seriously because we connect with the writer. The presentation is, indeed, generally coherent. There is strong control of language and sentence structure. The essay also follows a logical structure and paragraphing and it exhibits a reasonably strong grasp of writing conventions, even though it has a misspelled word here or there and a clause that should probably be attached to an independent clause.

Just as important, this writing sample is missing a fully developed argument that connects up all the ideas from paragraph to paragraph. The first paragraph takes a stand against a standardized justice system because we are all different, the second paragraph provides evidence of how we are all different, and the third paragraph argues that we get what we deserve. The writer has omitted the transitions that would guide the reader from point to point. The essay also needs a stronger concluding paragraph that could pull the whole argument together. The argument as a whole is inherently sound, but the writer has to make it clear to the reader.

Think/Write #3

Did you agree with the authors' evaluation of the student sample? Why or why not? Bring a middle school or high school paper to class and apply the rubric drawn up by the State of Michigan. Meet with other students and discuss how you evaluated the paper. Where are the most difficult points of agreement?

Tailored Rubrics. As one can see from the rubrics above, it is easy to set up one-size-fits-all criteria with some variation from assignment to assignment. But there are other approaches as well. Primary trait scoring rates the writer's ability to perform a given compositional task in relation to the abilities of other writers accomplishing the same task. The key to a successful rubric for primary trait scoring is to reflect the specifics of content and genre so that student writing is shaped by the generic requirements of that assignment. Composition professor Charles R. Cooper argues persuasively for genre-centered instruction through which students examine the strategies and features that each genre uses. When Cooper defines the genres, he does not restrict his definition to Standard English class genres such as poetry, descriptive essays, or narrative writing. He is including more specialized kinds of writing such as reports, case studies, explanations, job applications, thank-you notes, essay tests, and the many other situations or occasions that we have for writing in a literate society. Cooper makes the case that we should "broaden and deepen this education [of genre awareness] if students are to learn to write a wide range of genres that will then be available to them for learning, civic participation, and work" (Cooper and Odell 27). One example (not Cooper's) might be a rubric for news writing. When a class is asked to draft a typical news report on a recent event for broadcast on their local radio station, the rubric might look something like this (point values have been omitted):

> The report covered the essential who, what, when, where, and whys of the story;
>
> The event was reported accurately;
>
> The language of the news report used phrases typical of that station's broadcasts;
>
> The news report was no longer than the average story at the top of the hour;
>
> The sign-off used the station's standard format for reporters;
>
> A paragraph followed the news story that included the following details—the name of the station, the intended audience for the story, and a short description of their broadcast style that would lead to choices about language in the report, length of story, and sign-off format.

Notice how the rubric encourages students to analyze the rhetorical strategies of the genre and asks them to devise the means for adopting the strategies. The criteria would be significantly different if the teacher asked students to analyze the radio station's news report for bias and accuracy or if she asked students to compare that station's reporting of a news event to a newspaper's coverage of the same event. The specialized rubric enables students to reach beyond the standard criteria of writing for clarity, organization, and punctuation, features that are assumed in the assignment. It concentrates, instead, on the more narrowly defined set of critical thinking processes—analysis and judgment—that conditions students to become attentive users of language and more thoughtful critics of their own writing processes. Furthermore, it teaches them how to generalize on real writing and use its lessons for those purposes.

Writing for In-class Essay Exams

A very practical genre that is often overlooked in composition classes is preparing students for writing answers to essay questions in science, history, or even English class. Nearing the end of each semester, the teacher should give students practice runs in preparation for exam week.

The most important starting point is with the test itself. Teachers in all subjects across the curriculum should help students decode key words that are likely to crop up in their area exams. In English and many other subjects in the humanities, some of these words are

Analyze—break topics into pieces or parts

Compare—show the similarities

Contrast—show the differences

Define—give a precise definition, one that is specific to the topic at hand

Describe—offer general impressions; usually not a list of physical characteristics

Discuss—show off what one knows in a brief and organized way

Evaluate—establish a hierarchy for ranking things

Explain—clarify; often it refers to a cause-and-effect sequence

Justify—defend a point of view

Outline—discuss by hitting only the high points of a topic

State—lay out an argument clearly

Summarize—state briefly, much like "Outline," but generally shorter

Trace—follow a logical sequence, usually chronological

The teacher might also check to see what features the other teachers in his school generally employ on essay tests, but here is a sample rubric:

Rubric for Answering an Essay Test Question

_______ **1.** Writer has followed the instructions (especially the key words).

_______ **2.** Writer's answer gets to the point in the first sentence or two.

_______ **3.** Writer has allowed major points in the answer to stand out by supplying white space around the items, by underlining key words and phrases, or by listing and numbering key items.

_______ **4.** Writer has supported each of the points with brief elaboration and/or a quick example or detail from the text or teacher's notes.

_______ **5.** Writer has not padded or used irrelevant argument, but has stuck to the question throughout the discussion.

_______ **6.** Writer's answer has made sense.

Discussions of evaluation and grading linked to commonly assigned genres may also be found in Chapters Three and Six. Appendix D contains a rubric for grading a research paper.

Whether the teacher uses analytic or primary trait scoring will depend on his objectives for assigning the writing. More to the point is the importance of varying his writing assignments so that students are graded not only on the process of writing, but are also encouraged to explore a variety of genres for different audiences and purposes. He can do this by assigning many smaller, more focused tasks that assess the students' ability to think about the writing processes of others and to adapt to new strategies for writing. The best prepared student is one who can write expressive essays, thesis-oriented expository essays, narratives, thank-you notes, bad news letters, as well as a wide range of other compositional tasks. The elements of various rubrics may be instrumental in making this happen.

Think/Write #4

Consider this simple rubric below. Is the teacher using a process or product approach to teaching poetry? Is she using primary trait or analytic scoring? How would you assign points to each of the items? How would you improve on the rubric either by adding explanations to the criteria or by adding more items to the list? How would your changes alter the focus or approach presented here?

Poetry Evaluation

_______ Format

_______ Length

_______ Descriptive Language or Metaphor

_______ Creativity

_______ Clarity

Portfolio Assessment

When one of us recently assigned a final portfolio project in our undergraduate writing class of pre-service teachers this semester, some students were skeptical: "What's the purpose—just a way of collecting our stuff over the semester?" "How will I know which pieces I want to showcase?" "Do you mean we're not going to get grades on our writing until the end of the semester?" All questions that are reminiscent of the skepticism expressed by secondary students as well. Initially our students saw this as a mere collection of their work, although by the end of the semester they were eager to try out the system in their own future classrooms.

Purposes of Portfolios

Skepticism may be warranted if the portfolio is merely a receptacle for student writing, but we see it as having a much richer function than that. If our assessment of student writing is going to be based on anything more than an averaging of grades based on a collection of papers, the portfolio provides the means for much more meaningful assessment. Some teachers who use portfolio assessment have a folder system for collecting all of the student's work, including jottings, rough drafts, and final drafts. It is a collection of student writing, some of which can be used for further development, revision, and editing, and others of which may remain untouched. What distinguishes a portfolio from a file of student writing is that a portfolio is organized by the writer to demonstrate her growth as a writer. It includes selected materials rather than all the writing done, and it has a final reflective piece that asks the writer to reflect on her work over the semester. The portfolio, in essence, gives students an opportunity to organize the major pieces for final evaluation.

Portfolio assessment requires careful planning and thought before it is implemented. If the portfolio is to be more than a collection of student writing, teachers and students together must consider the following issues: Are they designed to show the student's progress over time? To represent only the student's best work? To demonstrate the student's range of writing experiences during a given period of time? And how will the portfolio be evaluated—holistically or piece by piece? How the portfolio is implemented will be determined by the answers to these questions (Wolcott and Legg).

We recommend that teachers consider the following purposes and uses for portfolios in their classes:

Showcasing work. One of the purposes of portfolios is the opportunity to showcase student writing, in some cases their best work. The public display often provides students with a strong incentive to produce final products worthy of public scrutiny, and those pieces often undergo considerable revision in the process.

Building ownership of writing. An argument we've made throughout this book is that student ownership of writing is critical if students are going to see themselves as writers and be willing to invest effort in the process of writing. Selection of portfolio pieces affords students greater ownership in their writing because they have some control over the pieces they wish to display. Even when teachers require that a certain set of pieces be included—one position paper, one reflective piece, one creative piece, and one expository piece, for example—students can have a choice of which ones in these categories to showcase or which additional pieces to include as well. Students can also be given some choice in how they will display their writing. Even our undergraduates were eager to provide an attractive portfolio whose presentation was an important part of the process.

Demonstrating the range of writing over a variety of genres. In some writing classes, students are expected to write in a variety of genres, some of which they are uncomfortable with because of a lack of experience. Our own students, used to writing academic papers, approached their three-genre assignment with some trepidation. We asked them to write on a topic related to their interest in becoming teachers of English but using different genres, with different audiences and purposes. One student, angry over how her essays in another course were being graded primarily on mechanics with no mention of quality of ideas or content, wrote a letter to the professor, an editorial for the student newspaper, and a poem using iambic pentameter to be anthologized for posterity. Difficult to write out of the traditional essayist form, these pieces were nevertheless showcased in her portfolio precisely because they illustrated her range of genres and her successful ability to deal with their stylistic difficulties.

Providing opportunities for revision. Sometimes the best writing emerges when students have a chance to set the piece aside for awhile, to reflect on it over time, and to then revise the piece with greater understanding of what needs to be done to improve it. Writers can keep the teacher's comments on earlier drafts in the working portfolio to come back to it at a later time for further revision. Looking at a piece with fresh eyes—a re-visioning of the piece—is an invaluable part of the portfolio process.

Documenting growth in writing over time. Writing development is difficult to ascertain if we look at our writing piece by piece, but reviewing our writing over a period of time enables both the evaluator and the writer to see growth in writing development. Our own students have commented as they surveyed their range of writing over the semester that they now see how much stronger their writing is, how their use of language is more effective, how they've gained control of the use of the colon and the semi-colon, how they have better ideas for organizing papers, and how their own thinking as writers has evolved. Without the looking-back/looking-forward opportunities, these insights would likely have been lost.

Developing metacognitive awareness of writing processes. Every portfolio, we argue, should contain a piece of writing that asks students to reflect on their own writing and their writing processes, an activity that flows naturally from re-visioning their writing over time. One of our students said, "Looking back at how my writing has changed, I now am much more able to see . . . how my pieces of writing demonstrate my growth as a writer throughout the semester. They reflect a significant change from strictly academic writing to a more unique style of writing." Another said, "I am showcasing my writing philosophy piece because it was the most difficult to write, but also the most satisfying because it demonstrates how far I've come as a writer."

Developing writers' ability to evaluate their own work. An important aspect of reflection is the writers' developing ability not only to see where they have come in their writing but also to know where they still need to go, what needs improvement, and how revision can be successfully accomplished. That self-evaluative ability comes only when writers have developed a degree of metacognitive awareness about themselves as writers.

Adjusting the role of teacher from authority to guide. Giving students more choice and asking them to take more responsibility for their own writing and revision encourages teachers to step aside and turn the work over to the student. No longer armed with red pens for deciding final paper grades, teachers use formative assessment—comments and suggestions for content, ideas, organization—and begin to guide and coach students through the process of drafting, revision, and editing. The portfolio, in other words, allows for a more long-range assessment process, and this allows teachers to take on very different roles. As Sandra Murphy and Mary Ann Smith assert, portfolios

> . . . are a means for teachers to reposition students from the sidelines to the center of their schooling: to intensify students' efforts, ownership, and experimentation. Consequently, portfolios have the potential to change the student's and, therefore, the teacher's role in education. When students own their work, teachers act less as conduits for externally prescribed content, and more as expert guides for students who have a personal investment in their education (325).

Implementing Portfolios

We offer the following suggestions for making a portfolio work effectively.

- Require students to write introductions to their portfolios and provide a table of contents as a guide for the reader.
- Establish together with students beforehand the goals and purposes of the portfolio, the grading procedures, the time frame for revision, and the presentation format of the portfolio at the end of the semester.
- Provide suggestions for the organization of the portfolio.
- Ask students to write a final reflective piece on their writing processes, on what has been successful and what has not, on what they still need to accomplish as writers. They can also write a short reflection on each of their polished pieces, discussing such things as why they chose this topic, the purpose and audience for the piece, and how they feel about it now.
- Provide scoring rubrics or grading criteria with students at the beginning of the portfolio project, and make decisions about the following issues:
  a) How will extra pieces count toward the final grade?
  b) Will everything in the portfolio be considered?
  c) Will showcased pieces be weighted differently from others that have not gone through extensive revision?
  d) Consider requiring that writers do a self-evaluation of individual pieces or of the portfolio as a whole. What role will writers' self-evaluation play in the final grade?

e) Will individual pieces be graded as they go into the portfolio? Teachers might consider giving tentative grades on some pieces of writing or holding individual conferences with students to give them a ball-park figure of how their writing measures up at this point in time. Students are notoriously concerned about grades, and a tentative grade or conference with the teacher can ease their anxiety by indicating where the writing is before revision takes place.

f) How will the following "dimensional" criteria (Murphy) be considered in the grading of the portfolio?

- The range and breadth of the writing
- The substance and content of the writing
- The writer's metacognitive awareness of his or her writing processes and the ability to be self-reflective about the writing
- The writer's growth over time
- The writer's technical and stylistic competence

Our own experiences teaching writing and working with writing teachers in the schools have led us to advocate portfolios as the preferred method of assessing writing because of the opportunities it gives for students to see themselves as writers, to grow, and to develop the habit of self-reflection.

See Figures 7.4 and 7.5 for examples of portfolio directions for students.

FIGURE 7.4 *Directions for Final Portfolio*

I. Organize all the work you did in this class this term in the following way:

For each of the five major papers, put all the work, drafts, revisions, comment sheets for a paper together, the best version on top. You should have five "packets" held together with a paper clip or separated in some way if you are using a loose-leaf notebook.

Arrange these so that the two "best pieces" you used for your final revisions are on top. Write a short "reflection" for each of these two revisions after you complete it. This reflection should be about a page in length, typed, double-spaced. Put the reflection for each piece on top of the final draft of that piece. A reflection can discuss any or all of the following: How you came to write this piece. The process you used in writing the piece. Why you selected this piece for one of your final revisions. What this piece shows about you as a writer. How you feel about this piece now that it is revised. Anything you might want to say about the topic, the piece of writing itself, the work you put into it, or your feelings as you worked on it.

Put any short, informal writings and responses to readings together in a separate grouping and put this behind the five formal papers.

If you want to tell me anything special about individual pieces or label your work in any way, use post-it notes or colored ink so I am sure to see these messages when I read through your portfolio.

II. Write your final self-reflection and put it on top of all your writing as an introduction to your work. See the attached page for guidelines.

III. Prepare a Table of Contents to use as the first page of your portfolio.

FIGURE 7.5 ***Final Self-Reflection: Looking at Yourself as a Writer***

The final piece of writing for this class is an analytical paper in which you describe and discuss your work in this class and analyze your growth as a writer. As you prepare your portfolio and review your work in this class, think about the following questions and jot notes to help you when you write the self-reflection. This final paper should be two to four pages in length, typed, double-spaced.

1. Consider your past experiences with writing before you entered this class. What are the most important writing skills or strengths you brought with you to this class when it first started in September? Write about this and try to document it with examples from your early papers.
2. Tell about the effects of this class on your writing. What did you learn? Talk about:
   - changes or lack of change in the quality of what you write—the content of the writing, your ideas, and your ability to get them down on paper in ways that meet the needs and expectations of readers;
   - changes or lack of change in how you write—the process you follow to arrive at a final draft;
   - changes or lack of change in your attitude and feelings about writing and about yourself as a writer.

   Document this part of your paper with specific examples from your own work. Quote bits of your own writing or discuss and describe what you see as you examine your writing from day one of the term to the present time and from draft to draft of individual papers.
3. What are you most proud of about your own effort or accomplishment in the class? What are you not satisfied with, or what do you want to work on improving?
4. What has been the greatest challenge to you in this class?
5. What has been the most important thing you've learned in this writing class? What do you feel will be most helpful to you in the writing you will do in the future?
6. Conclude this final self-reflection by writing about your progress toward the goals we set at your mid-term conference. How far have you come toward meeting those goals? Refer to your own writing or to anything you have already discussed in this paper to document your points.

High-Stakes Assessment and the Politics of Testing

Classroom assessment of student writing is generally considered to be "low-stakes/high yield" (Lee Shulman). Low-stakes because individual pieces of writing are not likely to carry a significant amount of weight, and the evaluation of which tends to be formative rather than summative. High-yield because students can learn from the teacher's evaluation, may have opportunities for revision, and can then proceed to other pieces of writing, using their accumulating knowledge of how to craft good pieces of writing. The quality of the evaluation lies in its specificity to a particular piece of writing and to the student's capabilities as a writer, based on a specific classroom assignment. The high-yield form of assessment will ideally lead to appropriate intervention and help through guided instruction by the teacher and to the student's increasing awareness of how to improve her writing. The grade or score on an individual paper will not be the one single factor in a student's overall writing assessment for the semester but will be one of several instances of writing—an indication of the student's progress and potential as she continues to write.

High-stakes/low yield assessment, on the other hand, uses an evaluation often based on a single piece of writing for making high-stakes decisions—being placed in a particular course or program, getting certified, passing a state-mandated writing test for earning a high-school diploma, receiving a monetary stipend—but with no opportunity to improve one's writing as a result of the assessment. In fact, students in high-stakes testing situations rarely see which answers they got wrong, what specific aspects of their writing were praised or criticized. Much of the current push in educational institutions is in this direction—preparing students to take a battery of tests that are high stakes not only for the students themselves but for the teachers and the institutions whom the students are representing.

The Push for Accountability

Standardized tests for assessment of student learning are part of the educational landscape. For many years they seemed innocuous, given sporadically with little obvious effect except for placement purposes—essentially low-stakes/low yield. School systems were not compared and funding was not dependent on the scores. Teachers administered these tests, students took them, and the test scores were often set aside without much impact on either instruction or the reputation of the school system. Times have changed, as any newly-graduated senior can tell you. Students in all American high schools today take a large battery of tests, some designed at the local level but many increasingly mandated and designed by state departments of education, given frequently and with high stakes. Virtually all states have assessment programs in place for determining grade promotion, graduation fulfillment, or passage of competency levels in the major subject areas of math, science, reading, and writing. Sometimes there are monetary awards for high scores for both teachers and students, sometimes scores determine the kind of diploma the student will receive, and increasingly the scores are used to compare school districts across the state in some kind of educational "quality-control." Some states—Michigan, Illinois, and North Carolina, for example—even make decisions about takeovers of school districts based on the test scores of their students. Testing in this country has never been a more serious—or more lucrative—enterprise.

The most apparent reason for the current emphasis on high-stakes testing is the national concern for educational reform, with the assumption that accountability will improve the quality of the education provided by school districts. States, therefore, have developed content standards and benchmarks in the major content areas that serve as the basis of their assessment programs. Educators support the concept of accountability: teachers and administrators rightfully believe that they must be accountable to their students, the parents, and the public for the education they provide.

National and state-wide assessments do, however, raise questions that are frequently overlooked: What are the underlying motives for the push for high-stakes testing beyond the improvement of education? What is the nature of the assessments, and how valid are they for measuring student ability? What are they designed to do, and will they advance learning? This section focuses on these issues in general and with specific reference to writing assessment.

The Politicizing of Assessment. Politicians and public officials who lobby for reform measures in education rarely focus on the complicated issues underlying accountability or assessment. Rather, they tend to view educational reform through the lens of numbers and statistics, even if what is being measured isn't easily reducible to quantification. Political and public debate is less likely to focus on accountability issues of validity, purpose of assessment, or the connections between assessment and learning, and more on how scores can be used for comparison purposes among school districts and schools within districts. Issues too often become oversimplified for soundbite purposes, resulting in efficiency as the key criterion for an accountability measure at the expense of best practice in the teaching and assessing of writing. Support for assessments that use quantifiable data also comes from an inherent belief among many Americans that numbers are not only an adequate means for rating educational excellence or inferiority but that they provide an objective measure of quality. If this is the case, then, accountability is a simple matter of testing students' skills as efficiently as possible. As testing critic Alfie Kohn says, numerical forms "seem reassuringly scientific. . . . Concepts such as intrinsic motivation and intellectual exploration are difficult for some minds to grasp, whereas test scores, like sales figures or votes, can be calculated and tracked and used to define success and failure. Broadly speaking, it is easier to measure efficiency than effectiveness, easier to rate how well we're doing something than to ask whether what we're doing makes sense" (3–4).

Contributing to the call for efficient assessment measures is the fact that major testing companies achieve their financial success by providing readily accessible, easy-to-administer assessments along with study guides and materials. It's often the worst tests that are the most appealing to school systems because testing companies more interested in profits than in valid accountability measures have little incentive to replace easily scorable tests with "more meaningful assessments that require human beings to evaluate the quality of students' accomplishments" (Kohn 3).

The consequences of efficiency at the expense of authentic assessment are far-reaching. First, because what gets tested on a high-stakes test is likely to be the focus of instruction, many important abilities like creativity and critical thinking remain untested and therefore untaught. In a number of states where the focus of testing is math, writing, and reading, other subjects in elementary schools, for example, like science, are marginalized and ignored. The curriculum doesn't have room for those subjects not being assessed. Teachers increasingly find their curriculum curtailed and their instructional decisions altered by the demands of assessment programs, in terms of time management, content, and pedagogical decisions.

Assessment experts agree that assessment should primarily be used for making instructional decisions and for improving teaching, in which case state-mandated assessment programs are extremely limited: they provide little feedback besides a numerical score and are incapable of suggesting how instruction should or can be altered. Scores provide no written feedback about areas of strength or weakness and no indication of where students need further work in the content area. Yet these same assessments are imbued with the power to make or break school districts and the students' graduation status within them. Low or mediocre scores, therefore, suggest only that teachers need to do a better job in some global sense of teaching to the test. They have no instructional value.

High Stakes, Validity, and Writing Assessment

Kohn's reference to bad assessment tests is particularly true for the assessment of writing, which is more complicated than in many subject areas where traditional multiple-choice tests are used. Writing is a performative act that demands a performance assessment. Grammar and usage tests sometimes used as the means of assessing writing are incapable of indicating a writer's ability to organize a piece of writing or to articulate an issue: they focus on surface issues of writing, not the ability to think critically or develop ideas. But many states compromise on sound principles of assessment design by using multiple choice tests that are "cost effective" and "efficient" to administer and score. Statistics and quantifiable data may work for quality control in the manufacture of bolts for airplane engines, but they are much less accurate for assessing the quality of writing. Just as a multiple choice test is not an adequate measure of a painter's ability to create a piece of art, a musician's skill at playing an oboe solo, or a tennis player's facility on the tennis court, it is inadequate for determining a writer's ability to write. These abilities can be assessed only over time, from multiple perspectives, in a variety of settings in which the student is actually performing and demonstrating his ability.

Not all performance assessments are equal, however. If a writing assessment is going to be valid, it should reflect the kinds of writing tasks students do in the classroom. Because strong writing programs use tasks that are multiple, assessing a writer's ability in only one style—the argumentative essay, for example—may ignore the other forms of writing the student is proficient in using. Writing tasks are also complicated by purpose and individual perspective; a writer who sees possibilities for a more creative approach to a writing prompt because of how she conceives of the audience may be discouraged from doing so because of the strictures set up within the guidelines of the writing prompt. A writer, on the other hand, trained in the essayist style may have difficulty writing more personally to an audience—a friend, for example—that seems artificial and unreal.

All of these examples point to the problem of authenticity. Writing a letter to the local city council to lobby for a recycling program at the school is authentic writing if it's a topic selected by the student for the purpose of getting something done. When the audience is real, the purpose is real, and the writing can be revised and edited with audience and purpose in mind, the writing provides a sense of agency for the writer. Prescribed writing for large-scale assessment that is required to be completed in one sitting, timed, and with little choice of topic, genre, or sense of audience, is highly inauthentic and unnatural, as educator Sheila Fitzgerald suggests, because it is totally decontextualized. Timed writing, with pre-determined topic and an unknown reader, whose sole purpose is the assessment of the writer's ability, is perhaps the most inauthentic writing exercise students are ever asked to do.

The Negative Impact of High-Stakes Writing Assessment. In theory, writing assessments should improve instruction. Unfortunately, performance measures of writing just described can shape the writing curriculum negatively. Essays written in one sitting without revision or rethinking may encourage writers to pay attention to surface features of writing for the sake of the assessment. Essays written to an inauthentic audience for an artificial testing purpose may discourage writers from demonstrating voice or commitment to a topic. Perfunctory writing is unanimated, distant writing, and writers rarely perform their best under such circumstances. Such assessments are at best partial perspectives on writing ability and at worst contradictory to the principles of good writing instruction. Authenticity and standardization, in other words, are in a constant state of tension in the world of testing. Assessment programs walk a delicate line attempting to negotiate these two ends of the spectrum, and far too often the focus favors standardization at the expense of authenticity.

If writing assessment distorts writing processes or narrows the instruction in order to focus on what is being tested, the long-term effects of high-stakes writing assessment may be detrimental. While there is some evidence that in Michigan, writing teachers are having their students do more drafting and revising as a result of the assessment procedures, the assessment program has impacted some classroom instruction negatively. At the moment in the state of Michigan a number of school systems have been accused of cheating on the state-mandated MEAP (Michigan Educational Assessment Program given to all fifth, eighth, and tenth graders annually) because student answers from different school districts appear to be quite similar. School personnel are defending student answers by explaining how they prepare students for the tests. First of all, test-preparation suggestions to student writers include repeating terms in the question as part of the answer, using certain transitional phrases, using patterns of organization that are appropriate to the kind of essay being required. Second, until recently the test allowed students to discuss test topics and revise their writing before completing a final draft. Both practices are likely to result in similar answers. For example, on the Grade 8 social studies MEAP, the first prompt for a two-part question first asks students to place three events in a time-line ("Lansing Requests Separate MEAP Investigation"):

A. The U.S. buys the Louisiana Territory from France
B. Oliver Perry defeats the British at the Battle of Lake Erie
C. The XYZ Affair causes problems between France and the U.S.

The two items already listed in the timeline presented in the test are:

The Embargo Act cuts off trade with England and France
Andrew Jackson leads Americans to victory at the Battle of New Orleans

The second prompt asks students to describe the cause and effect relationship between the Embargo Act and the Battle of New Orleans. The following answer was provided by several students:

> The XYZ affair causes problems between France and the United States. The Embargo act cut off trade with England and France. The effect was Andrew Jackson leads Americans to victory at the Battle of New Orleans.

The irony is that because students followed directions and used the language in the prompt, the schools were accused of cheating. Teachers are doing what they are expected to do: teach students how to succeed on these tests by giving them the linguistic and rhetorical tools for writing acceptable essays. They've been told to prepare their students, and yet they are reprimanded for doing so. At a recent hearing on the issue in the state of Michigan, one teacher said, "How can you not expect standardized answers when we are forced to prepare students for a standardized test?"

While these teachers and districts are likely to be exonerated, what remains is still problematic and potentially detrimental to good writing practice. Even performance assessments can demand cookie-cutter approaches that produce artificial, unimaginative, and uninspired writing. It may get students passing scores, but it sets a poor standard for the kind of writing that should be valued in our schools. Why teach students to write creatively, imaginatively, and interestingly if that writing is not recognized and tested? Some researchers go so far as to say that this kind of assessment, ill-conceived in its construction and destructive to students and school districts who don't measure up, in fact reverses any gains over a traditional multiple choice test that a performance assessment might have initially accomplished.

States have developed a range of performance assessments of writing from essays written during one period of time without opportunity for revision, to essays with revision opportunities over two consecutive days, to portfolio assessments of a collection of individual students' writing. Revision time certainly provides students with greater opportunity to rethink, reshape, and edit, making the second alternative a more legitimate writing experience than the first, and yet it is void of the authenticity of portfolio assessment. This last alternative is undoubtedly the best reflection of a student's ability to write under a variety of circumstances, to a range of audiences and for different purposes. Most portfolios are assessed by teachers, and the assessment occurs over a range of writings each student has produced (see our discussion of portfolio assessment earlier in this chapter). But because portfolio assessment is the most costly and complicated, it isn't surprising that most states opt for a simpler, more "efficient" assessment of a single essay scored holistically.

Superior to non-performance assessments of writing, a single writing assessment is nevertheless limited for all the reasons just discussed. Perhaps the most insidious cost to its usefulness as an assessment is the message it sends to students about writing—that the process is mechanical and perfunctory, that traditional forms of writing are valued, and that the purpose of writing is for demonstrating a narrow range of skills.

> ***Think/Write #5***
> What high-stakes writing tests have you taken? What were your responses to these tests? Did you learn anything about writing from these tests? What would you change in the system, if anything?

Issues of Equity in Writing Assessment

Central to our consideration of the assessment of writing is the issue of equity, a concern that should be present in both large-scale assessments and in individual teachers' assessments of their students' writing. Issues of equity center on two major aspects of writing: the specific language differences that students bring with them to the classroom and the cultural assumptions about rhetorical structures and patterns appropriate for writing that may differ from mainstream assumptions about written English.

Language Differences. The nature of high-stakes writing assessment imposes its own limitations on students' ability to produce "acceptable" standard written prose. Holistic scoring is usually based on a set of criteria—the rubric developed for the assessment of a piece of writing—that as a whole determines one final score. Usually the student's ability to write Standard English prose is one criterion out of four or five. But depending on the degree to which the raters are trained to keep usage features in proper perspective, that criterion may be given particular emphasis by raters who lack knowledge or experience with vernacular forms of English. Non-standard features may draw the attention of the rater away from the writer's ability to express ideas clearly or to organize his writing well to a greater focus on the form and the surface features. In large-scale assessments this focus on surface features becomes all the more problematic because the evaluation is usually based on a single piece of writing, without additional knowledge of the student's abilities, and without an opportunity to see other pieces of the student's writing. A high-stakes writing assessment is therefore based on less authentic writing because the writer is producing a single text to be evaluated, under constraints that are more severe than in a classroom. These dialect features may become the significant factor in determining the score, regardless of the paper's other strengths. There is considerable evidence that people unfamiliar with vernacular dialects or harboring linguistic bias against users of the vernacular or against ESL speakers often give unwarranted emphasis to surface features of the writing in the final determination of the score, overlooking logical organization, original voice, and verbal wit (Haswell). The validity of a holistic score, then, is only as strong as the training of the scorers who understand the difference between surface features and more substantive indications of writing ability. Of course, classroom teachers, too, must deal with this issue as they read student papers, but teachers, at least, have the luxury of using the writing for feedback to the student for further revision, and teachers have a wide range of a student's writing on which to make a final assessment of writing ability.

Sometimes the high-stakes writing event itself will trigger other kinds of language difficulties. The concern for correctness under high-stakes testing situations may complicate the writing process. Premature editing, as Sondra Perl (1997) refers to it, occurs when writers who are so conscious of using "correct" grammatical forms allow editing to occur before ideas are fully developed. Focusing on the correctness of surface features, writers may actually be distracted from a focus on ideas or organization—a kind of blocking of the larger composing processes (Wolcott and Legg). While this is likely to be a problem for all writers to some degree, it is particularly troublesome for writers whose linguistic backgrounds have made them especially conscious of getting their writing "right" and "correct."

Writing problems for students from diverse linguistic backgrounds may go well beyond not knowing all of the Standard English features expected in school writing. For most student writers, in fact, moving from elementary school writing to middle school writing, or from middle school to high school writing and beyond, demands a sophistication and an awareness of academic discourse that takes some time to develop. Composition specialist David Bartholomae suggests that inexperienced writers may not fully understand academic expectations for structure, for argumentation, or for the complexities of voice. Difficulties with these aspects of writing are further complicated by the discipline-specific nature of academic discourses. Students in the sciences need to learn to write like scientists, students in history like historians, students in the arts like artists. The forms and registers of academic writing take longer to approximate and are less amenable to direct instruction. Students in a discipline need to live and think in that discipline before the writing takes on a feel of authenticity.

To compound the issues of writing for students from diverse linguistic backgrounds, a number of cultural differences complicate the production of standard academic "school" prose. Researcher Arnetha Ball cites cultural discourse patterns in African American vernacular speech that often find their way into the writing of these students. For example, they will sometimes use ritualized forms of oral expression that are not often found in academic discourse, they may make use of narrative as part of argumentation or exposition, and they may have a preference for coherence devices that assume a common knowledge on the part of the listener/reader, whether that knowledge exists or not.

ESL speakers often struggle with English discourse patterns because discourse patterns in any language are imbued with political and ideological beliefs. Many Americans, who put great stock in logic, order, and argumentation, prefer essayist writing that states a thesis followed by points of support, perhaps reflecting

Americans' views of the importance of individualistic perspectives and ideologies. While American culture favors explicitness, many ESL students from Asian countries favor indirectness, and their writing may reflect these cultural/rhetorical beliefs (Leki). Chinese students, for example, prefer forms of discourse that indicate an unwillingness to be too direct, using rhetorical questions, metaphor and simile, analogy, and illustrative anecdotes to imply their point of view, unlike Americans who are often told to be direct—to state what they are going to tell the reader, then to tell the reader, and finally to tell the reader what they've told them (Cai). Preferred Chinese organizational patterns and forms of self-expression reflect the sociopolitical contexts of the importance of harmony and community at the expense of individualism and directness.

Topic choice may also be culturally problematic, according to Wolcott and Legg. ESL students from cultures in which community takes precedence over the individual may be uncomfortable with personal topics and may find the personal essay often favored in American classrooms foreign and awkward to write. Some cultural groups in American society also object to writing that is personally revealing. So the assumption that a personal topic is one that all students will be able to relate to or feel comfortable writing about ignores cultural differences among students that may, in fact, affect the quality of the writing negatively.

Individual classroom teachers who are aware of these issues relating to linguistically and culturally diverse students in their classrooms will be able to more richly modify assignments and broaden rubrics for evaluation. First they will understand that the grammatical problems that some students exhibit in their writing may be reflections of the speech community from which they come, that they are surface features only, which should not detract from other strengths of the writing. And second, they will understand that the language difficulties in producing standard written English may not be the only difficulties ESL or vernacular dialect speakers encounter in writing assignments. Classroom teachers have opportunities, therefore, to modify writing assignments and evaluation procedures that can accommodate cultural differences.

High-stakes performance assessments of writing are more complicated, particularly if the assessment is based on a single piece of student writing. The writing prompt, if it is going to be equitable, must be culturally unbiased, and the rubric for holistic evaluation must be developed with linguistic and cultural differences in mind. Most testing companies attend to issues of equity in test design but are rarely able to accommodate all the linguistic and cultural differences represented in the population of students taking the test. Again, the implication of these difficulties is the need for a more authentic assessment program like portfolio assessment, which can accommodate cultural diversity more easily.

Points to Remember

Grading may be the part of teaching writing that teachers like the least, but teachers can reduce the burden with alternative approaches to grading every paper and with the use of rubrics and portfolios. The goal of the classroom teacher is to do more formative rather than summative evaluation. Formative responses—self-evaluation, peer response, teacher conferences, and teacher comments on drafts—all guide writers toward higher quality final drafts, which in itself makes grading easier. Also, teachers should not be grading everything students write; much writing should be considered "practice." We recommend that grading be reserved for selected pieces that have gone through the full writing process and are adequately revised and edited.

Rubrics should be tied to the goals of the lesson(s). Whether the teacher is designing a day's lesson plan, a unit, or a year's set of plans, she needs to think about how she will be assessing the students as she draws up the lessons. She also needs to think about why she is assessing and weight the points accordingly. For the year's planning she might draw up a generic rubric that she can modify unit by unit or day by day. The best rubrics will guide student attention to what's important in the lesson and modify writing behavior, so rubrics should be thoughtful and well-designed.

Portfolios provide a means for more meaningful assessment by serving not only as a collection of students' writing but as a means of building ownership, encouraging greater awareness of the writing process, and offering opportunities for on-going revision. Portfolios also demonstrate writing growth over time in ways that other forms of writing assessment don't.

Classroom assessment is primarily formative rather than summative, unlike state-mandated assessment programs that provide little help with instructional planning. High-stakes assessment is too often based on single pieces of writing, ignoring developmental and situational issues of writing so important to the writing process. What is at stake in high-stakes writing assessment is a view of the teaching and learning of writing that acknowledges its complexity and its development over time. Writing development is part of a rich literacy, not essentialized into narrow forms and structures. When high-stakes assessments are designed for number crunching and cross-district comparisons, good writing instruction—and therefore appropriate assessment—becomes secondary.

Randy Bomer goes so far as to suggest that high-stakes testing is a failure of democracy: it presents unequal structures of opportunity, it closes off inquiry, it allows the corporatization of education, it disenfranchises the people most affected by it because the public sphere is no longer available, and it creates an oppressive school environment. Regardless of where teachers stand on the issues of high-stakes assessments, they are here to stay. It is up to teachers and educators who value writing and its instruction to work together to ensure that the assessment reflects good writing practice and teaching.

For Further Reading

Atwell, Nancie. *In the Middle*. Portsmouth, NH: Boynton/Cook. 1st ed. 1987, 2nd ed. 1998.

Black, Laurel, Donald Diaker, Jeffrey Sommers, and Gail Stygall, eds. *New Directions in Portfolio Assessment: Reflective Practice, Critical Theory, and Large-Scale Scoring*. Portsmouth, NH: Boynton/Cook, 1994.

Cooper, Charles R. and Lee Odell, eds. *Evaluating Writing: The Role of Teachers' Knowledge about Text, Learning, and Culture.* Urbana, IL: National Council of Teachers of English, 1999.

Hewitt, Geof. *A Portfolio Primer: Teaching, Collecting, and Assessing Student Writing.* Portsmouth, NH: Heinemann, 1995.

Kohn, Alfie. *The Case Against Standardized Testing: Raising the Scores, Ruining the Schools.* Portsmouth, NH: Heinemann, 2000.

State of Michigan Michigan Educational Assessment Program. Revised Model of the Assessment for Writing in 1998. http://www.mde.state.mi.us/off/meap

Tchudi, Stephen, ed. *Alternatives to Grading Student Writing.* Urbana, IL: National Council of Teachers of English, 1997.

Tierney, Robert, Mark Carter, and Laura Desai. *Portfolio Assessment in the Reading-Writing Classroom.* Norwood, MA: Christopher-Gordon, 1991.

Wolcott, Willa, and Sue M. Legg. *An Overview of Writing Assessment: Theory, Research, and Practice.* Urbana, IL: National Council of Teachers of English, 1998.

8

A History of Composition Pedagogy

A quick overview of this history reveals that through the last two centuries no single pedagogy has emerged to meet all the composition policies and needs in our schools. Indeed, pedagogical decisions about teaching reading and writing have reflected the political and economic demands of their times. The reasons for teaching composition have thereby evolved, as classroom methods have reflected the needs of each new generation of learners. In each new political and economic era over the last 100 years of America's history, principals and teachers have listened to concerns about the "failing school systems" and established new directions for composition education. Complaints about the literacy crisis have tended to become most acute when economic conditions required new skills to meet the challenges of innovations in technology. For example, loud complaints were brought against America's lack of changes in reading and writing pedagogy at the end of the nineteenth century, when America's dying agrarian economy was being replaced by the up and coming manufacturing age. At that time a "crisis" in secondary school teaching surfaced when the English faculty at Harvard gave the first entrance examinations in 1874. They were shocked that the graduates of the best American preparatory schools were writing essays with mechanical errors in punctuation, spelling, capitalization, and syntax. Their discovery led to the first remedial English program and direct grammar instruction. This era was later followed by a report in 1892 by Harvard's Committee of Ten on the Teaching of Secondary English, which recommended limiting grammar instruction in the final years of high school because technical grammar was not serving composition improvement.

Complaints have again arisen about a "crisis in our schools" and this one corresponds to the economic changes in the last 25 years when rote, assembly line jobs in manufacturing were being replaced by computer age jobs. America has discovered a need for more computer literate people on the assembly lines, readers of software manuals, and writers of e-mail. We also need more literate office workers who can manipulate software programs and mid-level people who can generate print ready manuscripts. So the pedagogical needs for reading and writing are again being re-evaluated by legislators, Chambers of Commerce, school boards, and parents responding to larger historical, economic, cultural, and social forces.

Literacy statistics, however, tell us that the public's expectations are unrealistic. Given the complicated and diverse network of teachers, textbooks, students, and administrative concerns, American schools as a whole are powerfully resistant to change. Some teachers and schools systems might experiment with reading and writing pedagogies, but few reforms will be adopted wholesale because one size does not fit all. One educational reform in literacy cannot possibly be appropriate for every school district because the various regions of the country have their own economic and cultural needs and their needs are complex. Many factors determine literacy: religious concerns, opportunity and expectations for children, class attitudes, and the need to master other kinds of literacies—mathematic, scientific, visual, and aesthetic literacies. These are just a few of the variables that determine whether the rates of reading and writing make a difference in the community. Additionally, educator Ira Shor argues that critical or social literacy—the ability to "go beneath surface meaning, first impressions, dominant myths, official pronouncements, traditional clichés, received wisdom, and mere opinions to understand the deep meaning, root causes, social context, ideology, and personal consequences"—holds the most promise for converting reading and writing to meaningful practice (Ira Shor quoted by Graff 1995, 335). He is talking about the ability to see through false patriotism or to take a skeptical step back from a popular film to look at its subtexts. Social literacy is explored in a section of this chapter on the Socio-epistemic approach to composition and in an earlier chapter on alternatives to the research paper.

In this chapter, our discussion also follows the history of rhetoric with its twists and turns from the Greeks of fifth century B.C. to the Current-Traditional essay of the present day. We will pick up Expressivism, a second movement in composition inspired by Romanticism of the nineteenth century, and we will review its adoption by progressive educators in the 1960s. We will discuss the Socio-epistemic school of composition, another strain of composition theory that was adopted in the twentieth century. We will conclude with another view of composition through the perspective of literacy. Throughout, we suggest the economic, cultural, and political forces that shaped the history, but bowing to the restraints of space and reader interest, we touch only briefly on these issues. For the preservice teacher, our objective is to review the foundations of composition and to heighten an awareness of the variety of communication models. We will also address current NCATE/NCTE standards outlined below.

2.6 The impact that culture, societal events and issues have on teachers, students, the English language arts curriculum, and education in general;

3.1.2 The evolution of the English language [in composition] and the historical influences on its various forms;

3.7.1 Research and theory related to English Language arts.

Once in awhile we English teachers wonder if current trends in pedagogy are the wisest course we can take and whether some lost practice or another might work any better. Once in awhile we are curious about what brought us to this point of English teaching practices. Once in awhile we would like to try something new. Through an understanding of our past and the movements that have shaped present day practices, we are better equipped to reflect on what we are doing in the classroom and why. Such reflection allows us choices and confidence in the decisions we must make daily while writing our lesson plans.

Think/Write #1
What were the practices that shaped your high school compositions? Did the teacher use the writing process? Did you write five-paragraph essays? Did you also do informal writing? Did you choose your own topics based on events in your community? Did your English teachers discuss the writing process?

The Beginnings of Rhetoric

The history of composition stretches back to fifth century B.C. Greece when educators, aware of the need for deliberative speakers in the new democratic assemblies, began to teach students in the arts of philosophy and debate. With the rise of city states and the system of representative government in Athens, the senators of Greek city states were called upon to generate ideas, search for the truth, question authority and custom, and validate practice. Since there were no professional lawyers at the time, people learned to defend ideas and themselves. The training of the young was threefold—to groom ceremonial orators who could preside at state and family dinners, to sharpen legal orators (or forensics), and to prepare civic leaders. Students were taught persuasion with ethical, rational, and stylistic components. The main thrust of their program was contestatory. Students learned how to debate as a way of discovering ideas; but more to the point, they learned how to win people to their side in an argument. By 335–350 B.C., Aristotle and others had laid out a system of rhetoric describing well established practices that would continue to influence more than 1,500 years of oratory and composition in the western world. We still use textbooks today that name persuasion and argument as two of the most important basic genres of composition. We still recognize in advertising as well as in political speeches and composition, three forms of persuasive appeal—to reason (*logos*), to emotion (*pathos*), and to the speaker's authority (*ethos*). The persuasive and argumentative forms of these appeals are so embedded in speech and composition classes that contemporary high school teachers expect them to be included in their textbooks.

Greek influence is evident in other ways as well. The time-honored arrangement of the argument—an introduction with the thesis, points of discussion with supporting evidence, and a conclusion—draws on rules developed by the ancient rhetoricians, particularly the Sophists who organized their arguments into the exordium or prooemium (the introduction), narration (the basis of the argument), proofs (the evidence), and peroration (the conclusion). In each phase of the argument, ancients chose a strategy from a range of approaches, depending on their relationship to the audience. Were the listeners friendly? If so, they could state the argument at the outset. Hostile? They might have eased them into an argument with a long introduction and convincing evidence. In doubt? They could win them over with agreed upon points. Or they might have opened with a fair-minded, not hasty introduction, demonstrating goodwill. Or they might have shown rage and indignation. For proofs (evidence) of the argument they could have strived to impress or entertain or convince with quiet restraint.

In any case, the Greeks had a range of choices for arguments as well as proofs for evidence, and the options were studied in great detail. In Aristotle's day, the orator's evidence was based primarily on syllogistic reasoning. A typical syllogism is

All men are mortal.
Socrates is a man.
Therefore Socrates is mortal.

Oral arguments were thus structured on a series of statements in which two premises led to a conclusion. By the eighteenth century, however, rhetoricians had altered the discipline of that process by inserting tricks of tropes, metaphor, and wit to win over the audience. The four-part standard arrangement—introduction, proof, evidence, conclusion—based on the deductive model of argument was eventually expanded into the familiar five-paragraph essay found in many high schools today. The logical progressions established by the Greeks and the clever strategies developed by rhetoricians in later centuries continue to be discovered anew or re-invented by today's speakers and young writers for business letter writing, political persuasion, and advertising, to name just a few applications.

Aristotle's Contributions to Rhetoric

Aristotle's systematic discussions in the *Rhetoric* are still deemed invaluable by rhetoricians because his study established the subject headings for the table of contents for many of today's composition textbooks—organization, audience analysis, and style. His greatest contribution was a thorough examination of topic selection and discovery (heuristics). His use of logic-tested argumentative proofs (syllogisms and enthymemes), examples, and maxims—a practice used widely by the ancients—likewise continues to influence the authors of composition texts in the form of advice about how to structure a sound argument. Indeed, the combination of philosophy and rhetoric has proven perennially useful since it was first explored in ancient Greece and Rome by Gorgias, Cicero, Isocrates, Quintilian, and others (Crowley, *Ancient Rhetorics*).

Although we often treat the ancients as a monolithic group, they clashed and were divided among themselves on serious philosophical grounds over many points. Like Plato, Aristotle was concerned with using rhetoric to test truths and achieve rational dialog during argumentation. But Plato was more suspicious than Aristotle about the potential of rhetoric to defraud, and Plato's concern is still reflected today in connotations of the word *persuasion* as a means of selling something through underhanded suggestion or flim-flam techniques. Aristotle placed more faith in the desire of the speaker to be logical and in the power of the word as a vehicle for playing out the rational order and knowledge about things. For him, correct reasoning begins with logos, the word, and the strict mode of thinking through rhetorical proofs based on common sense assumptions and formal logic.

The classical strategy for teaching and learning to write, one that dominated Western education from 400 B.C. through 1800 A.D. was imitation. Passages written by the masters were usually memorized, paraphrased, and emulated by students. They copied the passages, defined the vocabulary, and dissected the rhetorical style. They committed the passages to heart, then borrowed the phrases and stock rhetorical devices for their own essays. The topics for writing borrowed from the classical models became standard over the centuries. In Aristotle's day they debated the values of goodness, justice, honor, and other such concerns. Their arguments were fresh and meaningful in the matters of Greek political policy. By the nineteenth century, however, these topics became weather worn and abstract, divorced from discussions that effect legitimate changes in the state's democratic practices. Students wrote about assigned topics for the sake of *copia,* that is fluency, rather than to settle burning contemporary issues. Topics spun around such questions as "What is joy?" or "When do our actions serve the greater good?" and so forth. Recognizing that these topics had grown stale, teachers eventually turned to the sciences, medicine, math, and the arts for additional themes. The shift towards more relevant material was promising. Although students were encouraged to hold forth as fully as they could, they still had little opportunity to write personally however (Connors). Contemporary composition assignments, particularly the research paper, have slightly modified these "commonplaces" (topics) to make them more concrete and timely. Explorations based on contemporary issues such as global warming, gun control, or school vouchers owe their pedagogical origin to the ancients and many students today are encouraged to connect these topics in some way to their own experiences.

Rhetoric in the Eighteenth and Nineteenth Centuries

Classical methods in composition were used in one combination or another in America and England until the eighteenth century when it was clear that the Greek method of encouraging students to argue controversial issues in preparation for activism was deemed inappropriate for most American colonial school rooms. For one, most Americans believed that children should be "seen and not heard." Young students were therefore not encouraged to think for themselves or to argue against authority. Secondly, formal rhetoric was regarded by many as a luxury for the student body who were soon to become farmers. Since many students only attended school through the sixth or eighth grades, simple drills and skills in reading and writing were considered sufficient in elementary education. Spelling was taught in these lessons, although not standardized until the late eighteenth century, when Noah Webster brought out the first American dictionary with our own national spellings.

Paper was in such short supply that writing was sometimes done on other materials (such as birch bark). Students wrote with goose quills, so every word had to be well chosen. Even ministers were often hard pressed to obtain sufficient writing materials because the good paper had to come from Holland. In country schools, children used copy books made of foolscap, a 13" × 16" sheet of paper. They were carefully shaped into books with sewn binding and ruled by hand. Ink was manufactured at home by steeping bark in water and adding copperas. A poor ink was made with vinegar, water, and ink-powder, but it usually dried out quickly or clotted. Slates were not found as commonly as the children's stories might lead us to believe.

Children who left school early continued to read and write at home with some older tutelage, creating diaries, letters, and commonplace books. The commonplace book had blank pages that children filled with memorable quotations from books they had read and admired and often memorized. Sometimes the copied passages were appended with sweet commentary or dutiful religious thought. As ever, the children of wealthier homes had greater opportunities for education at boarding schools and with tutors at home. Except in Quaker schools, where they received equal treatment, the poor, the girls, and ethnic minorities generally received less education than white, middle-class boys. Argumentation—appealing to the boys' preferences in English classes—therefore took priority over the Belles Lettres and creative writing, which were regarded as more pleasing to the girls. (See Alice Morse Earle's *Child Life in Colonial Days* for further description of early American schooling.)

The Contributions of Blair, Whately, and Campbell to Rhetoric. With a growing national literature and intellectual community in the late eighteenth century, Belles Lettres were nevertheless added to the curriculum at the college level and literary criticism as well as poetry, fiction, and essay writing became the subjects of post-secondary examination alongside the sterile subject matter in composition that remained standard in every teacher's syllabus. The best known names in eighteenth century composition were the Scottish rhetoricians Hugh Blair, Richard Whately, and George Campbell who developed the classical pedagogies that we employ today—the rhetorical modes of discourse, the importance of unity and coherence, and correctness in style and grammar. Since information on the teaching methods in secondary schools is scant, we have to assume that most of the methods that were designed for college composition also applied to secondary education at that time. As far as we can tell, many of the college practices that we describe here were also adopted by teachers in the lower grades. Harvard's program in composition was an exception in that it was more innovative with a mix of personal writing,

writing about literature, and writing about ideas. Personal writing consisted largely of sketches describing a mood, a place, or a moment rather than a psychological self-examination, but Harvard did honor the individual's perspective and some creative nonfiction writing. At the University of Michigan, students were encouraged to connect ideas to real experience. A literature-based writing course, which began in 1870 at Yale, Cornell, Wisconsin, and Vassar, also experimented with literature in their composition courses.

Many of the less prestigious and smaller colleges in the East and South adopted the conservative advice of Blair, Whately, and Campbell (Brereton 14). Blair's *Rhetoric* (1783) arbitrated in matters of taste, polish, eloquence, and he connected style to reason and morality. He wrote about stylistic points and correctness, and what to say to raise passions and pathos. Whately's *Rhetoric* (1828) and Campbell's *Philosophy of Rhetoric* (1762) linked scientific argument and rhetoric. Their discussions were concerned with the logical principals behind composition. It's a mystery why their books were popular since they contained long disquisitions about logic and style and descriptions of good writing, however, less advice about how to write than one would expect. These men were the last word in composition for 200 years.

The Role of Grammar in Eighteenth- and Nineteenth-Century Rhetoric. Rather than teach grammar, writing teachers of the eighteenth century referred students to the study of Latin. This had been the practice since Archbishop Robert Lowth (175) took on the task of standardizing the English language by aligning it with the structures of Latin, even though the match was imperfect. Lowth attempted to assign Latin cases to English nouns, although the possessive (genitive) case is the only one that applies, and he tried to match English and Latin verb tenses, even though Latin does not use some of the verb tenses found in English (e.g. the progressive tense). Lowth's insistence that English should be as logical and consistent in structure as Latin continues to influence composition teaching today. Composition teachers still subscribe to some of Lowth's rules, even when the rules make little sense. For example, they warn students never to end a sentence with a preposition, never to split infinitives, and never to say "It is me" in order to maintain strict use of the nominative case. All of these were Lowthisms borrowed from his admiration of the Latin language (Thomas and Tchudi 172–80).

Reduced to petty rules of ornament, grammar, and correctness, rhetoric declined into a test of class membership for an established social order. Eloquence in diction and syntax were tickets to polite debate societies that turned on men-only discussions in colleges and universities where the students were preselected largely by wealth and status. Because of linguistic snobbery, the mispronunciation of certain words (such as *subtle*) could prove deadly to someone trying to gain entry into certain circles. Rhetoric prepared young men to be articulate in medicine, law, and the ministry and afforded them social and political connections. Prescriptive practices in language gave rise in the regions to a demand for "pronouncing dictionaries, hard-word dictionaries, error-hunting grammars, and tracts on elocution" (Bizzell 649). As restricting as they sound, the classical rules for composition in both Great Britain and America were not altogether stultifying, since many of the writings produced by American statesmen of that period—notably Thomas Jefferson, Cotton Mather, and William Byrd II—were eloquent and formative in shaping our national consciousness and destiny. Nevertheless, a number of the most articulate spokespeople of that period—Ben Franklin and Thomas Paine, to name two—were trained in the streets, and a few women of the eighteenth century were self-educated (Connors, *Composition-Rhetoric 40*). To this day, many self-educated Americans remain suspicious of formal training, especially if it hints at "elitist" classical—meaning, Latin and Greek—roots.

Think/Write #2
Have we lost some knack in our ability to write with a flourish? To express ourselves eloquently? Should we bring back some exercises that promote wit, taste, polish, and metaphor into our students' writing? Or do you think that our democratic, simple style is best?

The Influence of John Locke on New Composition Practices. American education and, concomitantly, composition were deeply influenced by the Enlightenment up till about 1865, the end of the Civil War. It was John Locke (1632–1704) who slowly altered the way scholars thought about the link between language and thinking. Educators took this to mean that words representing our ideas are idiosyncratic and personal in meaning. This line of argument gave credence both to the primacy of reason in learning and the importance of the individual mind, thus shifting the burden for understanding to the learner's ability to collect and sort data. Locke called attention to the individual powers of observation. Moreover he explicitly condemned Aristotle's syllogisms and the rules of formal logic as useless to the development of thinking. Having said this, Locke still did not abandon the usefulness of reason. In his discussions of irrational thought, he reasserted the supremacy of reason in the human mind with its ability to organize ideas and overcome the pressures of nonrational urges. Nevertheless, his insistence on learning from experience opened up education to progressive ideas about individual expression, the cultivation of individuality, and a more relaxed attitude towards control of children's minds—ideas that influenced John Dewey's educational philosophy, which became the cornerstone of liberal education today.

Under the influence of Locke and the Enlightenment, American universities seized enthusiastically on the authority of humans to produce and to situate the production of ideas within the individual mind. For composition and the common man, this meant that writers put more trust in their own ability to interpret what they observed and it validated their personal perspectives in composition. Rhetoricians began to think more broadly about the links between composition and how knowledge can be developed through the discipline of discourse, written and oral. They could see how important speaking and writing were in the formation of reasoned knowledge.

Even though self-exploratory writing was still not encouraged, Locke's more liberal approach to education opened the way for shaping the structures of new genres and for teaching methodical ways of presenting knowledge. Science writing, for example, grew in the eighteenth century (see Berlin's *Writing Instruction in Nineteenth Century American Colleges* for a more complete discussion). Locke's emphasis on observation and sensation justified empirical approaches to scientific discovery in astronomy, navigation, map-making, surveying, medicine, mathematics, and the natural sciences. Scholars found new confidence in self-reliance and initiative, already endorsed by a commercial-minded, growing middle class.

Modern technology and technical writing began to catch hold as well. Values of self-reliance were embraced by Americans in spite of their Puritan beliefs, because at a time of rising economic opportunity, the notion of free enterprise expanded to cover workers, whose potential through sobriety and diligence translated into increased productivity. Affluence for the middle and working classes undermined the effects of privilege and servitude, giving rise to the myth of the classless society. Economic growth and opportunity opened up new demands on literacy, affording composition a new importance. Indeed, new practices in secondary reading, writing, and mathematics were now preparing the growing commercially-minded middle classes. Secretaries needed to be trained in the etiquette of communication. Newly invented typewriters meant an even greater emphasis on standards for spelling, grammar, and basic business forms.

By the 1880s, educators were also designing curricula to address the growing influx of American immigrants. Immigration was to affect educational policy into the third and fourth decades of the twentieth century as schools helped newcomers to acculturate and to train in Standard English. Migrants needed to assimilate, most of all, into the workplace and to become articulate in the expanding fields of sales and advertising, two fields that blossomed at the turn of the century.

Rhetoric and the Current-Traditional Essay

Although only fragments of the old Greek and Latin form of education remained in the 1920s, classical rhetoric did not die out by any means, since its offspring in the form of current-traditional practice has lived on to become the most prominent method of teaching composition in our time. The current-traditional essay is the one we associate with high school English classes—the "My Summer Vacation" essay. It has been widely adopted because it could be taught to a large number of students in school and could be standardized in preparing students for the business world. Today, the approach is still embraced by teachers who worry about preparing their students for national and state standardized tests.

Assuming that children are not capable of original thought, proponents of the current-traditional method believe that children have little need to discover new ideas through writing. Instead, the young writer is expected to observe and report her findings in a detached manner without personal interpretation or insertion. She is discouraged from pitching a meaningful argument or showing independent thinking, so her thesis is secondary. Her purpose is to reiterate what she generally knows to be true and to use language that best reflects the facts of the experience. The audience for her essay is not important, since the writer's main purpose is to write for the teacher's grade.

The best examples of this writing are the *five-paragraph essay* and its many guises. The current-traditional essay invariably begins with an introduction, in which a proposition or thesis statement is explicitly given, and then the essay's topic is narrowed, supported by three pieces of evidence, usually one paragraph each and usually one argument per paragraph. Individual variation from this sequence is discouraged. Since the topic is often assigned, invention (discovery of topic) exists largely in the narrowing of the topic through definition or analysis and the careful selection of evidence for supporting arguments. Her conclusion is usually a reiteration of the opening with some variation.

Any teacher wanting to reinforce the construction of the current-traditional composition can also teach the structure of the complete sentence (with subject and verb) and the perfect paragraph built with a prescribed sequence of complete sentences. Many composition and grammar books such as John Warriner's *English Grammar and Composition* still include a chapter on how each well-honed paragraph ideally forms a miniature essay when the first sentence introduces the topic, two or three related sentences expand on the topic in the middle of the paragraph, and a "clincher" rounds off the idea and brings it to a close. It is all very neat. (See Figure 8.1 A Model Student's Paragraph using the Current-Traditional Model.)

The current-traditional composition represents an amalgamation of the eighteenth century's logical arrangement and the Enlightenment's clearly reasoned statement. After the Scots Blair, Whately and Campbell had fully explored stylistic matters, later scholars turned to matters of organization. They drew on the

FIGURE 8.1 ***A Model Student's Paragraph Using the Current-Traditional Model***

[1]Our government guarantees rights to all individuals regardless of race or creed. One right is the chance to practice a faith without prejudice. [2]The Islamic community in our small town, for example, should be able to meet and pray in peace. So should any other recognized religious group. We must learn that religious prejudice is still very prevalent in America, although most Americans do not like to be reminded of the fact. Then we must recognize that we make a mistake when we discriminate against the families of that community. [3]Profiting from our mistakes, we can determine that we will never take such a discriminatory action again. Thus, by trying to improve ourselves, we can gain lasting self-respect for ourselves and the democracy we represent.

Key to the Paragraph

1. Introduction
2. Body of the paragraph with an example and supporting argument
3. Conclusion with a "clincher" sentence

work of the Scots who argued that rhetoric shapes the thinking of the audience and that the reader could be manipulated as a passive and static recipient of ideas. It was thought, for example, that the reader's mind worked naturally from individual items to categories of things and then to laws and principles. The writer had only to trigger these processes of natural scientific thinking through forms of discourse and language well chosen to make the reader give a predicted response. A later Scot, Alexander Bain, added to the rules of expository writing. He explained the way that sentences could be chained to build paragraphs and he emphasized unity, coherence, and focus as part of the arrangement. Many American rhetoricians wholeheartedly adopted the idea that each part of a composition should be recognizable and that arguments should flow mechanically from an efficient model of methodical order and clarity. They also embraced the features of close observation, scientific prose, use of research materials, and empirical data and liked to see them presented in an orderly and predictable outline. Soon this mode of formulaic writing outweighed persuasion and other rhetorical forms, such as narration or descriptive writing, in the classroom.

Throughout the nineteenth century and into the twentieth century, college composition textbooks reasserted the value of argumentation, analysis, and amplification using the directives first laid out by Aristotle and later extended by the eighteenth century Scots. Texts for K–12 education picked up these rhetorical points and provided the last bastion of support for the current-traditional essay. Thanks to this line of educators, current-traditional genre theory was eventually reduced into a few specific types of invention—Exposition, Description, Narration, and Argument—a foursome so commonly accepted by teachers as the outline for the course that Sharon Crowley in her excellent book on the current-traditional essay reduced them to the acronym EDNA. Although Exposition is sometimes subdivided into cause-and-effect and comparison-contrast essays and Argument is often broken down into inductive and deductive essays, these basic genres still crowd out most other types of writing from the curriculum. History, biography, autobiography, and letter writing, for example, have all but disappeared from the English classroom, especially in K–12 education.

After decades of the current-traditional essay, many teachers believe still that it is the only way to write a composition regardless of audience or authorial purpose because the message is easily developed, and organizational logic and clarity are heavily weighted. Reducing the writing process to a formula lightens the teaching load. Teachers have a list of tried and true topics and students recognize what to do when one or two topics are assigned on Friday afternoon/due Monday. Given this routine, teachers and students have clear guidelines for what to expect week after week when essays are assigned. Very little additional instruction is needed. Grading is also easy: a standard checklist with points for each solid paragraph, for organization, coherence, spelling, and grammar. Occasionally, points are also awarded for the logic of the argument or to style or colorful examples, but from essay to essay, paper marking is fairly predictable. Although dull, the current-traditional essay was considered a marked improvement over the nineteenth century essay, which often recycled memorized text or canned prose from the ancients. Most practitioners in the late nineteenth century championed the essay model for its order, its clarity, and the examples from the students' own social and cultural experiences. It is still used as a basis for science reports, essay exams, and as a skeleton outline for longer, factual writings—theses and dissertations, for example, because it is the most efficient and least taxing model to employ.

Opposition to the Current-Traditional Essay. The problem with the current-traditional approach is that it favors method and arrangement over the writer's ideas for the material, and it denies the natural and self-evident connection between fact and the author's need to claim his own ideas. Emphasis on correctness and form overrules the need of the writer to write from his own convictions or to choose a tone or a genre appropriate to the message he wants to convey. Without an opportunity to communicate from a personal viewpoint, the writer is also divested of responsibility for holding a serious opinion or ethical stance. Over the years, educators have attacked the current-traditional essay with discussions about the importance and role of various parts of the writing process. The fact remains that the processes of composition should and can aid the writer in discovery of learning through the interplay of ideas on paper, the opportunity to brainstorm for ideas, and time for revision. Attempts to shortchange this write-to-learn process have proven counterproductive.

Opposition to the current-traditional essay also questions the notion of a sufficient and convincing, "disinterested" argument. The pretense of the current-traditional essay to achieve meaningful argumentation has been problematic since it is not actually used to explore scientific truths or to arbitrate political debates. What strategies do we have for testing truths anyway? In recent years, it has also been generally conceded that the writer's bias *inevitably* influences selection and interpretation of evidence. It is difficult for anyone to maintain with conviction that facts are facts. Impersonal and detached argumentation is therefore questioned since studies based on so-called incontrovertible facts are often considered flawed and limited in application. Even so, traditionalists and back-to-basics educators continue to dismiss the personal writer in favor of teaching the formulaic essay as a means of reporting what are thought to be empirical truths.

Although many composition theorists try to put the current-traditional essay behind them, teachers of composition cling to the old five-paragraph essay even while it suppresses imagination, the value of the individual voice, and individual commitment to values. It betrays our understanding of how children must write to think for themselves, to problem-solve, to be responsible for satisfying their own curiosity, and for testing the truth of their own ideas. While it serves some purpose in showing children how to organize their thoughts, current-traditional rhetoric loses more than it gains when it ignores what we learned through Romanticism, a nineteenth century movement that privileged inspiration and personal exploration through writing.

The Nineteenth- and Twentieth-Century Expressivist Essay

Romanticism was a movement in the nineteenth and twentieth centuries that freed the artist and writer from the rigid rules of the classical era. Best known for the writer's exploration of the inner self, the movement grew slowly in reaction to eighteenth century rationalism and exploded with the British preoccupation with psychology and the workings of the human imagination. All sorts of psychological states of mind were explored—love, morbid melancholy, mental illness, unrestrained imagination, primal mind, and the nature of the self as an extension of nature and the environment. Romanticism led to Expressivism, one of the most important revolutions in composition and a response to the current-traditional approach to writing. From this movement rooted in the upheaval of the 1960s grew a whole new resurgence of interest in studying writing through self-examination, beginning with one's personal knowledge.

The Rise of the Individual and the Expressivists

Following the American Civil War, teaching at all levels turned professional. Concurrent with the rise of an institutional self-awareness in education came a shift in the way Americans thought about disciplining children. Building on the liberal and democratic ideas of Locke and other thinkers of the time, educators began to regard children not as short adults but as a special class of innocents whose pure and malleable ideas were worth nurturing. Much of the turn in thinking came from at least two influences—Jean Jacques Rousseau (1712–1778) and Ralph Waldo Emerson (1803–1882). Rousseau's theory was that society represented all that was corrupt and immoral, but children—born in a natural state and free of society's artificialities—could be brought up pure and self-fulfilled if they were led to discover and experience the natural world. Basking in the glow of the French influence on the Revolution and heavily influenced by English Romanticism, Americans warmed to Rousseau's theories. Emerson, and other like-minded New Englanders such as Bronson Alcott (Louisa May Alcott's father) applied Rousseau's philosophy toward developing an optimistic and humanistic understanding about child rearing. He proposed that the young scholar would learn through nature and books, then translate his understanding into practical tasks. Liberal Protestant churches such as the Methodists, Unitarians, Quakers, Congregationalists, and Episcopalians, who underplayed the role of original sin and Satanical forces, laid the foundation for the discovery of knowledge and a child-centered curriculum that challenged the lessons commonly taught through authoritarian drill. Emerson's insistence on self-love, the essential worth and dignity of the individual, became an ethical principle in the life and education of a young nation.

The K–12 curriculum was gradually reshaped to reflect the newly formed ideals of childhood development and the growing importance of individual expression. Recognizing that young writers must be free to explore through writing, to express their own voice and pursue understanding through argument, the Expressivist movement arose in the 1960s. Although it never fully challenged the current-traditional movement in the first half of the century, it functioned as an alternative approach used by K–12 progressive schools. In the 1960s, it was adopted by post-secondary educators looking for approaches to replace the current-traditional model, a pedagogy that seemed to have run its course. In her exploration of nineteenth century texts for K–12 education, Lucille Schultz discovered more innovative approaches to secondary composition than those practiced in the American colleges. She found "self-reflection, irony, and humor" in the writings of school-age students who tell stories based on lived experiences and an emphasis by the schools on composition for lifelong learning. For invention, she found texts that used illustrations to develop themes and personal student response and some texts even used student-generated compositions as models, journal entries, and free writing, ideas for composition that were rediscovered in the 1960s. She also found early versions of peer editing and revision, techniques that would be adopted anew. These were apparently early seeds of the shift that was to come.

The Dartmouth Conference and Its Aftermath

Following the Dartmouth Conference of 1966, a gathering to discuss the dismal state of composition studies in both British and American colleges, a new awareness emerged in composition pedagogy. The consensus was that something new was needed. Student essays were widely recognized as boring, teaching methods advocated by Warriner's handbook were considered bankrupt, and teachers felt that the new breed of student was hungry for a more liberating curriculum. The conference had been preceded by heated discussions about mediocrity in the education of the 1950s, a radical school reform movement instigated by educators at the University of Chicago. The National Defense Education Act of 1958, an upsurge of interest in the College Entrance Examination Board results, and a landmark report by Albert Kitzhaber on effective composition at Dartmouth added to that agitation. The Dartmouth Conference's sense of the discipline's serious contribution to education was given legitimacy by Jerome Bruner's theories on the nature of thinking and learning. Bruner's approach was essentially cognitive; he emphasized learning through discovery in combination with creative guesswork that showed students how to use their intuition productively. Bruner also proposed a K–12 classroom climate that would enable a more considered approach to the writing process. Students would be enticed to use inductive reasoning and creative exploration to find their individual approaches to writing. They would raise their own questions and write in response to them. They would also observe and analyze their own writing practices to fine tune their own methods.

Later known as the Expressivists, educators at the Dartmouth Conference discussed a self-exploratory model of teaching composition based on a personal growth model. They agreed to encourage students to write about themselves as subject matter and they would gradually move students through their own experiences towards a more public awareness of the world around them, much like

James Britton's discussion of the move from personal to more public forms of writing. The purpose was a more natural model of composition that mimics what professional writers actually do. Proponents such as Ken Macrorie and Donald Murray, cherishing language and delight in detail, encouraged play and imagination using the specifics of everyday life. At the center of their assumptions was authenticity established by honesty of expression and concrete instance. Many teachers in the public schools enthusiastically embraced the model as both innovative and sound based on the experiential education proposed by John Dewey as an extension of the child's everyday life. They found ways to combine the personal focus with reading and field experience to expand students' horizons. Journal writing as a response to literature is an example of this approach. Often these first impressions are expanded into a thoughtful essay with argumentation and/or quotations from the literature. Another example of the Expressive essay might be a letter written from one historical figure to another, say from George Washington to Betsy Ross talking about the meaning of the flag. These writings combine the child's imagination and experience with fact in an organized composition. Other examples are explained in Chapter Three on the writing process.

The writing process as delineated by the Expressivists begins with pre-writing, a form of the classical invention that triggers inquiry and a search for meaningful insight. Writers learn more about what to do next by rereading their own piece of writing and responding to it. Content is determined by finding a balance between the data collected and the connections that must be made between fact and the writer's understanding of them. The writing process ends when the writer is reasonably satisfied with the insights she has gained and the effectiveness of the communication. Little of the writing process can be directly taught because it is neither straightforward nor formulaic. It is a process that touches on all the classicists' concerns with invention, arrangement, style, and audience, and yet it begins with an emphasis on exploration and authorial intention, and it moves toward self-conscious polishing and refinement. The contribution of the Expressivists to the history of composition pedagogy lies not only in the articulation of the writing process, but also in the privileging of self as subject, the student-centered curriculum, the emphasis on making meaning as the work unfolds, and the de-emphasis on form and mechanics. As a pedagogical approach to composition, it has found wide acceptance in the English classroom during the latter half of the twentieth century.

The Cognitivists, Neo-Rhetoricians, and the Socio-Epistemists

Critics of the Expressivists have objected at various levels of disagreement with the writing process, which they associate with the Expressivists. While most camps of theorists support the basic approach of the writing process, they all prefer to stress aspects of composition, which they regard as underdeveloped. The various camps of opposition have arisen primarily from a neo-rhetorical school of composition. They are the Cognitivists, the Neo-rhetoricians, and the Socio-epistemists (term used by James Berlin). All but the Socio-epistemists oppose Expressivism, based on some aspect of the new rhetorical model of composition. A short description of each group follows.

The Cognitivists

The *Cognitivists* are those who endorse the basic principles of traditional composition, but they also examine the interactions between thinking and writing. Their contemporary proponents are Linda Flower and John Hayes. They use empirical studies to observe the composing process at all levels, to dissect a writer's thinking paragraph by paragraph, to study the developmental stages of growing writers, or perhaps to catalog errors, and they focus on one aspect of writing, such as voice, using ethnographic methods. Their primary concern echoes Locke's arguments in observing how the mind works to shape writing, how a conscious engagement of the thinking processes can inform and enrich the writing process and how the structures of language shape thinking. Language is used as a window on the mind and as a way of organizing the world's information for the thinker. Feelings and self-fulfillment are less real than the rational and the metacognitive (the ability to watch oneself think) for the purposes of their research. Their objection to the writing process might be that free writing is good for getting words on paper, but it is just the beginning. To the Cognitivist, self-exploration is best reserved for journals and letters. It is considered less productive for composition than goal setting and problem solving, which are necessary constituents of clear and purposeful writing.

The Neo-Rhetoricians

Neo-rhetoricians such as Janet Emig, Anne Berthoff, Sharon Crowley, and Peter Elbow also have much in common with the Expressivists, particularly in their endorsement of the writing process as a way of learning and discovery. While they too describe the various stages of writing as non-linear, they emphasize a more conscious use of invention techniques to start and focus the topic, deliberate choices for building coherence, organization, and audience considerations, and a more direct instruction for maintenance of such conventions as grammar and mechanics. Neo-rhetoricians object to Expressivists for their inattention to persuading the audience through textual organization. For them, the text is a product of the interaction between writer and reader, given the topic and intentional aims of the writer and the discourse community to which he is writing. For the Neo-rhetorician, expressive writing is only one type of discourse along with persuasion and referential writing. To assist in the organization of student information, the teacher directly teaches one of the classical modes of discourse—description, narration, persuasion, or exposition.

Among the Neo-rhetoricians are also specialists such as Stephen Toulmin who believe that all writing is somehow argumentative and that composition theory should take us back to a greater concentration on logical demonstration, fallacies, and proofs. For Toulmin, personal topics are largely irrelevant. The Neo-rhetoricians claim that with direct instruction, students are less mystified by unstated expectations and therefore they have less need for multiple drafting, which can frustrate the young writer. They additionally argue that expressive writing is weakest when the student is exploring academic topics, because the naturally self-absorbed child does not easily build bridges, that is transcend his own interests to the world beyond himself. They contend that if the young writer is to outgrow his egoism, he needs plenty of direct instruction and firm rules. There is some merit in this argument.

The Socio-Epistemists

Socio-epistemists such as James Berlin and Ira Shor bear the harshest criticism for the Expressivists. Their strongest objections charge the Expressivists with an undue emphasis on the individual at the expense of communal awareness. They contend that an understanding of self can best be appreciated by considering one's own cultural climate, one's own place in history and one's own political views. Above all, the Socio-epistemist believes that the employment of language shapes our conception of the world and our selves. To assert something in words is to give it some sort of reality, even if it is not fully true. Language is the vehicle by which meaning is made. It is a direct reflection of what we know and what our community believes. Writers who would like to know how their words and phrases belong to their culture and historical time and place can begin by asking about the assumptions of the community.

- What are the phrases that are used often to express communal truths?
- Who benefits from this version of the truth?
- How are the benefits distributed?
- Will these statements create conflict? for whom?
- What powers will accrue and to whom?
- How can the writer respond with social action?

In short, the Socio-epistemic approach demands that students recognize their place in the social and economic system and take responsibility for it by acting on it with self-reflection and social commentary. Clearly this approach demands sophisticated thinkers who have been trained to analyze the economic and historical forces around them, so it is more commonly taught at the college level. But teachers can steer students toward thinking about the power of language and the concrete ways it does indeed shape our material reality. Examples abound in the media's representation of ideas through image, sign, and symbol. All students can become savvy consumers as they learn to read the messages in the advertisements they see every day, the variants in news reporting, and the subtle shadings of words that tell a story first one way, then another. They can examine the discourse of their own community and compare it to others. For instance, they could look at the ways that supermarkets sell their goods in the different sections of town. Or they can look at letters written by people in authority in order to get cooperation. Students are fascinated by questions of power and how they are manipulated in a culture where the young enjoy very little power of their own. High school students, especially at the upper levels, are hungry to assume responsible roles in the community; an exploration of the self in relation to the community is a first step. Whatever the curriculum, the Socio-epistemist wants to add self-awareness of language and political power into the writing process in hopes that students will position themselves in the world and write for social change.

Composition Literacy

This brief history of composition has followed two key strands of theory—rhetoric from the Greeks to the present variant in current-traditional composition and Expressivism from the Romantics to the present manifestation in the writing process. What has been omitted in our narrative is the place of composition in a larger discussion of literacy. For a long time, we measured America's literacy rate by counting the percentage of personal signatures on land contracts and other legal documents. Later, scholars measured literacy by the ability of people to cope with daily literacy requirements—to find a job by reading the classified ads, to fill out an employment application, to pass a written driver's exam, or to read a company's warranty and enforce its promises. Today's literacy demands more than the simple ability to read and write to meet the economic and social needs for surviving in one's job and community. Focused on the minute effects of teaching this prewriting technique or that stylistic feature, composition theorists often overlook who is learning to write and the reasons we teach writing for meeting both in- and out-of-school tasks. The result is a fragmentation of composition methods into skills or processes or products without regard for the most critical goals of schools in a democracy: to help students from diverse cultures and classes to function in school, to move all students into the world of work, to provide opportunities for wholesome leisure (such as reading), to include all students as viable members in the school's communities, and to become informed and active participants in our democracy.

In the absence of a composition model that finds a compromise among these theorists or purposes, a new approach that synthesizes the two positions (the Rhetorical model and the Expressivist), the authors of this book would like to step back and reiterate the function of composition literacy in the academy. We believe that all writing—regardless of purpose—should be meaningful and relevant to learners. Students should be able to summon their writing skills for their own needs as well as for the academic community, particularly to make meaning and to communicate from their own experience and knowledge as well as through newly acquired information. Through language, students should be able to create meaning of their own by seeing relationships and the contexts of their ideas. They should be able to engage in active exploration, analysis, comparison, and synthesis of ideas. They should have a chance to talk to others about their ideas, to read for enrichment, and to listen to competing views before, during, and after writing. The writing process should be nurtured—not as a fixed set of steps that writers must take—but as an exploratory and recursive process in which the writer, moving forward and backwards into and out of the material, takes risks with provisional ideas and backtracks into sharper and more confident statements.

Having said that, we acknowledge that many of our fondly held composition practices have failed with non-elite populations, largely because school-based literacies dominate all others. Exposure to mainstream, middle-class uses of literacy is not empowering to non-mainstream students, unless the home, school, and community value multicultural uses of language. Teachers need to seek the ways and means to help students stand up to the dominance of academic language and composition. Students—mainstream and minority—should be able to learn the language of standard speakers as well as achieve a critical distance on the social and cultural ideologies that support the language.

Social Literacy and Composition

What is it that literacy can do? One of the latest theorists in literacy, James Paul Gee, answers that question with the wry observation, "Literacy has been used, in age after age, to solidify the social hierarchy, empower elites, and ensure that people lower on the hierarchy accept the values, norms, and beliefs of the elites, even when it is not in their self-interest or group interest to do so" (1996, 36). Gee argues that exaggerated claims have been made for school literacy, holding out the hope of upper mobility for those who master the discourse in exchange for obedient behavior and a commitment to the school literacy. But acquiring the skills to read and write is not enough. Students need also to understand the social context in which the words are produced so they can use the language in the manner of insiders. In this sense, Gee is much like the Socio-epistemists in his thinking. As an analogy, he gives the example of a person who walks into a biker bar and asks his "leather-jacketed and tattooed drinking buddy" an academic's question, "May I have a match for my cigarette, please?" Gee concludes that the outsider knows the words but not the language. Taking in the social setting, he should have said, "Gotta match?" In short, mouthing words is not enough for success in or out of school. The speaker of the language has also to be aware of his "identity kit" or the discourses that types of people speak as well as the cultural models that generate that language in that particular group. Without an insider's mastery of the language, without being able to use it as other speakers of that community, one remains at a disadvantage, even while understanding the words.

Gee distinguishes, therefore, between acquiring a language and learning it. A student will mistakenly believe that language is little more than words or grammar, until he becomes familiar with the nonverbal implications of the communication. It is not enough to write or speak like a lawyer or an Indian or a Southerner unless one also understands the "acts, values, beliefs, attitudes, and social identities, as well as gestures, glances, body position and clothes" of that group (1996, 127). These are the elements that point to a Discourse with a capital "D." They signal the words and phrases that identify the features of membership in a particular community. He writes, "A Discourse is a sort of identity kit which comes complete with the appropriate costume and instructions on how to act, talk, and often write, so as to take on a particular social role that others will recognize" (127). Most students understand this phenomenon when they try to imitate the mannerisms of the "popular group" for the first time. They soon learn that using the word "cool" is not enough to induct them into the cool crowd.

Gee and others would agree that it is through an appreciation of language and its larger context that composition must function. Emphasizing audience awareness, rhetoricians claim to address the larger context, but their interest in group-sharing language seems more aimed at the academic community than any other group. The Socio-epistemists take the high ground on this issue with their emphasis on promoting social literacy and on placing the writer in his own community of beliefs as opposed to the mainstream. But composition teachers may have to guard against the possibility that students positioning themselves against a norm work to create mistrust and factionalism. Their strongest approach may be to acknowledge the pluralism of discourse communities—both in and out of school—and to enlarge the acceptable modes of discourse in the classroom. They will have to help students learn respect for a wide variety of ways to say things and to express one's self. Writing often and writing for different purposes is a way to begin. Offering students the possibility of writing for a variety of discourse communities and to imagine themselves transformed by their larger cultural understanding may also bring new awareness to their use of language. Other features of a language-aware classroom might include the following:

- Writers should be aware that language of writing varies, both as the same writer attempts different kinds of writing and as different writers attempt the same kind of writing. Writers should be able to see how others—professional and peers—wrestle with these various forms by sharing models in the classroom.

- Opportunities to write for all sorts of in and out of classroom purposes and discourse communities. Students should be able to attempt many different voices and to write often. This includes everything from recording conversations overheard beyond the classroom walls, to Expressive writing, to following the strictures of the narrowly rhetorical current-traditional essay, or writing for the sciences and history and math.

- Students should be able to hear and talk about the sounds and ideologies of different discourse communities as reflected in these writings.

- Talking about exclusion and inclusion on the basis of verbal and non-verbal language may reinforce these practices. As Gee points out, meta-knowledge about one's discourse and about discourses in general can provide the "foundation of resistance and growth" (1996, 191).

- Making meaning. Throughout all the composition exercises, students should be committed to their own ideas.

Think/Write #3
Given this brief list of composition theories, can you now identify the approach that your high school English teachers took in class? What practices would you try to use in your own classroom? What practices would you drop? What would the key features be of your composition methodology?

Points to Remember

Looking back over the history of composition, we can conclude that one purpose for writing has been and continues to be effective and clear communication in print. Theorists seem to agree on that much. But historical pressures have dictated many new shifts in emphasis as theorists attempt to solve the perennial difficulties of addressing problems inherent in student writing from the Greeks to the present. Clarity is not the only goal. Each new generation has had to meet its community's expectations for literacy. The Greeks identified the need for clear-speaking leaders to strengthen their budding sense of democracy. The Expressivists' reaction to the current-traditional approach might never have registered had it not been for the Civil Rights movement, the Free Speech Movement, and protests to the Vietnam War, which encouraged self-expression and the demand to express one's moral commitment. Student attraction to personal writing was acute in those years. Computer literacy, the value placed on technical writing, and writing for e-mail and chat rooms are forcing still new rhetorical practices. Electronic mail has certainly changed our standards for timely replies, punctuation, capitalization, and other conventions. Thoughtful letter writing is on the wane and the fragmentary statement in correspondence has gained wide acceptability.

We have also suggested how two key pedagogical strands—rhetoric in its many guises and Expressivism—have been shaped by cultural and economic pressures of history, and we have demonstrated how the Socio-epistemic school of composition in cultural studies teaches students to read their own culture, to ask questions of it, and to leave the classroom better prepared to identify the cultural conflicts and power struggles in the world. Neither conventionally rhetorical nor Expressivist, the Socio-epistemic approach to composition teaches literacy through social reform. Gee suggests the strongest approach yet, a thorough exploration of all sorts of writing styles and discourse communities. Given the many choices for composition pedagogy, the classroom teacher today has to continue examining his own practices and reflecting on what seems to be effective in his particular classroom with his own student needs.

For Further Reading

Berlin, James. *Writing Instruction in Nineteenth-Century American Colleges.* Southern Illinois University Press, 1984.

Bizzell, Patricia and Bruce Herzberg, eds. *The Rhetorical Tradition: Readings from Classical Times to the Present.* Boston: Bedford Books, 1990.

Brereton, John C., ed. *The Origins of Composition Studies in the American College, 1875–1925: A Documentary History.* University of Pittsburgh Press, 1995.

Bruner, Jerome S. *The Process of Education.* Cambridge, MA: Harvard University Press, 1966.

Connors, Robert J. "Personal Writing Assignments." *College Composition and Communication* 38.2 (1987): 166–182.

Crowley, Sharon. *The Methodical Memory: Invention in Current-Traditional Rhetoric.* Southern Illinois University Press: 1990.

———. and Debra Hawhee. *Ancient Rhetorics for Contemporary Students.* 2nd ed. Allyn & Bacon, 1999.

Earle, Alice Morse. *Child Life in Colonial Days.* Stockbridge, MA: Berkshire House Publishers, 1993. First published in 1899.

Graff, Harvey J. *The Labyrinths of Literacy: Reflections on Literacy Past and Present.* University of Pittsburgh Press, 1995.

Hobbs, Catherine. *Nineteenth Century Women Learn to Write.* Charlottesville, VA: University of Virginia Press, 1995.

Kitzhaber, Albert R. *Themes, Theories, and Therapy: The Teaching of Writing in College.* McGraw-Hill, 1963.

Murphy, James J., ed. *A Short History of Writing Instruction: From Ancient Greece to Twentieth-Century America.* Davis, CA: Hermagoras Press, 1990.

Schultz, Lucille M. *The Young Composers: Composition's Beginnings in Nineteenth Century Schools.* Southern Illinois University Press, 1999.

Shannon, Patrick. *The Struggle to Continue: Progressive Reading Instruction in the United States.* Portsmouth, NH: Heinemann, 1990.

Toulmin, Stephen Edelston. *The Uses of Argument.* Cambridge (England) University Press: 1964.

Appendix A

A Hassle-Free and Cheap Method for Having Students Create Their Own Individual Books

Supplies

1 paper cutter

1 hole punch

1 manila folder *per student*

Books of wallpaper samples—large size, approximately 12" by 17" (free for the asking at any wallpaper store)

Elmer's glue or the equivalent—enough for class use

Scissors—enough for class use

Lined white paper for student writing

Solid white paper for illustrations

Solid colored paper for lining insides of covers

Fasteners: colored turkey rings or Chinese jacks; paper fasteners; ribbon; yarn

Teacher Preparation Before Books Are Made in Class

1. Cut each manila folder 7" by 8" on paper cutter; each half of the folder becomes one side of the cover, front or back.
2. Cut each wallpaper page into two pieces, each 8½" by 10", on paper cutter. One piece will cover the front; the other will cover the back.
3. Cut solid colored cover liners for inside of front and back covers 6½" by 7½" on the paper cutter.

4. Cut lined writing paper and white solid illustration paper 6½" by 7½" on the paper cutter. Punch with 2 holes along the longer side.
5. Gather the following for students to use in class as they make their covers:
   scissors
   glue
   a hole punch
6. Make enough copies of the Directions for Creating a Book for each student to have one to refer to in class as you guide them through book making.

Suggestions

A beautiful handmade book cover is a wonderful motivating device for student writing. To capitalize on this desire to "publish," teachers might have students select their own wallpaper samples from a large pile of pre-cut pieces and create the covers before writing the pieces that will go into the book. Once the covers are made, they can be set aside while students write, revise, edit, and proofread the pieces that will go into the books. When each student's piece has gone through all the steps of the writing process and both teacher and student agree that it is ready for publication, the student can be given the 6½" by 7½" lined and unlined pages for final copy and illustrations. Don't assemble the book until the final copy is finished.

Display these in the library, share them with other classes, send them home as gifts to parents or friends. Create one yourself to see how satisfying this writing activity can be.

Directions for Creating a Book

1. You will need the following for each book:
   2 pieces of matching wallpaper 8½" × 10"
   2 pieces of manila folder 7" × 8"
   2 pieces of colored paper 6½" × 7½"
   2 fasteners
   lined and unlined paper 6½" × 7½" for writing and illustrating your book
   scissors, glue, a hole punch
2. To make the front and back covers do the following for each cover:

STEP ONE

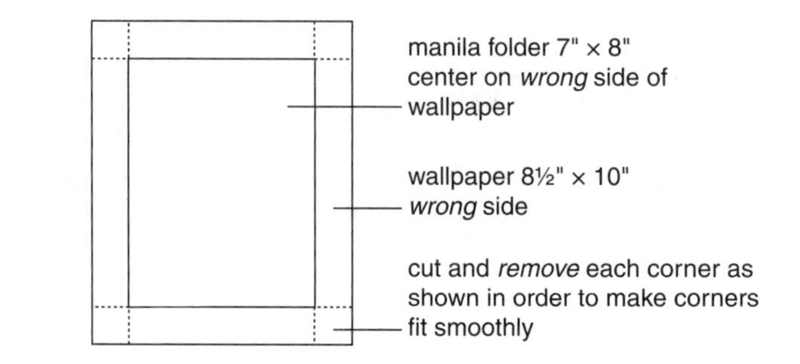

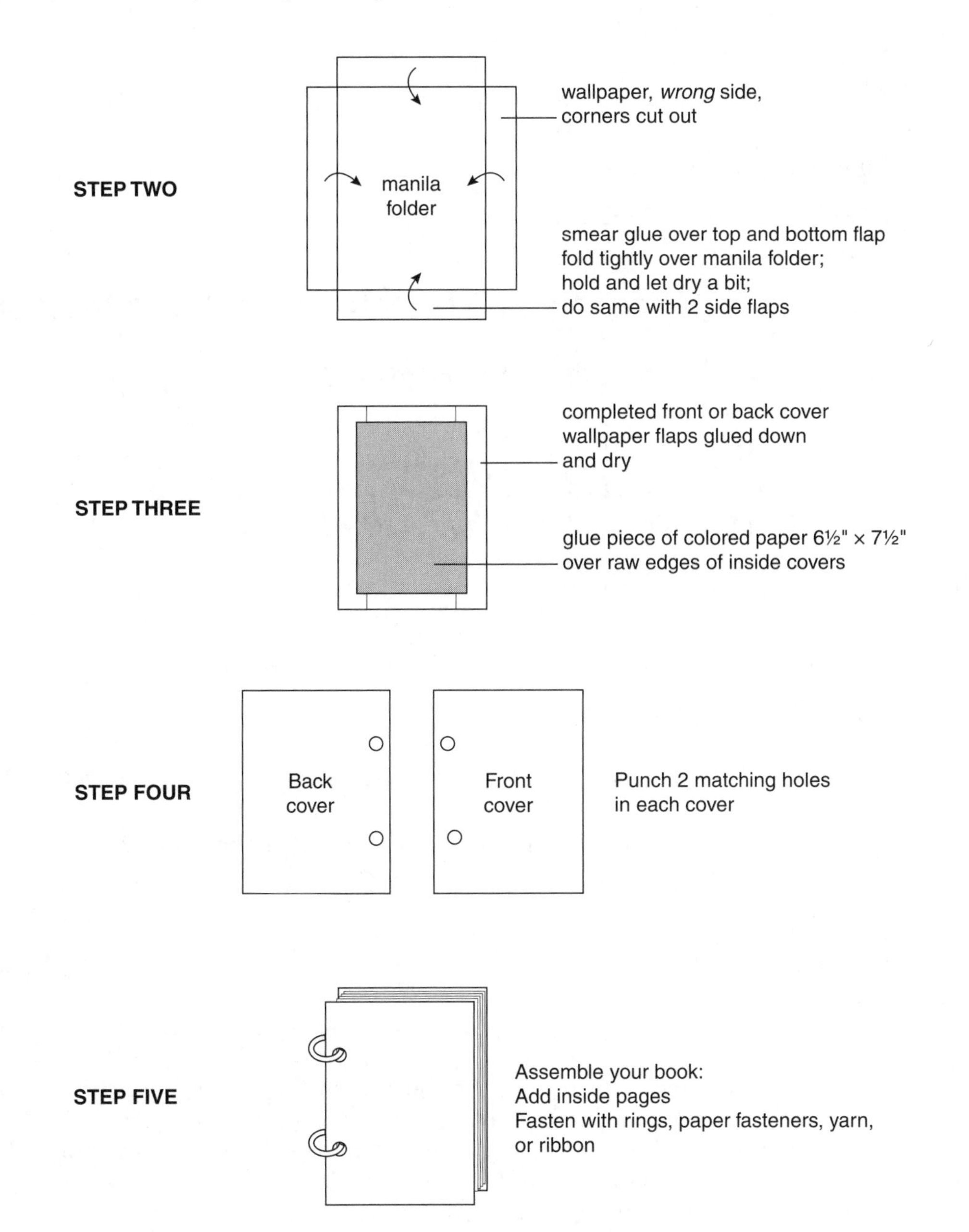
STEP TWO
manila folder
wallpaper, *wrong* side, corners cut out
smear glue over top and bottom flap fold tightly over manila folder; hold and let dry a bit; do same with 2 side flaps
STEP THREE
completed front or back cover wallpaper flaps glued down and dry
glue piece of colored paper 6½" × 7½" over raw edges of inside covers
STEP FOUR
Back cover
Front cover
Punch 2 matching holes in each cover
STEP FIVE
Assemble your book:
Add inside pages
Fasten with rings, paper fasteners, yarn, or ribbon

Appendix B

Developing a Beginning Framework for Writing Workshop

Laurie Lee
Imlay City Middle School, Michigan
Seventh Grade Language Arts Classroom

Focus

1. Prepare the classroom for writing workshop prior to the start of the school year.
2. Plan the first few weeks of writing instruction to begin writing workshop with the students.

Objectives

The students will:

- Become familiar with the components of the writing workshop—including mini-lessons, writing/conferring time, group sharing.
- Maintain writing folders—one with their collections of unfinished drafts and pieces, another with finished work.
- Develop an ongoing list of topics.
- Become familiar with questions and guidelines for conferencing with other students.
- Plan for how they will use their writing time.

(Laurie Lee adapted this workshop approach from Nancie Atwell's *In the Middle* and from ideas generated as a result of her participation in the Flint Area Writing Project.)

- Understand expectations for seventh grade writing.
- Demonstrate ability to respond to students' writing in conferences.
- Begin to view themselves as writers.

Pre-School Preparation

1. Gather supplies: folders, writing tools, etc.
2. Set up room:
   - **a.** Create Writing Center on back table in room with supplies and reference materials.
   - **b.** Set up trays:
     "To Be Edited"
     "To Be Photocopied"
   - **c.** Set up file cabinet for permanent writing folders.
   - **d.** Designate private, quiet, writing table.
   - **e.** Set up peer conference corners: four areas isolated from the rest of the classroom, equipped with conference guidelines and peer response forms.
   - **f.** Set up group share area.
   - **g.** Prepare posters and guidelines to display in room.
   - **h.** Run copies of writing sheets:
     "Titles and Dates of Finished Pieces"
     "My Ideas for Writing"
     "Things __________ Can Do as a Writer"
   - **i.** Set up teacher's record keeping:
     - Status-of-the-Class sheets on clipboard to record each student's daily plan for the workshop period.
     - Conference journal with several pages set aside for keeping notes about each student.
   - **j.** Set up file box for mini-lessons.

Week One

Day One: Introduce Three Writing Workshop Components

A. Mini-lesson—Topic Modeling/Topic Search.

Topic Modeling—Teacher models possible stories he/she could write, talks about various topics, tells personal anecdotes that could be turned into a piece of writing.

Topic Search—Students think about their own possible stories to tell, list topics, share with peers. Students volunteer possible stories for writing; teacher comments on them.

B. Writer's Workshop.

Introduce procedures (have on poster):

1. No erasing.
2. One side of paper.
3. Save everything.
4. Date, label everything.
5. Skip lines.
6. Quiet voices.
7. Work really hard.

Begin writing—teacher writes for ten minutes, then begins to confer with students as they continue writing.

C. Group Share.

Discuss "leads"; students find the "lead" in their pieces.

Day Two: Introduce Status-of-the-Class Form

1. Mini-lesson: Status-of-the-Class form.
   - List of each student's name with a grid for each writing workshop day to be filled in by teacher or student; used to keep daily record of how each class member plans to spend writing workshop time.
   - Explain purpose and teach students how to use it.
2. **A.** Students think, decide plan for the day.
   B. Students tell topic and today's plan; this is noted on Status-of-the-Class form.
3. Writing time/teacher conferences.

   Teacher circulates with clipboard containing sheets of "Guidelines for Effective Conferences" and "Questions to Use in Writing Conferences" to guide him/her in these early conferences. (See Chapter Three for examples of these materials.)
4. Group Share (5–7 minutes before period ends).

Day Three:

1. Mini-lesson: Expectations for Grade Seven Writing.
2. Status-of-the-Class form filled out.
3. Writing time/teacher conferences (use conference notebook).
4. Group Share (model PQS—response, questions, suggestions).

Week Two

Day One:

1. Mini-lesson: Students write about their own writing skills, experiences, and attitudes. Some whole class sharing.

2. Status-of-the-Class form filled out.
3. Writing time/teacher conferences.
4. Group Share.

Day Two:

1. Mini-lesson: The Writing Process (use chart and leave posted on wall). Discuss process; show use of this process in teacher's own writing.
2. Status-of-the Class form filled out.
3. Writing time/teacher conferences.
4. Group Share.

Day Three:

1. Mini-lesson: Writing Folders.

   Discuss two types—one for in-process writing; one for completed work.

   Show where and how to store these in the classroom.
2. Status-of-the-Class form filled out.
3. Writing time/teacher conferences.
4. Group Share.

Week Three

Mini-lessons:

Day One: Topic List, generating ideas for writing; store list in in-process folder.

Day Two: What is Revision? Model with teacher's own writing or that of student volunteer.

Day Three: Tips for Revising.

Workshop time spent as above with students working on their writing, conferring with the teacher, revising, starting new pieces using their Topic Lists.

Week Four

Mini-lessons:

Day One: Introduce Peer Conferencing.

Teacher models good and bad examples with student volunteers.

Day Two: Guidelines for Content Conferences with Peers.

Discuss handout with guidelines, more modeling, discussion.

Day Three: Conference Corners.

Use of Peer Response Forms; how to give helpful feedback. (See Figure 3.9 for examples of these forms.)

Workshop time spent as in weeks one and two with students working on their writing, conferring with the teacher, revising, starting new pieces using their Topic Lists. This week students also begin peer conferencing.

**Mini-lessons will be adapted to the needs of the students. If an issue comes up that needs to be addressed in a mini-lesson, it will be discussed in the next session.

Resources

1. Writing supplies—folders, paper, pens, pencils, white-out, stapler, glue, etc.
2. References—dictionaries, thesauruses, reference books.
3. Forms for conferences, etc.
4. Posters—make or buy.

Evaluation

Students will be evaluated in the following ways:

1. Discussing and demonstrating writing workshop procedures.
2. Maintaining writing folder with all work, developing a topic list, maintaining a skills list of "Things _____ Can Do As a Writer" and a finished piece list.
3. Demonstrating ability to conference using "respond, question, suggest" during group share, peer conference, and teacher conference.
4. Doing daily planning for writing during status conference.
5. Demonstrating understanding of writing workshop expectations through discussion and observation of student during writing workshop time.
6. Making progress toward the writing requirements for the marking period.

Appendix C

Schedule for Persuasive Essay

Elaine Porter
Linden High School, Michigan

Day One

1. Students do role-playing on how to argue:
   Teacher gives them a situation such as convincing their parents they can go to a concert on a school night. Students play the parents. The student must convince his/her parents he/she should be able to go.
2. Class discussion follows on how to argue your points.

Day Two

1. Students fill out a form listing concerns they have with their high school.
2. Discussion: find the most common concerns of the students.
3. Students pick a topic for their persuasive paper. Common topics are open lunch, longer time between classes, tardy policy, attendance policy, athletic policy, etc.
4. For homework, students list the arguments they might use for their topic.

Day Three

1. Students get into groups to explain their arguments. The other members of the group must come up with the counter-arguments.
2. Class discusses how to find support for their arguments, such as gathering information from other school districts, interviewing fellow-students, etc.
3. For homework, students develop a thesis for their paper.

Day Four

1. Discuss possible formats for writing the paper.
2. Writing workshop day.
3. Teacher conferences with students as needed.

Day Five

1. Writing workshop day.
2. Discuss problems students are encountering with their papers.
3. Teacher conferences with students as needed.

Day Six

1. Rough draft due.
2. Peer response groups: students break into small groups; read their papers to their group; group members fill out peer response forms and discuss each paper.

Day Seven

1. Students fill out a form concerning the progress of their papers.
2. Class breaks into small groups and students try to help each other with their concerns.
3. Main concerns are discussed by teacher and whole class.

Day Eight

1. Revised draft due, typed.
2. Peer editing in pairs.
3. Hand out and discuss self-evaluation sheets.

Day Nine

1. Final revised, edited paper due along with self-evaluation sheet.
2. Sharing papers in small groups.
3. Volunteers read theirs aloud to the whole class for discussion.

Appendix D

Teaching the Research Paper in Senior English

Elaine Porter
Linden High School, Michigan

The theme for this unit on the research paper was "political correctness." After some introductory readings and class discussions on the theme, each student selected a topic of special interest within this theme for research and writing. Earlier in the school year, students wrote shorter papers using sources and were taught such techniques as how to paraphrase, summarize, use quotations, and cite sources. Review was done as necessary, sometimes on an individual basis, as students did research and wrote.

Day One

Talk about writing a research paper on political correctness.
Read "Taking Offense" by Jerry Adler.
Students write a response to the article.
Share responses.
Assign "Battle Widens over College Affirmative Action" by Julian E. Barnes for homework. Read and write a response.

Day Two

Discuss Barnes article and responses.
Read "Affirmative Action on the Edge" by Mike Tharp.
Break into groups to discuss article.
Groups brainstorm possible research topics.
Groups share topics with entire class.
Assign "Thought Reform 101" by Alan Kors for homework.
Students list 3 topics they are interested in researching and fill out form, "Finding a Topic."

Day Three Discuss Kors article.
Students break into groups to discuss their topics.
In groups, students help each other narrow their topics.
Groups discuss best way to complete the research.

Day Four Research in Media Center/Library.
Teacher conferences with students about their topics.

Days Five through Eight
Students continue research in the Media Center/Library.
Teacher works with individual students as needed.

Day Nine Work in classroom.
Discuss possible formats for paper.
Assign for homework: develop a "working" thesis statement.

Day Ten Writing workshop day.
Teacher conferences with students over thesis statement and direction of paper.
Assign for homework: bring in 3 great Internet sites related to political correctness to share with the class.

Day Eleven Students break into groups and share information on Internet sites.
Discuss in groups problems students are encountering with the paper.
Class discussion: try to solve these problems.
Assign "Research Paper Update" due next class session.

Days Twelve through Fifteen
Writing workshop
Teacher conferences with students over drafts.

Day Sixteen First draft of research paper due.
Peer response; students exchange drafts and fill out "Peer Response Form for Draft of Research Paper" on each other's papers to guide content revision.

Day Seventeen
Students work in small groups discussing papers and reader responses from "Peer Response Forms."

Day Eighteen
Revision workshop day.
Conferences with teacher and/or peers as needed.

Day Nineteen

Typed draft due.
Peer editing of drafts using "Peer Editing Sheet for Final Draft of Research Paper" (See Figure 4.5 for one example of this form.)
"Self-Evaluation Form" handed out.

Day Twenty

Final paper due.
"Self-Evaluation Form" due.
Presentations and discussions in small groups.

Works Cited

Adler, Jerry, et al. "Taking Offense." *Newsweek* 24 Dec. 1990:48–54.
Barnes, Julian E. "Battle Widens over College Affirmative Action." *U.S. News & World Report* 22 Dec. 1997.
Kors, Alan Charles. "Thought Reform." *Reason* Mar. 2000.
Tharp, Mike. "Affirmative Action on the Edge." *U.S. News & World Report* 13 Feb. 1995:32–47.

Elaine Porter's Handouts

Finding A Topic

List three topics related to political correctness that interest you.

1.

2.

3.

You have the most knowledge about which topic?

Which topic do you know the least about?

Which topic interests you the most?

Choose one topic:

What is the focus of your paper?

What questions do you want answered about your topic through your research?

1.

2.

3.

4.

5.

Before you begin your research, state your feelings on this topic.

What do you already know about this topic?

How are you going to research your topic (possible sources, primary and secondary)?

How can I help you with this paper? What concerns do you have with this topic?

Do you feel comfortable with documentation and writing a Works Cited page? Do you need additional information to refresh your memory?

Research Paper Update

Working thesis:

What are your main points?

How is the research progressing?

What problems are you encountering?

Are you finding the time you need to write this paper?

Peer Response Form for Draft of Research Paper

Writer:

Peer Responder:

1. What is the thesis of this paper? Where is the thesis? Is it stated or implied?

2. In what style is the paper written? (informative, persuasive, argument analysis, pro/con)

3. How is the paper organized?

4. What type of introduction does the writer use? How effective is it?

5. What are three main points of the paper?

6. What is the strength of the paper?

7. How many direct quotations are used in the paper? Who are these experts? Why are their opinions important?

8. What questions still need to be answered?

9. Do you have any problems following or accepting the writer's position? Would you make any changes in the logic of the writer? Are the conclusions the writer draws based on valid information?

10. Make at least one suggestion that would improve this paper.

11. Does the writer present enough evidence to support his/her theories? Put stars wherever more evidence is needed.

12. Are there at least three documentations from three different sources?
    Yes No

13. Is there a strong conclusion?
    Yes No

Self-Evaluation Form

Writer:

1. What is the strength of your paper?

2. What did you find difficult when writing this paper?

3. How do you feel about this paper now that it is completed?

4. Did you have enough time to write this paper? Explain.

5. Do you think we should have scheduled more classes related to research? More writing days?

6. Did you spend as much time as you should have on this paper? If not, why?

Grading Sheet for Research Paper

Name:

Grade:

Total Points Possible: 150	Points Received
Introduction (20 points) Thesis clearly states purpose of paper Main points of the paper are presented Background information Clever and interesting opening—grabs the reader's attention	_______
Political Correctness Research (70 points) Thoroughness of research Position supported with facts and statistics Logical development of topic Three sources used Three documentations from three different sources Information relates to topic Focus remains clear throughout paper	_______
Style of Writing (20 points) Use of transitions Smoothness of writing Vocabulary Clarity Rich language	_______
Mechanics and Spelling (20 points) Few errors in mechanics and spelling, and they do not detract from the total effect of the paper	_______
Conclusion (10 points) Logical conclusion to paper Leaves reader with writer's final message	_______
Format (10 points) Heading Works Cited Page Pagination Documentation	_______

Comments:

Works Cited

Adkison, Stephen and Stephen Tchudi. "Grading on Merit and Achievement: Where Quality Meets Quantity." *Alternatives to Grading Student Writing.* Ed. Stephen Tchudi. Urbana, IL: National Council of Teachers of English, 1997. 192–208.

Andrasick, Kathleen. "Independent Repatterning: Developing Self-Editing Competence." *English Journal* 82 (February 1993): 28–31.

______. *Opening Texts: Using Writing to Teach Literature.* Portsmouth, NH: Heinemann Boynton/Cook, 1990.

Andrews, Larry. *Language Exploration and Awareness: A Resource Book for Teachers.* Mahwah, NJ: Lawrence Erlbaum Associates, Publishers, 1997.

Apple, Michael. *Ideology and Curriculum.* Boston: Routledge & Kegan Paul, 1979.

Applebee, Arthur N. Writing in the Secondary School: English and the Content Areas. Urbana, IL: National Council of Teachers of English, 1981.

______, Judith A. Langer, and Ina V. S. Mullis. *Understanding Direct Writing Assessments: Reflections on a South Carolina Writing Study.* Educational Testing Service, May, 1989.

Atwell, Nancie. *In the Middle: Writing, Reading, and Learning with Adolescents.* Portsmouth, NH: Boynton/Cook, 1987. 2nd ed., 1998.

Baines, Lawrence, Colleen Baines, Gregory Kent Stanley, and Anthony Kunkel. "Losing the Product in the Process." *English Journal* 88 (May 1999): 67–72.

Ball, Arnetha F. "Evaluating the Writing of Culturally and Linguistically Diverse Students: The Case of the African American Vernacular English Speaker." *Evaluating Writing: The Role of Teachers' Knowledge about Text, Learning, and Culture.* Eds. Charles R. Cooper and Lee Odell. Urbana, IL: National Council of Teachers of English, 1999. 225–248.

Bartholomae, David. "Inventing the University." In *Cross-Talk in Comp Theory: A Reader.* Ed. Victor Villanueva, Jr. Urbana, IL: National Council of Teachers of English, 1997. 589–619.

______. "The Study of Error." *College Composition and Communication* 31 (October 1980): 253–269.

Barton, David. *Literacy: An Introduction to the Ecology of Written Language.* Oxford, UK: Blackwell, 1994.

Beach, Richard W. "Evaluating Students' Response Strategies in Writing About Literature." *Evaluating Writing: The Role of Teachers' Knowledge About Text, Learning, and Culture.* Eds. Charles R. Cooper and Lee Odell. Urbana, IL: National Council of Teachers of English, 1999. 195–221.

Bean, John C. *Engaging Ideas: The Professor's Guide to Integrating Writing, Critical Thinking, and Active Learning in the Classroom.* San Francisco: Jossey Bass, 1996.

Berger, Mary. *Teach Standard, Too: Teacher's Manual to School Talk/Friend Talk Scripted Lessons.* Chicago: Orchard Books, 1996.

Berkenkotter, Carol. "Decisions and Revisions: The Planning Strategies of a Publishing Writer, and Response of a Laboratory Rat—or, Being Protocoled." *College Composition and Communication* 34 (1983): 156–72.

Berlin, James A. "Contemporary Composition: The Major Pedagogical Themes." *College English* 44 (December, 1982): 765–77.

______. "Rhetoric and Ideology in the Writing Class." *College English* 5 (September, 1988): 477–94.

______. *Rhetoric and Reality: Writing Instruction in American Colleges, 1900–1985.* Carbondale: Southern Illinois University Press, 1984.

______. *Writing Instruction in Nineteenth-Century American Colleges.* Southern Illinois University Press, 1984.

Berthoff, Anne. *Forming/ Thinking/Writing: The Composing Imagination.* Rochelle Park: Hayden, 1978.

______. *The Making of Meaning: Metaphors, Models, and Maxims for Writing Teachers.* Portsmouth, NH: Boynton/Cook, 1981.

Bizzell, Patricia. *Academic Discourse and Critical Consciousness.* University of Pittsburgh Press, 1992.

______, and Bruce Herzberg, eds. *The Rhetorical Tradition: Readings from Classical Times to the Present.* Boston: Bedford Books, 1990.

Bloom, Alan. *The Closing of the American Mind: How Higher Education Has Failed Democracy and Impoverished the Souls of Today's Students.* New York: Simon and Schuster, 1987.

Bomer, Randy. Discussion at the National Council of Teachers of English Conference. Baltimore, MD, 19 November 2001.

Braddock, Richard, Richard Lloyd-Jones, and Lowell Schoer. *Research in Written Composition.* Urbana, IL: National Council of Teachers of English, 1963.

Brereton, John C., ed. *The Origins of Composition Studies in the American College, 1875–1925: A Documentary History.* University of Pittsburgh Press, 1995.

Britton, James, Tony Burgess, Nancy Martin, Alex McLeod, and Harold Rosen. *The Development of Writing Abilities 11–18.* Urbana, IL: National Council of Teachers of English, 1975.

Bruner, Jerome S. *The Process of Education.* Cambridge, MA: Harvard University Press, 1966.

Cai, Guanjun. "Texts in Contexts: Understanding Chinese Students' English Compositions." *Evaluating Writing: The Role of Teachers' Knowledge about Text. Learning, and Culture.* Eds. Charles R. Cooper and Lee Odell. National Council of Teachers of English, 1999. 279–297.

Chomsky, Noam. *Rules and Representations.* New York: Columbia University Press, 1980.

Connors, Robert J. *Composition-Rhetoric. Backgrounds, Theory, and Pedagogy.* University of Pittsburgh Press, 1997.

______. "Personal Writing Assignments." *College Composition and Communication* 38 (May, 1987): 166–183.

Cooper, Charles R. "What We Know about Genres, and How It Can Help Us Assign and Evaluate Writing." *Evaluating Writing: The Role of Teachers' Knowledge about Text, Learning, and Culture.* Eds. Charles R. Cooper and Lee Odell, National Council of Teachers of English, 1999. 23–52.

______. "A Writing Program Certain to Fail." *Writing in the Secondary School: English and the Content Areas.* Arthur N. Applebee with Anne Auten and Fran Lehr. Urbana, IL: National Council of Teachers of English, xi–xiii, 1981.

______, and Lee Odell, eds. *Evaluating Writing: The Role of Teachers' Knowledge About Text, Learning, and Culture.* Urbana, IL: National Council of Teachers of English, 1999.

Cordeiro, P. "Children's Punctuation: An Analysis of Errors in Period Placement." *Research in the Teaching of English* 22 (1988): 62–74.

Crowley, Sharon. *The Methodical Memory: Invention in Current-Traditional Rhetoric.* Southern Illinois University Press: 1990.

______, and Debra Hawhee. *Ancient Rhetorics for Contemporary Students.* 2nd. ed. Boston: Allyn & Bacon, 1999.

Daiker, Donald, Andrew Kerek, Max Morenberg, and Jeffrey Sommers. *The Writer's Options: Combining to Composing.* 5th ed. New York: HarperCollins, 1994.

Delpit, Lisa. "Skills and Other Dilemmas of a Progressive Black Educator." *Harvard Education Review* 56.4 (1986): 379–385.

______. "The Silenced Dialogue: Power and Pedagogy in Educating Other People's Children." *Harvard Educational Review* 58. 3 (1988): 280–298.

Dewey, John. *Art as Experience.* New York: Capricorn Books, 1934.

Didion, Joan. "On Keeping a Notebook." *Slouching Towards Bethlehem.* New York: Dell, 1968.

Diederich, Paul. *Measuring Growth in English.* Urbana, IL: National Council of Teachers of English, 1974.

Dillard, Annie. "The Fixed." *Pilgrim at Tinker Creek.* New York: Harper and Row, 1974.

Dixon, John. *Growth through English.* Yorkshire, England: National Association for the Teaching of English, 1967.

Donovan, Timothy R. and Ben W. McClelland. *Eight Approaches to Teaching Composition.* National Council of Teachers of English, 1980.

Dornan, Reade, Lois Matz Rosen, and Marilyn Wilson. *Multiple Voices, Multiple Texts: Reading in the Secondary Content Areas.* Portsmouth, NH: Boynton/Cook Heinemann, 1997.

Dunning, Stephen and William Stafford. *Getting the Knack.* Urbana, IL: National Council of Teachers of English, 1992.

Earle, Alice Morse. *Child Life in Colonial Days.* Stockbridge, MA, Berkshire House Publishers, 1993. First published in 1899.

Elbow, Peter. *Embracing Contraries: Explorations in Learning and Teaching.* New York: Oxford University Press, 1986.

______. *Writing without Teachers.* New York: Oxford University Press, 1977.

______, and Pat Belanoff. *A Community of Writers: A Workshop Course in Writing.* 2nd. ed. New York: McGraw Hill, 1989.

______, and Pat Belanoff. *Sharing and Responding.* 2nd. ed. New York: McGraw Hill, 1995.

Elly, W. B., I. H. Barham, H. Lamb, and M. Wiley. "The Role of Grammar in a Secondary School English Curriculum." *Research in the Teaching of English* 10 (May): 5–21.

Emig, Janet. *The Composing Processes of Twelfth Graders.* National Council of Teachers of English Research Report No. 13. Urbana, IL: National Council of Teachers of English, 1971.

Fagin, Larry. *The List Poem: A Guide to Teaching and Writing Catalog Verse.* New York: Teachers and Writers Collaborative, 1992.

Fitzgerald, Sheila. "Facing Up to the New MEAP Writing Assessments." *Language Arts Journal of Michigan* 12: 2 (1996): 63–69.

Flower, Linda. *Problem-Solving Strategies for Writing.* 2nd ed. San Diego, CA: Harcourt, 1985.

Gee, James Paul. "Literacy, Discourse, and Linguistics: Introduction and What Is Literacy?" *Journal of Education* 171.1 (1989): 5–25.

______. *Social Linguistics and Literacies: Ideology in Discourses.* 2nd ed. London: Falmer Press, 1996.

Goodman, Ken. *What's Whole in Whole Language?* Portsmouth, NH: Heinemann, 1986.

Graff, Harvey J. *The Labyrinths of Literacy: Reflections on Literacy Past and Present.* University of Pittsburgh Press, 1995.

______. *The Literacy Myth: Literacy and Social Structure in the Nineteenth-Century City.* New York: Academic Press, 1979.

Graves, Donald. "An Examination of the Writing Processes of Seven-Year-Old Children." *Research in the Teaching of English* 9 (Winter, 1975): 227–41.

Greene, H. A. "English—Language, Grammar, and Composition." *Encyclopedia of Educational Research.* Rev. ed. Ed. W. S. Monroe. New York: Macmillan, 1950. 383–396.

A Guide to the Teaching of English Composition Grades 7 to 12 (Tentative). Curriculum Office, Philadelphia Public Schools, 1958.

Gutek, Gerald L. *Education in the United States: An Historical Perspective.* Englewood Cliffs, NJ: Prentice-Hall, Inc., 1986.

Hagemann, Julie. "A Bridge from Home to School: Helping Working Class Students Acquire School Literacy." *English Journal* 90 (March 2001): 74–81.

______, and Melvin Wininger. "An Ideological Approach to Grammar Pedagogy in English Education Courses." *English Education* 31.4 (July 1999): 265–294.

Harris, Mickey. *Teaching One-to -One: The Writing Conference.* Urbana, IL: National Council of Teachers of English, 1986.

Hairston, Maxine. "The Winds of Change: Thomas Kuhn and the Revolution in the Teaching of Writing." *College Composition and Communication* 33 (1982): 76–88.

Haswell, Richard. "Dark Shadows: The Fate of Writers at the Bottom." *College Composition and Communication* 39: 303–315.

Hayes, J. R. and Linda Flower. "A Cognitive Process Theory of Writing." *College Composition and Communication* 32 (December 1981): 367–87.

______. "Identifying the Organization of the Writing Process." *Cognitive Processes in Writing.* Eds. L. W. Gregg and E. R. Steinberg. Hillsdale, NJ: Erlbaum, 1980.

Haynes, Elizabeth. "Using Research in Preparing to Teach Writing." *English Journal* 67 (January 1978): 82–88.

Heath, Shirley Brice. *Ways with Words: Language, Life, and Work in Communities and Classrooms.* Cambridge (England): Cambridge University Press, 1983.

Henderson, Kathy. *The Young Writer's Guide to Getting Published.* Cincinnati, OH: F & W Publications, Incorporated, 2001.

Hillocks, G., Jr. *Research on Written Composition: New Directions for Teaching.* Urbana, IL: ERIC Clearinghouse on Reading and Communication Skills and the National Conference on Research in English, 1986.

Hirsch, E. D., Jr. *Cultural Literacy: What Every American Needs to Know.* Boston: Houghton-Mifflin, 1987.

______. *What Your 6th Grader Needs to Know: Fundamentals of a Good Sixth-Grade Education.* New York: Doubleday, 1993.

Hobbs, Catherine. *Nineteenth Century Women Learn to Write.* Charlottesville, VA: University of Virginia Press, 1995.

Hult, Christine and Thomas Huckin. *The New Century Handbook.* Boston: Allyn & Bacon, 1999.

Hunt, K. W. *Syntactic Maturity in Schoolchildren and Adults.* (Monographs of the Society for Research in Child Development, No. 134). Chicago: University of Chicago Press, 1970.

Iser, Wolfgang. *The Act of Reading: A Theory of Aesthetic Response.* Baltimore: Johns Hopkins University Press, 1978.

Jackson, Philip W. *John Dewey and the Lessons of Art.* Yale University Press, 1998.

James, Sharon. *Normal Language Acquisition.* Boston: Allyn & Bacon, 1990.

Killgallon, Don. *Sentence Composing: The Complete Course.* Portsmouth, NH: Boynton/Cook, 1987.

King, Laurie and Dennis Stovall. *Classroom Publishing: A Practical Guide to Enhancing Student Literacy.* Hillsboro, OR: Blue Heron Publishing, 1992.

Kirby, Dan and Tom Liner with Ruth Vinz. *Inside Out: Developmental Strategies for Teaching Writing.* 2nd ed. Portsmouth, NH: Heinemann Boynton/Cook, 1988.

Kitzhaber, Albert R. *Themes, Theories, and Therapy: The Teaching of Writing in College.* New York: McGraw-Hill, 1963.

Koch, Kenneth. *Rose, Where Did You Get That Red?* New York: Vintage Books, 1993.

Kohn, Alfie. *The Case Against Standardized Testing: Raising the Scores, Ruining the Schools.* Portsmouth, NH: Heinemann Boynton/Cook, 2000.

Krishna, Valerie. "The Syntax of Error." *The Journal of Basic Writing* 1.1:43–49.

Kroll, Barry M. and John C. Schafer. "Error-Analysis and the Teaching of Composition." *College Composition and Communication* 29 (October 1978): 242–248.

Lane, Barry. *After THE END: Teaching and Learning Creative Revision.* Portsmouth, NH: Heinemann Boynton/Cook, 1993.

Langer, Judith. "Learning Through Writing: Study Skills in the Content Areas." *Journal of Reading* 29 (Feb. 1986): 400–406.

______, ed. *Literature Instruction: A Focus on Student Response.* Urbana, IL: National Council of Teachers of English, 1992. "Lansing Requests Separate MEAP Investigation." *Lansing State Journal* 16 June 2001: 1A, 5A.

Larvick, Jeanne. "Poetry Video Unit." Lansing Catholic Central High School. Lansing, MI. March 1997.

Lee, Laurie. "Developing a Beginning Framework for Writing Workshop" and "Writing Folder Requirements Based on a Point System." Imlay City Middle School, Imlay City, MI. Fall 2001.

Leki, I. *Understanding ESL Writers: A Guide for Teachers.* Portsmouth, NH: Heinemann Boynton/Cook, 1992.

Lyons, Bill. "Well, What Do You Like About My Paper?" *Iowa English Newsletter.* September 1978.

Macrorie, Ken. *The I-Search Paper: Revised Edition of Research Writing.* Portsmouth, NH: Heinemann, 1984.

______. *Telling Writing.* New York: Hayden Book Company, 1970.

______. *Writing to Be Read.* New York: Hayden Book Company, 1968.

Madraso, Jan. "Proofreading: The Skill We've Neglected to Teach." *English Journal* 82 (February 1993): 32–41.

Matsuhashi, Ann. "Pausing and Planning: The Tempo of Written Discourse Production." *Research in the Teaching of English* 15 (1981): 113–34.

McCloud, Scott. *Understanding Comics: The Invisible Art.* HarperCollins, 1995.

McQuade, F. "Examining a Grammar Course: The Rationale and the Result." *English Journal* 69 (1980): 26–30.

Miller, James E. Jr. *Word, Self, Reality: The Rhetoric of Imagination.* New York: Dodd Mead & Co., 1972.

Moskowitz, Breyne A. "The Acquisition of Language." *Language: Readings In Language and Culture.* 6th ed. Ed. V. Clark, P. Eschholz, and A. Rosa. New York: St. Martin's Press, 1998.

Moulton, Margaret. R. "The Multigenre Paper: Increasing Interest, Motivation, and Functionaltiy in Research." *The Journal of Adolescent and Adult Literacy.* 42 (1999): 528–238.

Murdick, William. "What English Teachers Need to Know about Grammar." *English Journal* 85 (November 1996): 38–45.

Murphy, James J., ed. *A Short History of Writing Instruction: From Ancient Greece to Twentieth-Century America*. Davis, CA: Hermagoras Press, 1990.

Murphy, Sandra. "Assessing Portfolios." *Evaluating Writing: The Role of Teachers' Knowledge About Text, Learning, and Culture*. Eds. Charles R. Cooper and Lee Odell. Urbana, IL: National Council of Teachers of English, 1999. 114–135.

______, and Mary Ann Smith. "Creating a Climate for Portfolios." In *Evaluating Writing: The Role of Teachers' Knowledge about Text, Learning, and Culture*. Eds. Charles R. Cooper and Lee Odell. Urbana, IL: National Council of Teachers of English, 1999. 325–343.

Murray, Donald. *Crafting a Life in Essay, Story, Poem*. Portsmouth, NH: Heinemann Boynton/Cook, 1996.

______. "Teach Writing as a Process Not Product." *Cross-Talk in Comp Theory: A Reader.* Ed. Victor Villanueva, Jr. Urbana, IL: National Council of Teachers of English, 1997.

______. *Write to Learn*. 5th ed. Fort Worth. TX: Harcourt Brace, 1984.

______. *A Writer Teaches Writing: A Practical Method of Teaching Composition*. Boston: Houghton Mifflin Co., 1968.

Myers, Miles. Changing Our Minds: Negotiating English and Literacy. Urbana, IL: National Council of Teachers of English, 1996.

National Council of Teachers of English (NCTE). *Students' Right to Their Own Language*. Urbana, IL: National Council of Teachers of English, 1974.

Neeld, Elizabeth Cowan. *Writing*. 3rd ed. Glenview, IL: Scott, Foresman/Little, Brown Higher Education, 1980.

Nielsen-Williams, Elling. "Clustering and Writing Process." East Lansing High School, East Lansing, MI. Winter 2002.

Olds, Bruce. *Raising Holy Hell: A Novel of John Brown*. Penguin, 1995.

Owston, Ronald D., Sharon Murphy, and Herbert H. Wideman. "The Effects of Word Processing on Students' Writing Quality and Revision Strategies." *Research in the Teaching of English* 26 (October 1992): 249–276.

Padgett, Ron. *The Teachers and Writers Handbook of Poetic Forms*. New York: Teachers and Writers Collaborative, 1992.

Parsons, Michael. *How We Understand Art: A Cognitive Developmental Account of Aesthetic Experience*. Cambridge (England) University Press, 1987.

Perl, Sondra. "The Composing Processes of Unskilled College Writers." *Cross-Talk in Comp Theory: A Reader.* Ed. by Victor Villanueva, Jr. Urbana, IL: National Council of Teachers of English, 1997. 17–42.

_______. "A Writer's Way of Knowing: Guidelines for Composing." *Presence of Mind: Writing and the Domain Beyond the Cognitive*. Eds. Alice G. Brand and Richard L. Graves. Portsmouth, NH: Heinemann Boynton/Cook, 1994. 77–87.

Pinker, Steven. *The Language Instinct: How the Mind Creates Language*. New York: HarperCollins, 1994.

Porter, Elaine. "Schedule for Persuasive Essay," "Peer Editing Sheet for Final Draft of Research Paper," and "Teaching the Research Paper in Senior English." Linden High School, Linden, MI. Fall 2001.

Powell, David. *What Can I Write About? 7000 Topics for High School Students*. Urbana, IL: National Council of Teachers of English, 1981.

Resh, Celeste. "A Study of the Effect of Peer Responding on the Responder as Writer-Reviser." Ph.D. Diss., Michigan State University, 1994.

Reyes, Maria de la Luz. "Challenging Venerable Assumptions." *Harvard Educational Review* 62 (Winter 1992): 427–446.

Rico, Gabriele Lusser. *Writing the Natural Way.* Los Angeles, CA: Tarcher, Inc., 1983. Romano, Tom. "The Multigenre Research Paper." *Writing With Passion: Life Stories, Multiple Genres.* Heinemann Boynton/Cook, 1995.

Rose, Mike. "Rigid Rules, Inflexible Plans, and the Stifling of Language: A Cognitivist Analysis of Writer's Block." *College Composition and Communication* 31 (Winter 1980): 389–400.

Rosen, Lois. "Afloat upon a Sea of Talk." *Language Arts Journal of Michigan* 8 (1992): 1–20.

______. "Developing Correctness in Student Writing: Alternatives to the Error Hunt." *English Journal* 76 (1987) 62–69. Rev. and updated version in *Lessons to Share: On Teaching Grammar in Context.* Ed. Constance Weaver. Portsmouth, NH: Boynton/Cook Heinemann, 1998.

______. "Responding to Student Writing: Case Studies of Six High School English Teachers." Ph.D. diss., Michigan State University, 1983.

Rosenblatt, Louise M. "Literature—SOS!" *Language Arts* 68 (October 1991): 444–448.

______. *The Reader, the Text, the Poem: The Transactional Theory of the Literary Work.* Southern Illinois University Press, 1978.

Rottenberg, Annette T. *The Structure of Argument.* Boston, MA: Bedford Books, 1997.

Russell, David. "Activity Theory and Writing Instruction." *Reconceiving Writing, Rethinking Writing Instruction.* Ed. Joseph Petraglia. Mahwah, NJ: Lawrence Erlbaum, 1995.

Schieffelin, Bambi and Marilyn Cochran-Smith. "Learning to Read Culturally: Literacy Before Schooling." *Awakening to Literacy.* Eds. H. Goelman, A. Oberg, and F. Smith. London: Heinemann Educational Books, 1984.

Schultz, Lucille M. *The Young Composers: Composition's Beginnings in Century Schools.* Southern Illinois University Press, 1999.

Shannon, Patrick. *The Struggle to Continue: Progressive Reading Instruction in the United States.* Portsmouth, NH: Heinemann Boynton/Cook, 1990.

Scribner, Sylvia, and Michael Cole. *The Psychology of Literacy.* Cambridge, MA: Harvard University Press, 1981.

Searles, J. R., and G. R. Carlson. "Language, Grammar, and Composition." *Encyclopedia of Educational Research.* 3rd ed. Ed. C. W. Harris. New York: Macmillan. 454–470.

Shaughnessy, Mina P. *Errors and Expectations.* New York: Oxford University Press, 1977.

Shor, Ira. *Critical Teaching and Everyday Life.* University of Chicago Press, 1980.

______. *Empowering Education: Critical Teaching for Social Change.* University of Chicago Press, 1992.

______. *A Pedagogy for Liberation: Dialogues on Transforming Education.* South Hadley, MA: Bergin and Gargey, 1987.

Shulman, Lee. Discussion at Michigan State University. East Lansing, Michigan 12 December 2001.

Slack, Delane. "Fusing Social Justice with Multigenre Writing." *English Journal* 90.6 (2001): 62–66.

Smith, Frank. *To Think.* New York: Teachers College Press, 1990.

Smith, T. V. and Marjorie Grene. *From Descartes to Locke: Philosophers Speak for Themselves.* University of Chicago Press: Phoenix Books, 1957.

Sommers, Nancy. "Revision Strategies of Student Writers and Experienced Adult Writers." *College Composition and Communication* 31 (1980): 378–88.

State of Michigan. Michigan Educational Assessment Program. Revised Model of the Assessment for Writing in 1998. <http://www.mde.state.mi.us/off/meap>

Street, Brian. *Social Literacies: Critical Approaches to Literacy in Development, Ethnography and Education.* New York: Longman, 1995.

Strong, William. *Sentence Combining and Paragraph Building.* New York: McGraw-Hill, 1981.

______. *Creative Approaches to Sentence Combining.* Urbana, IL: ERIC/RCS and the National Council of Teachers of English, 1986.

______. *Sentence Combining: A Composing Book,* 3rd. ed. NY: McGraw-Hill, 1993.

Tchudi, Stephen, ed. *Alternatives to Grading Student Writing.* Urbana, IL: National Council of Teachers of English, 1997.

______, and Diana Mitchell. *Explorations in the Teaching of English.* 3rd ed. New York: Harper-Collins, 1989.

Teasley, Alan B. and Ann Wilder. *Reel Conversations: Reading Films With Young Adults.* Heinemann Boynton/Cook, 1978.

Thomas, Lee and Stephen Tchudi. *The English Language: An Owner's Manual.* Boston: Allyn & Bacon, 1999.

Thomas, Sharon and Michael Steinberg. "The Alligator in the Fishbowl: A Modeling Strategy for Student-Led Writing Response Groups," *Language Arts Journal of Michigan* 4 (Fall 1988): 24–35.

Vygotsky, Lev. *Mind in Society: The Development of Higher Psychological Processes.* Eds. M. Cole, V. John-Steiner, S. Scribner, and E. Souberman. Cambridge, MA: Harvard University Press, 1978.

Wade, Nicholas. "Researchers Say Gene Is Linked to Language." *New York Times,* 8 October 2001: A1, A20.

Warriner, John. *English Grammar and Composition: Complete Course.* New York: Harcourt, Brace & World, Inc., 1957.

Weaver, Constance. *Reading Process and Practice: From Socio-psycholinguistics to Whole Language.* Portsmouth, NH: Heinemann, 1988.

______. *Teaching Grammar in Context.* Portsmouth, NH: Heinemann Boynton/Cook, 1996.

______. "Teaching Grammar in the Context of Writing." *Lessons to Share: On Teaching Grammar in Context.* Ed. Constance Weaver. Portsmouth, NH: Boynton/Cook-Heinemann, 1998.

Wilhelm, Jeffrey. *"You Gotta BE the Book": Teaching Engaged and Reflective Reading with Adolescents.* New York: Teachers College Press, 1997.

Wolcott, Willa, and Sue M. Legg. *An Overview of Writing Assessment: Theory, Research, and Practice.* Urbana, IL: National Council of Teachers of English, 1998.

Zemelman, Steven and Harvey Daniels. *A Writing Project: Training Teachers of Composition from Kindergarten to College.* Portsmouth, NH: Heinemann, 1985.

Index